P9-BBT-272

THE GUN DIGEST® BOOK OF CONCEALED CARRY

MASSAD AYOOB

©2008 Massad Ayoob
Published by

Gun Digest® Books

An imprint of F+W Media, Inc.
700 East State Street • Iola, WI 54990-0001
715-445-2214 • 888-457-2873
www.gundigestbooks.com

Our toll-free number to place an order or obtain
a free catalog is (800) 258-0929.

All rights reserved. No portion of this publication may be reproduced or transmitted in any form or
by any means, electronic or mechanical, including photocopy, recording, or any information storage and
retrieval system, without permission in writing from the publisher, except by a reviewer who may quote
brief passages in a critical article or review to be printed in a magazine or newspaper, or electronically
transmitted on radio, television, or the Internet.

Library of Congress Control Number: 2008925074

ISBN-13: 978-0-89689-611-6
ISBN-10: 0-89689-611-0

Designed by Paul Birling
Edited by Ken Ramage

Printed in United States of America

Acknowledgments and Dedication

It is a pleasure to acknowledge the contributions of those who made this book possible. Gail Pepin, who took most of the photographs and was indispensable to the editing process on my end. Steve Denney, whose proofreading advice was invaluable, and who was kind enough to write the foreword. Herman Gunter, III who also helped me proofread. Harry Kane, the superb editor at *Combat Handguns* and *Guns & Weapons for Law Enforcement,* who gave me permission to blend into this book some things I had previously written for some of the Harris Publications titles he puts together so tirelessly. Thanks! I never would've made deadline without you!

I may have designed a couple of holsters and come up with a couple of techniques, but this book really comes to you from the countless number of people who have taught me and allowed me to pick their brains over the last nearly fifty years. They are holster designers and gun designers, gunfight survivors and survivors of horrors they were unarmed and helpless to prevent. They range from world handgun champions to novice handgun students, all of whom taught me lessons about how to help people prepare themselves and become ready to quell lethal violence at a moment's notice.

I was merely the conduit of their knowledge, the collecting agent who passed their collective learning experiences on to you, the reader of this book.

It is to all of them that this book is gratefully and respectfully dedicated.

■ Massad Ayoob,
December 2007

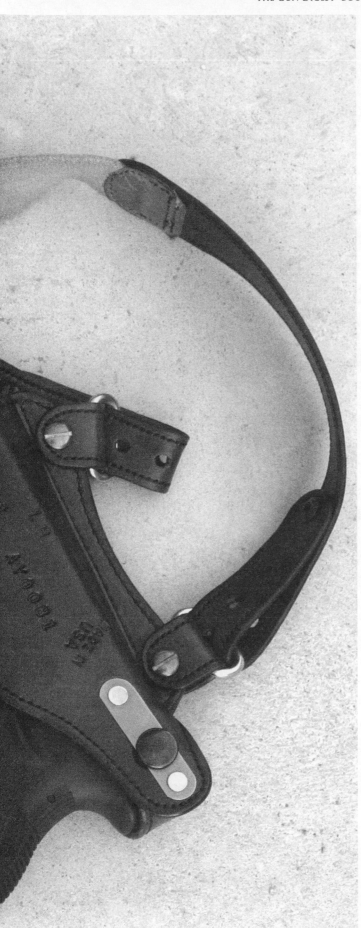

CONTENTS

FOREWORD

Spent casings are inches apart from ex-SWAT cop Steve Denney's new SIG P250 9mm as he tests it with a fast double tap.

I've been carrying concealed firearms since 1968, which was my first year as a sworn law enforcement officer. I was finishing the last year of my Criminology Degree at Florida State University and joined the Tallahassee Police Department as a Reserve Officer. Since then, I've learned a few lessons about concealed carry by trial and error, but my knowledge about firearms has been improved immensely by reading what the experts were saying. In the early 1970s, besides reading articles by people with names like Cooper, Gaylord, Askins, Skelton, etc., I started reading articles from a guy by the name of Massad Ayoob. I began to wonder, who was this Ayoob guy and, more importantly, why did what he wrote actually make sense, based on my own experience? My relationship with Mas' writing was strictly one-sided (he wrote and I read) from then until 1999, when I finally had the chance to take my first LFI course. Since then we have become good friends and I have become an instructor with him for his Lethal Force Institute. That has given me a precious opportunity to see how he acquires and uses the knowledge that he shares with others in his training classes, his writing and his case work as an expert witness. So when he said he was writing a book about concealed carry, I thought: "This has got to be good!"

Well, it is. I have been poring over the manuscript for the past week and I am happy to report that Mas has put together a winner. And a timely winner, at that. Concealed carry has been a hot topic in the world of gun ownership for the past two decades or so. More and more opportunities for decent, law abiding citizens to protect themselves by legally carrying concealed firearms have emerged as State after State has adopted more realistic concealed carry laws. Even so, only about two percent of the people eligible for a concealed carry permit actually apply for one. That is starting to change, however. Of course, September 11, 2001 started folks thinking more seriously about the subject. And most recently, the mass murder of students at Virginia Tech, the shootings in malls in Omaha and Salt Lake City and the armed attacks on religious centers in Arvada and Colorado Springs are causing people to reassess their vulnerability as they go about their daily lives. As more and more people come to the conclusion that they need to take realistic precautions against violent attack, the need for sensible concealed carry advice will continue to expand.

One of the things that has always impressed me about the way Mas works is that he is not just a teacher and not just a writer. He is a true student of firearms, their history and their use. This book reflects his serious research of the subject, as well as his ability to communicate with his audience. The references to many of the legendary names in the firearms world and many of the real-world case studies are not just academic. Mas has known most of the greats. And anyone who knows Mas also knows that he is always asking questions, always analyzing other people's views and always seeking more and more knowledge. It's not just the "names" either. I have been with him when he asked the ordinary man or woman what their impressions were on a particular gun or piece of gear. "How do you like that Beretta," he asked a young highway patrolman we were sharing a gas pump with during a fuel stop on a trip across the Great Plains. "How's that holster workin' for ya," to a Sheriff's Deputy we met at a convenience store. "What do you think they should do to improve that" is a common question we hear when he calls on us to help evaluate some gun or other gear that has been sent to him to "T & E." Beyond the equipment, Mas gathers real-life information about the use of firearms for self defense.

Certainly his case work as an expert has given him unique access to incidents from the streets. Some of them are high profile, some rather ordinary. Except to the people involved. Every case has its lessons. And, very often, his students have their stories. Stories that can make the hair on the back of your neck stand up, or bring a tear to your eye. Like the female student who had been the victim of two violent sexual assaults. The first time her attacker succeeded in raping her. The second attacker did not. The difference? The second time she was armed and prepared to defend herself.

Or the Roman Catholic priest, who grew up in a foreign country known for its civil strife. He has been shot five times and stabbed once, all in separate incidents. He now lives in the United States, carries every day, and when he quietly relates his story, he simply says: "Never again."

These are the sort of people Mas spends time with as both a teacher and as a student of the human experience. And that experience is what he willingly and skillfully shares with his students and his readers. In this book, he has compiled decades of experience in not just the carrying of firearms, but the shooting of firearms. Mas has been a competitive shooter since the old PPC days. He was a "regular" at the Bianchi Cup and other national matches. He still competes regularly in law enforcement competitions and International Defensive Pistol Association (IDPA) matches. In fact, Mas was one of the first IDPA Four Gun Masters and became *the first* Five Gun Master, when an additional revolver category was established by IDPA a couple of years ago. He is also an avid researcher of the history of carrying firearms and their use by police and ordinary private citizens alike. As such, he was a guest lecturer at a conference of writers and historians in Tombstone, Arizona, assembled to discuss probably the most famous gunfight ever, the shootout at the OK Corral. And, on a more contemporary note, he was requested to represent the "expert witness" point of view on a panel of American Bar Association legal experts who were making a Continuing Legal Education training tape for attorneys. The tape specifically addresses the investigation, prosecution and effective defense of people who have had to use deadly force to protect themselves or others.

In this book, Mas discusses both WHY we carry and HOW to carry. Mas explains the concepts behind the two styles of holsters he has designed, the LFI Rig and the Ayoob Rear Guard, and why holster selection is such an important part of your carry "system." He also explains the need to practice drawing from concealment, in order to quickly respond to any threat. He explains the rationale behind two drawing

Concealed carry has been a hot topic in the world of gun ownership for the past two decades or so.

methods that he developed: using the StressFire "Cover Crouch" to draw from an ankle rig and the Fingertip Sweep (he calls it "reach out and touch yourself") used to positively clear an open front garment for a smooth same-side draw. Mas began developing his "StressFire" shooting techniques back in the 1970's. By late 1981, at the suggestion of world champion shooter Ray Chapman, he established the Lethal Force Institute and has been instructing "certified card carrying good guys" there ever since. The Chief of Police of the department where Mas serves as a Captain, Russell Lary, has entrusted his son to Mas' tutelage to the extent that he has attended all of the LFI classes, LFI-I, II & III, and he just recently completed the most advanced class, LFI-IV. Yes, Mas really is a Captain in the Grantham, NH Police Department. I know the Chief, and he is delighted to have such a true "human resource" available to the residents of his community.

A lot has changed in the nearly 40 years since I started in this field. A lot happened before that, of course, but I see the next major steps coming in the immediate future. People are tired of being victimized by people who use guns and other weapons illegally. And people are tired of being victimized by anti-gun advocates and the laws and rules for which they are responsible. They have been shown to be worse than ineffective.

And, make no mistake, you are your own "First Responder."

They have put decent people unnecessarily at risk in "Gun-Free Zones," that are only gun-free to the law abiding. They continue to attempt to thwart efforts to make concealed carry by law abiding people a nation-wide reality. They have made people vulnerable at a time when they should be seriously thinking about, and preparing for, their own self protection. Not to become "vigilantes," but to be able to hold the line against violence, until the professionals can respond. And, make no mistake, you are your own "First Responder." Just as you would have a fire extinguisher in your home or car, or take a course in first aid and CPR, you need to consider how well you are prepared for the other kind of deadly threat that may suddenly present itself: a violent, criminal attack on you or those who depend on you. In this book, Massad Ayoob has brought together all the essential elements that you need to know if you are currently carrying concealed firearms or if you are considering doing so. This is your opportunity to take advantage of all of the research, knowledge and experience that Mas has accumulated over more than four decades. I can't think of a better teacher.

Steve Denney
Firearms and Defensive Tactics Instructor
Firearms Training Contributor to Officer.com
Former Police Supervisor and Ordinary Citizen of the USA

THE CCW LIFESTYLE

As Gail begins to give him a hug, Steve tucks his elbows into his body and will seem to be hugging back, but his forearm placement will prevent her from feeling the SIG 357 on his right hip or the spare magazine on his left.

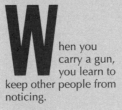

When you carry a gun, you learn to keep other people from noticing.

If you're reading this book, that tells me that you've either made the decision to CCW (Carry a Concealed Weapon), or are thinking about it. Either one is a good start to enhanced personal safety of oneself and loved ones.

It surprises some people to hear that from a guy who's been carrying a badge for three and a half decades. Surprise: there are more cops who feel the same way than you might think. Fact is, for the most part, the anti-gun cops fall into two narrow

If you carry, be competent with your gun. You don't need to be able to shoot this perfect qualification score with a Glock 30 and 45 hardball, but you want to come as close as you can. Confidence and competence intertwine, says Ayoob.

of my family to arrive in the USA, was an armed citizen who went for his gun when he was pistol-whipped in his city store by an armed robber. He shot and wounded the man. The suspect fled, only to be killed later that night in a shootout with the city police. The wound my grandfather inflicted slowed him down when he tried to kill the arresting officer, and the cops thanked him for that. My dad had been in his twenties when he had to resort to deadly force in the same city's streets. A would-be murderer put a revolver to his head and pulled the trigger; my dad ducked to the side enough to miss the bullet, but not enough to keep the muzzle blast from destroying his left eardrum. Moments later, my father's return fire had put that man on the ground dying from a 38 slug "center mass," and the thug's accomplice in a fetal position clutching himself and screaming.

It's no wonder that growing up in the 1950s, guns were a part of my life: in the home, and in my father's jewelry store. When I went to work there at age twelve, I carried a loaded gun concealed. There were strategically placed handguns hidden throughout the area behind the counter and in the back room, but Dad was smart enough to know that I wouldn't always be within reach of one when I needed it. The laws in that time and place allowed the practice.

I realized this was some pretty serious stuff, and set to learning all I could about the practice. My dad's customers included lawyers, judges, and his friend the chief of police. I picked all their brains on the issue. What I learned stunned me.

There were books then on gunfighting: how to do it, what to do it with, and how to develop the mindset to do it. Interestingly, there were *none* on *when* to shoot. My dad's lawyer friends told me that even kids like me could use a legal library; we didn't have to be attorneys or law students to get in there, and the librarian would show us how to find what we were looking for. I lived in the state capital, and the State Legal Library had the same rule. As I began that self-education, I found myself thinking, "Somebody ought to write a book about *this* for regular people! When I grow up, if nobody's written that book yet, *I* wanna write it!"

And I did. "In the Gravest Extreme: the Role of the Firearm in Personal Protection" hit print in 1979, and has been a best-seller ever since. And I've been carrying a concealed handgun since the year 1960, in public on a permit since the year 1969. By 1973, I had become a police firearms instructor, and from then to now have taken training as avidly as I've given it. I've been teaching and researching this stuff full time since 1981, when I established Lethal Force Institute (www.ayoob.com). That has included expert witness testimony in weapons, shooting, and assault cases since

categories. One is the chief appointed by an anti-gun mayor or city council, who serves at the pleasure of the appointing authority and can get busted back to Captain – the highest rank normally protected by Civil Service – if he doesn't make himself a mouthpiece for the politician(s) in question. The other is the young rookie who didn't have a gun of his own until he got into the Academy, and associates the weapon with the new identity into which he has invested so much of his time, effort, ego and self-image. It's not something he wants to share with the general public.

Give him time. My experience has been that the great majority of LEOs (law enforcement officers) in the middle of those two ends, the seasoned street cops who've seen the reality, have a more realistic view. A great many of them make sure they leave a gun at home for their spouse to use to protect the household while they're gone. They've learned that police are reactive more than proactive, and that the victim has to survive the violent criminal's attack long enough for law enforcement to be summoned and arrive.

I've carried a concealed handgun since I was twelve years old. My grandfather, the first generation

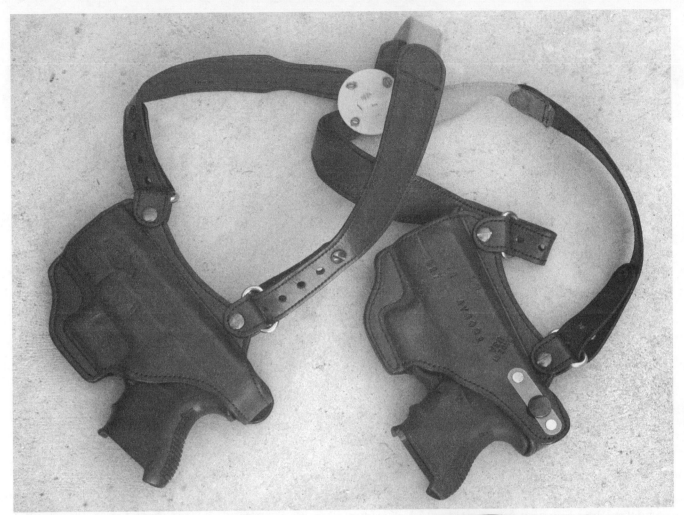

Many who carry guns have learned to carry two. Here, twin baby Glocks ride in double shoulder holster by Mitch Rosen.

1979. From 1987 through 2006, I served as chair of the firearms committee for the American Society of Law Enforcement Trainers, and have been on the advisory board for the International Law Enforcement Educators and Trainers Association since its inception. I've also had the privilege of teaching for the International Association of Law Enforcement Firearms Instructors inside and outside the US, and served a couple of years as co-vice chair, with Mark Seiden under Drew Findling, of the forensic evidence committee of the National Association of Criminal Defense Lawyers. I've had the privilege of studying the firearms training of the DEA, NYPD, LAPD, numerous state police agencies, and countless other law enforcement organizations. I've been able to study hands-on with such great shooting champions as Ray Chapman, Frank Garcia, Rob Leatham, and many more. I learned one-on-one from living legends like Charlie Askins, Jim Cirillo, Jeff Cooper, Bill Jordan, Frank McGee and more. Some of the "more" have asked that their names not appear in print, and I will respect that here.

It has been a long and educational road, and with a little luck, it won't be over anytime soon. The bottom line is, I'm not a super-cop as so many of those men literally were. In all these years, though I've had my

When you become accustomed to carrying, you learn to have at least one weak-side holster and ambidextrous gun so you can protect yourself and your loved ones if you sustain an injury to the dominant arm. This is one of author's Springfield Armory 1911s, with ambidextrous safety and left-hand High Noon concealed carry scabbard.

gun on a lot of people and was starting to pull the trigger a few times, I've never had to shoot a man. With a little luck, that will stay the same, too. I see my role – as an instructor and as the writer of this book – as a funnel of knowledge. You're at the receiving end of the funnel.

There have been tremendous advances in the last fifty years in holster design, handgun design, and ammunition design. We now have the finest concealed carry firearms, holsters, and defensive rounds that have ever been available. We likewise have techniques that have taken advantage of modern knowledge of the human mind and body that was not available to the famous gunfighters of old. (But the Old Ones have left their lessons to us, and many of those are timeless, too.)

"CCW"

Let's sort out the alphabet soup for those readers new to concealed carry. To those who practice it, CCW can describe the practice of (lawfully) carrying a concealed weapon. It can also be a shorthand noun, e.g., "My CCW is a Colt Commander 45." Unfortunately, to some the letters have a negative connotation. In many jurisdictions, police know them as the abbreviation for the *crime* of *illegally* Carrying a Concealed Weapon.

In some parts of the country, CCW refers to the permit to carry itself, as in: "I carry my CCW next to my driver's license, so I can hand both to the officer if I'm pulled over for speeding." But each state has its own terminology. That little laminated card might be a CPL (Concealed Pistol License), CWP (Concealed Weapons Permit), CHL (Concealed Handgun License), or some other acronym. We're talking about the same thing. Hell, in the state where I grew up and spent most of my adult life, it was known simply as a "pistol permit." (And, no, we're not going to use these pages to debate whether "license" or "permit" is the proper term. The book is about concealed carry, not what I've come to call Combat Semantics.)

The concealed carry lifestyle changes you. Most of the changes are positive. If you're new to the practice, what this book says will be helpful to you. If you've been doing it for as long as I have or longer, you might find a new trick or two, and at worst will have a book to back up your advice when *you're* sharing this knowledge with *your* students.

Changes

People who don't understand the lifestyle think a gun on your hip will turn you from Dr. Jekyll to Mr. Hyde, or make you "go where angels fear to tread." *Au contraire.* Those who've actually *lived* the CCW lifestyle can tell you that it's just the opposite.

When you carry a gun, you no longer have the

Concealed carry means several small changes of habit. If reaching to a high shelf might raise your outer garment and expose holster or gun …

option of starting fights, or even keeping the ball rolling when another person starts one with you. When you are armed with a lethal weapon, you carry the burden of what the Courts call a "higher standard of care." Because *you* know a deadly weapon is present, and *you* know that a yelling match or "mere fisticuffs" can now degrade into a killing situation, law and ethics alike will say that *you of all people* should have known enough to abjure from a violent conflict. This is why a phrase from science-fiction writer Robert Heinlein, popularized by Col. Jeff Cooper, has become a guiding light for CCW practitioners: "An armed society is a polite society." Answering a curse with a curse, or an obscene gesture with a one-finger salute, is no longer your option when you carry a gun.

Another saying among CCW people is, "Concealed

...you learn to reach with the other hand. Similarly, to pick up an object on the ground, you learn to bend at knees instead of waist so the gun at your hip won't "print" through your concealing garment.

certain that your shots fly true. Did you learn to shoot, perhaps even "qualify" with your weapon like a police officer? Or did you just buy it, strap it on, and think it would somehow protect you by itself? Did you become sufficiently skilled with it that, in a state of stress, you could be reasonably and prudently confident of hitting your target and not an innocent bystander? Did you carefully choose ammunition designed to incapacitate a violent attacker, and designed *not* to shoot through and through him and strike a bystander hidden from your view behind him? *Did you become familiar with the laws of your jurisdiction that govern the carrying of firearms and the lawful use of deadly force?*

It's critical that you *learn to draw expeditiously and safely.* A legal gun carrier not instantly recognizable as a Good Guy or Gal, the way a uniformed cop or security guard would be, risks starting a panic if drawing in public. An onlooker perception of "the cop has his gun out, get out of the way" becomes "good Lord, that psycho just pulled a *gun!*" This means that in "iffy circumstances," the plainclothes carrier may have to wait longer to react, putting a premium on drawing speed. In the following pages, we'll emphasize discreet "surreptitious draw" techniques that let you sneak your hand onto the still-hidden gun without frightening the crowds. For the same reason, lack of identifiability, you want

means *concealed.*" Only the rankest rookie cop or first-time permit-holder will allow the handgun to become visible in anything less than an emergency. In professional circles, people who don't follow this rule are sometimes known as gun-flashers, and are looked down upon with only slightly less opprobrium than the other kind of "flashers."

Responsibility comes with CCW. The responsibility to keep that deadly weapon secured from unauthorized children, incompetent guests in the household, and burglars. The responsibility to use the weapon as judiciously as, in the words of the Courts, "a reasonable and prudent person would do, in the same situation..."

If the gun must be drawn and fired to save your life or the lives of others, there is a responsibility to make

to be able to holster that gun smoothly, one-handed, by feel without taking your eyes off the danger in front of you if cops are arriving, because you don't want those tensely responding officers seeing "man with a gun, there now."

Going out and drinking to the point of intoxication in public is not your option if you're carrying a gun. There are places in America where setting foot in a bar stone sober – or, hell, even a liquor store – can cost you your permit and "buy you some time," the latter phrase not in the good sense. There are also places where it's technically legal to get smashed in a gin mill while packing a piece. But there is *no* place in America where that won't get you into very deep trouble if you have to draw the gun in self-defense in that condition.

We who carry guns in public are a minority. We have an unwritten covenant with the rest of society: "You can be assured that we will not endanger you." It's a covenant we must live up to in every way, if we're going to keep the attendant rights and privileges and preserve them for our children and grandchildren.

The practice of CCW comes with a commitment, if you're serious, and that commitment is that you will actually *carry* the damn thing! *Criminal attackers don't make appointments.* The mindset of "I'll only carry it when I think I'll need it" is a false one. I, and anyone my age who's been carrying guns as long as I have, can tell you stories all night of people whose lives were saved because they were carrying guns in places where they didn't think they'd need them. Criminals attack you precisely when you *don't* think you're in a situation where you'll be ready for them. That's what they do for a living. If you are serious, you'll carry your gun like you carry your wallet: daily, constantly, unless it's illegal to do so.

Which brings us to another responsibility: *make sure you're carrying legally!* As you'll see later in these pages, today's situation makes concealed carry legal for more people in more places than at any time in the memory of any living American. If you're in one of those places where legal carry is not possible, I have to advise you, *don't carry there.* Yes, there are people whose lives have been saved by guns they were carrying without benefit of permit. I became, at age 23, one of them. I know more now than I knew at 23, and today, I either wouldn't have been in that place, or would have found a way to legally carry there.

"They won't find out I'm carrying illegally unless I need to use it, and if I need to use it, getting busted for it is the least of my worries." You've heard that, right? Well, *it's a myth!* The likelihood of the gun being found on you after a car crash or medical emergency, the likelihood of it being spotted or felt by someone in contact with you, may be greater than the likelihood of your needing to draw it in self-defense. Remember that in many jurisdictions the first offense of illegally carrying a gun is a felony, often bringing a minimum/mandatory one year imprisonment. And where it's "only a misdemeanor," remember that "only a misdemeanor" means "*only* 364 days in jail." Not to

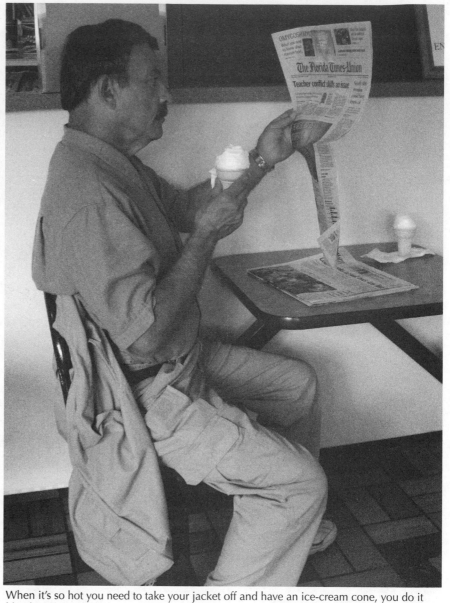

When it's so hot you need to take your jacket off and have an ice-cream cone, you do it like this. (Note that paper is held up to read, so head and danger scan aren't "buried.") Unless you need to stand and reach for it, no one will notice...

mention a firearms-related crime on your record.

Be smart. Be legal. Carry only where the law allows you to do so.

The Price of the Wardrobes

You don't just go to the pawnshop, buy the cheapest handgun they've got, stuff it in your pocket and go. If you are serious about this, there are wardrobes you'll have to acquire. Three wardrobes, in fact.

The wardrobe of clothing. This will be discussed at length in following chapters, but you will find yourself changing your clothing to "dress around the gun" if you're serious about CCW. I didn't get a big charge out of bringing my gun and holster into the tailor shop to get "court suits" made that would conceal a full-size handgun...but I'm glad I did. I don't especially like the look of Dockers-type sport slacks, at least on my body, but they do a great job of hiding guns, and they've become a staple of the "sport coat and tie" section of my wardrobe. When I see myself in the mirror wearing a vest with a short sleeve shirt, I see Ed Norton from the old TV show "The Honeymooners"... but when you carry a full-size pistol and spare ammo in hot weather, believe me, these garments become your new best friend. You learn to appreciate the extra pockets, too.

You'll discover the "two-inch waist range factor." If your waist size is 38, and you carry a handgun inside the waistband, you'll quickly gravitate toward size 40 for comfort. This will also keep you carrying the gun, since *without* that holster, your pants will feel as if they're going to fall down to your ankles. And the day will come when you gain some weight, and decide that an *outside*-the-belt holster is cheaper than a whole new wardrobe of trousers...

The wardrobe of holsters. This book will explain why different holsters work better in different situations. When I pack a suitcase and go on the road for a few weeks of teaching and/or testifying, there will be more than one holster per gun in the suitcase. The pocket holster for the snub-nosed 38 may bulge obviously in the side pocket of the tailored suit-pants, but that same gun may disappear under the "classic suit straight cuff" of the same trousers in an ankle holster. One inside-the-waistband and one outside-the-waistband hip holster will accompany the primary handgun, and if neither of those is ambidextrous, there will also be a weak-side holster in case I sustain an arm or hand injury on the road and can't use the dominant hand. (Been there, done that.) A belly-band holster that doubles as a money belt will go in the suitcase too, and I've been known to toss in a shoulder rig to allow for lower back injuries where I won't want weight on the hips, or a case of intestinal flu that might have me dropping my pants constantly in public rest rooms, a situation where hip holsters are tough (though not impossible) to accommodate.

The wardrobe of guns. I've gotten pretty good at gun concealment over the years, but I've learned that I can't hide a full-size 45 automatic in a swim suit. A good friend of mine carries a little Smith & Wesson J-frame Airweight 38 snub-nose revolver in his, though.

A snub-nose 38 is a great little carry gun, and it's a staple of any CCW "gun wardrobe." However, I've been in a lot of places where I was *way* more comfortable with something bigger, easier to shoot accurately and fast, that held more – and more powerful – ammunition.

You'll find yourself buying more firearms as you get into CCW seriously. Some will suit you, and you will keep them for carry. Some will turn out to be great guns but just too big and heavy, and you may keep them as home defense or even recreational weapons. Some will turn out to not be for you, and you'll trade them in for something that works better. That's all OK.

A small gun that will be there in circumstances where you just *can't* carry a bigger one may still save

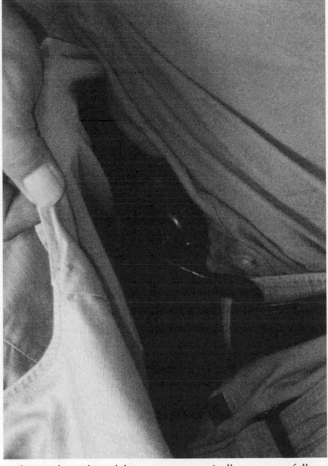

...that you have draped the garment strategically to cover a full-size Beretta police service pistol in a quick-access Dillon holster.

your life. There will be times when a larger gun will give you not only more confidence, but more capability. I've debriefed gunfight survivors who would have died if they'd had only a five-shot 38, but survived because they had something that carried more ammo and let them stay in the fight long enough to win it. So, as time goes on, you'll want at least one small CCW handgun and one larger one. Don't be surprised if, like so many professionals, you find yourself carrying both at once. It's a belt-and-suspenders, "same reason there's a spare tire in my car" kind of thing.

About This Book

This book is not about when you can shoot. That would be *In the Gravest Extreme*. It's not about how to shoot a handgun under stress. That would be *StressFire*. It's not about a total approach to personal safety and crime prevention. That would be *The Truth About Self-Protection*. All three are available from Police Bookshelf, PO Box 122, Concord, NH 03302, (www.ayoob.com). I recommend them, but hell, I *wrote* them, so take the recommendation from whence it comes.

The chapters on guns and holsters are generic. If I don't recommend a particular brand, it doesn't necessarily mean it's a piece of crap; it may just mean that I haven't worked with it long enough to give it a recommendation. Anything I recommend in here by name is something I've tested sufficiently to trust my own life to; I can't do that with every product. I've tested guns that were obviously designed by people who didn't carry them and didn't know how to shoot them, and holsters obviously designed by people who didn't carry concealed handguns. I don't have time to list the junk, nor do I have the time or the financial resources to fight nuisance suits by junk-makers who sue people for telling the truth about their products. If I say it's good, I'm putting my name and reputation on that fact. If I don't mention it, well, I'm just not mentioning it, but remember, there's good stuff out there that I probably just haven't tested yet.

I may be a funnel, but I can't funnel the whole industry.

Some points will be repeated in different chapters. I suppose that reflects a little of the instructor's mantra, "Tell 'em what you're gonna tell 'em; tell 'em; then tell 'em what you told 'em." I think it reflects more the simple reality that in an adult lifetime as an author, I've found that folks read novels straight front to back, but non-fiction books like this a chapter at a time, piece-meal, jumping back and forth. Some points need to be made in context for the sporadic reader.

TV and movie characters are mentioned here a lot. That's because such things have largely defined public perception about concealed carry methods. It needed to be addressed.

In some chapters, you'll see me drawing from under a transparent raincoat. No, I'm not recommending "transparent concealment"! It's a device I hit on to demonstrate concealed draw without hand and weapon being hidden from the learner's view.

In reading this book, it's important to maintain some perspectives.

The *raison d'etre* is important. Carrying a concealed handgun reflects serious understandings about predictable danger in Life, and it brings more serious understandings with it. We'll talk about that.

This book is laid out the way it is for a reason. **Rules of the Road** are important. We'll talk about where you can carry, and where you can't. When you should, and when you shouldn't.

Hardware is important. We'll discuss which handguns have proven themselves best suited for concealed carry for different purposes in different "dress code" situations. Hardware encompasses not only the guns but the holsters, the ammunition, the reloading devices, and other accessories.

Deployment is important. It's amazing, for instance, how many people have designed and sold belly-band holsters but obviously don't know the most effective

ways of either carrying them or drawing from them… not to mention how many people have carried ankle holsters for a career as an armed professional and never learned how to most quickly and efficiently draw from one. Let's see if we can't fix that…

I know it sounds complicated. That's because it *is* complicated. By the time you finish this book, you will have noticed that I've never invoked the currently popular weapons training buzzword that is the "KISS principle." KISS stands for "Keep It Simple, Stupid."

I can't utter that in good conscience, for two reasons.

se your power wisely. Keep your good people safe.

For one thing, I don't think you're stupid.

For another, I know for *damn* sure it ain't simple.

If anybody wants "simple," the simple fact is, a lot of people died for the lessons that were funneled into this book. Some of them were good guys and gals who died only because they didn't know the things the gunfight survivors and master gunfighters gave me to funnel into the words that follow. And we'll never know how many innocent victims died *because they didn't have a gun, right there and right then that they could have drawn from concealment and used to save their lives and others.*

And I think you know that, too, or you wouldn't be reading this.

Within a few days of my deadline for this book, a mass murderer in Colorado hit two religious institutions, and killed people at both. At the first location, he killed innocent people and sauntered away. There was no one there with the wherewithal to stop him.

At the second death scene, he opened fire in the parking lot, and then entered the building. He didn't get thirty feet before he was interdicted by one Jeanne Assam, a member of the church who was licensed to CCW, had her own gun, and knew how to use it. She shot him down like the mad dog he was, and in his last bullet-riddled moments the only person he could still shoot was himself. He died. No more innocent people did. Jeanne Assam had taught a lesson to us all.

On the pro-gun side, people started posting on the Internet the story of Charl van Wyck, a story I had put into this manuscript months before. I can only hope that the general public will look at both Assam's story *and* Van Wyck's, and the lessons that came before. I am sure – sadly sure – that similar lessons will be written in blood after this book is published.

Thank you for taking the time to read what follows. Thank you for having the courage to be the sheepdog prepared to fight the wolves back away from the lambs. I hope you find the following pages useful.

Use your power wisely. Keep your good people safe.

WHY WE CARRY

The question is constantly asked, "Why do you want to carry a gun?" Here are several proven answers.

Forty-eight of America's fifty states now have at least some provision for law-abiding private citizens to carry loaded, concealed handguns in public. This comes as a shock to many people in American society. Those responsible adults who choose to avail themselves of the concealed carry privilege will constantly be challenged as to this decision by friends, family, co-workers, and others who have not been educated on the issues involved. This is one reason it is always sensible to be extremely discreet about concealed carry, and to not broadcast the fact that one goes legally armed.

At the same time, the old phrase "forewarned

Why do we carry? Ask Dr. Suzanna Gratia-Hupp, photographed here while testifying for concealed carry legislation. She watched her parents murdered during the Luby's Cafeteria massacre in Killeen, Texas, helpless to stop the gunman only a few feet away, because law of the period forced her to leave her revolver outside in her car.

is forearmed" applies to the argument as well as the practice itself. Those of us who've had to debate the issue repeatedly, in forums ranging from State Houses where reform concealed carry legislation was on the floor to radio, TV, and print media, have learned that the best response is often a "sound bite." A good sound bite is short, memorable, and so logical that the listener tends to ask himself, "Why didn't I think of that?"

The following effective sound bite answers to the most common challenges against concealed carry have been proven to work time and again. As done here, always be able to back them up with more

A much younger Ayoob with one of his kids, today an adult and a parent herself. Here, she's learning about ammunition. In her late teens, she won a national handgun championship title…and not long after, used her legally-carried handgun to defend herself successfully against two large male rape suspects on a city street.

detail. Keep it logical, and always, *always* apply common sense.

> *"Why do you carry a gun?"*
>
> **Kathy Jackson said it best on her website (www.corneredcat.com): "I carry a gun because I can't carry a policeman."**

It is generally accepted that the population of this country is approximately three hundred million, and that there are only a bit over 700,000 currently serving police officers. By their nature, wolves attack sheep when the sheepdog isn't there, and criminals are careful to make sure there are no police officers in sight when they attack their victims. This leaves the victim alone to fend for himself or herself.

Carrying a concealed handgun in public is very much like keeping a small fire extinguisher in your car. Neither means that by possessing it, you become an official member of the public safety community. Neither means that you don't need public safety personnel from the fire department or the police department.

But the concealed handgun and the fire extinguisher are each emergency rescue tools designed to allow first responders to crisis to hold the line against death and injury, to control things and save lives, until the designated professionals can get to the scene to do what they're paid to do. That's all the responsibly

carried concealed handgun is: emergency rescue equipment for use by a competent first responder, who in this case, often turns out to be the intended victim of intentional, violent crime.

> *"But aren't you worried that if more people carry guns, more arguments will escalate into people being shot and killed?"*
>
> **No. Responsible gun owners are too practical to worry about things that don't happen.**

Ever since the 1980s, when Florida started the trend of reform legislation that replaced the elitism and cronyism of the old "discretionary" permit system with the modern, enlightened "shall issue" model, opponents of self-protection and civil liberties have made the argument that "blood would run in the streets." It hasn't happened yet. If anything, statistics show that violent crime against the person seems to go *down* after shall-issue legislation is passed.

In the wake of the recent confirmation of this by Minnesota's experience with their fledgling shall-issue permit system, my old friend Joe Waldron of the Citizens' Committee for the Right to Keep and Bear Arms (CCRKBA) put it as well as it's ever been said. The Committee had noted, "According to the (Minneapolis Star Tribune) newspaper, people with gun permits are far less likely to be involved in a crime, whether it is a physical assault, a drug crime or even drunken driving. Authorities have confirmed that the hysterical predictions about gunfights at traffic stops and danger to children simply have not materialized."

Commented Waldron, executive director of the CCRKBA, "You will not hear an apology or any kind of acknowledgement from the anti-self-defense crowd about the statistics. No doubt they will try to blame the law for crimes committed by people carrying guns illegally. But the newspaper did a good job of sorting out fact from fiction, and it has found that only a miniscule number of licensed citizens have been involved in serious crimes, and a tiny fraction of armed citizens have had their permits revoked.

"We knew all along what Hennepin County Sheriff Rich Stanek told the newspaper: the worst predictions of gun control advocates who bitterly fought to keep this law off the books just haven't come true. We're delighted that the press, which did not support the law, has at least acknowledged the public's right to know how the law is working.

"Minnesota is just one more state where people have been given the opportunity to pass a law and see how it really works. The state's legally-armed citizens have proven not only that they are overwhelmingly responsible with firearms, the data shows that providing the means for citizens to go armed is not a threat to public safety, and never has been."

Concluded Waldron, "The Personal Protection Act (in Minnesota) has succeeded in destroying the myth that legally-armed citizens are somehow a threat to the general public. We knew they were wrong, and now everybody else knows it, too."

> *"Why should a person who lives in a low crime area feel they had to carry a gun?"*
>
> **Famed combat small arms instructor John Farnam said it best. He was teaching an officer survival class to rural police when one officer asked him, "Hey, how often do you think cops get killed around here, anyway?" Farnam's reply was classic: "Same as anywhere. Just once."**

In the 19th century, Coffeyville, Kansas and Northfield, Minnesota were quiet, safe towns where no one might have thought ordinary citizens needed guns…until they were robbed by violent, professional robbery gangs from "out of town." One of those gangs was led by Jesse James and Cole Younger, and the other consisted primarily of the infamous Dalton brothers. Both gangs were shot to pieces by armed townsfolk acting in defense of themselves and their communities.

In the early 20th century, the automobile allowed criminals to range even more widely. The John Dillinger/Baby Face Nelson gangs made a specialty of robbing small town banks and escaping in their high-speed Hudsons and Ford V8s. They, too, felt the sting of armed citizens' gunfire. When robbing a bank in South Bend, Indiana, Baby Face Nelson and Homer Van Meter, both hardened cop-killers, were shot and wounded by a jeweler with a .22 target handgun. Nelson was saved by his bullet proof vest, and Van Meter, while knocked senseless by the bullet that ricocheted off his skull, would have been killed if the shooter's aim had been truer by an inch, or if the armed citizen had launched a more appropriate round. In another bank robbery, John Dillinger and accomplice John Hamilton were each shot in the right shoulder by a retired judge, armed with an antique revolver and firing from a window across the street.

Now, in the 21st century, little has changed. Criminals are highly mobile. They have learned that "the thin blue line" is thinnest in the hinterlands. Police in rural communities can tell you that many of their major crimes are committed by criminals from cities who "commute to the crime scene." And any small town cop can tell you that even "Mayberry, RFD" can grow its own violent criminals without any outside help.

The smaller the town, the more rural your location, the longer it generally takes police to respond to an emergency call. Thus, while in the big picture there may be fewer crimes committed in "low crime communities,"

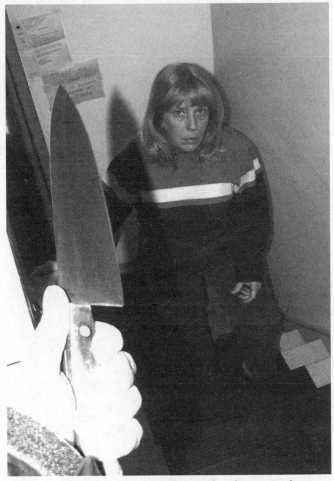

Why carry a gun? Suppose you're a petite female, coming home alone, and are confronted by a knife-armed attacker…

that doesn't make them safe by any means…and, more remote from police assistance, the potential victim in such an area has all the more need to be self-sufficient in terms of being able to protect self and loved ones from nomadic criminals.

> *"Why can't you face the fact that a study has proven that a gun in the home is 43 times more likely to kill a member of the household than a burglar?"*
>
> **Probably because, being logical people, most of us who carry guns detest having to look at such fact-twisting exercises in sophistry.**

"Discredited" is a strong word, but the study in question is indeed one of the most thoroughly discredited exercises in twisted statistics of the late 20th century. It compared all deaths by gunfire in two communities of similar size, one in Canada and one in the United States. Under "guns killing householders," it included suicides, many of which typically are the so-called "rational suicide." This is what happens

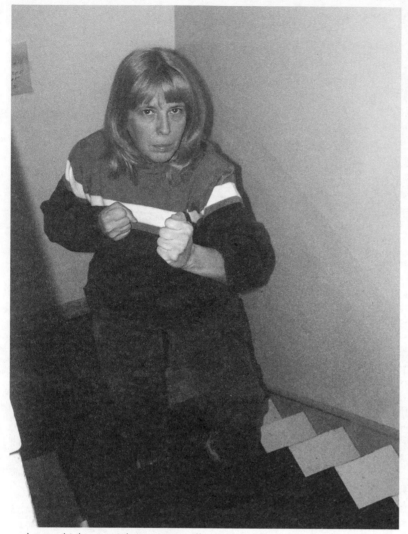

...do you think a martial arts stance will ward him off? Or...

each country in the "study" were not taken into consideration. There is simply less violent crime in Canada than in the US, by virtually every measurement, including measurements that factor out possession of firearms.

All told, then, the "43 times more likely" story will be remembered by history as a classic example of how to lie with statistics, how to conveniently manipulate the truth, and how to misinterpret reality. Its proper place would be in a book of "Dirty Debate Tricks That Won't Work in the Long Run," not in any logical discussion of concealed carry that is subjected to critical thinking and honest, fact-based debate.

> *"A review of strategy discussions on Internet gun boards reveals the fact that many people who are licensed to carry guns carry more than one. If this is not an indication of two-gun cowboy mentality, how else can it be explained?"*
>
> **Firearms instructor and author David Kenik was once asked, "Why do you carry three guns?" He calmly replied, "Because four would be ostentatious."**

when an individual diagnosed with a terminal disease that brings a long, agonizing death chooses to depart life with dignity. (In some foreign countries, this process is assisted by state-approved euthanasia, not an option in the USA.)

That study's use of human body count as the ultimate arbiter of a complicated social issue poisoned its results in and of itself. The fact is that most law-abiding citizens who confront criminals and take them at gunpoint, *don't* have to kill them. The latest studies, by Professor John Lott, indicate that in well over 90 percent of such incidents, the felon either flees or submits to citizen's arrest when taken at gunpoint by his intended victim, and none of his blood is shed. The oft-quoted bogus study interprets this benevolent lack of bloodshed 180 degrees away from reality, as if the object of the exercise had been to kill intruders and anything less than a "kill" didn't count for the "good guys." How ironic...a hypocritical attempt to measure safety from murder by body count.

The Federal government's own statistics, at this writing, show that the United States is at an all-time low in gun-related fatal accidents.

Gun ownership quite aside, the cultural mores of

The simple fact is, armed citizens to a large degree make their choice of defensive firearms based on the model of the domestic law enforcement sector. For generations, when the 38 Special revolver was the overwhelming choice of American police, it was also the overwhelming choice of armed citizens. Though freedom of choice allowed the citizenry to carry autoloading pistols before those guns became popular with police, the general replacement of the service revolver with the service pistol in American police work greatly increased the popularity of the semiautomatic pistol in the private sector.

Similarly, the last several decades have seen a vast increase in the number of police officers who carry backup handguns on duty. A number of police departments even issue a second handgun to all sworn personnel for just this purpose. Not surprisingly, the armed citizenry has modeled on this as well, and for the same good reasons.

Any firearm can run out of ammunition, malfunction, be dropped by a wounded "good guy," or be snatched from its legitimate user. In all those cases, recourse to a second handgun is the fastest avenue – and often the *only* avenue – to last-ditch survival.

Just off the top of my head, I can think of at least seven cases where recourse to another immediately-

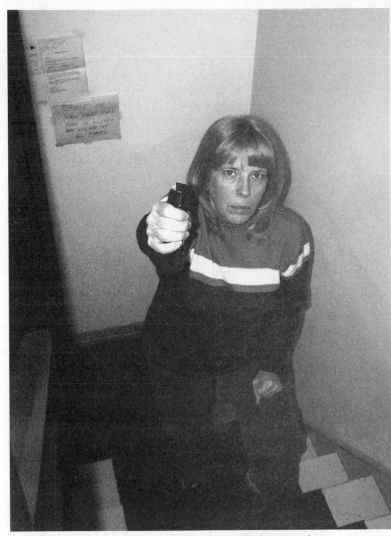

...perhaps this can of pepper spray? Or do you think just maybe ...

For example, at this writing I am spending time with my girlfriend in one of America's largest cities. This particular metropolis has many attractions, but it is also a notoriously high crime area. The lady in question is highly competent with a handgun, in fact is a current regional IDPA (International Defensive Pistol Association) champion, but as it happens, while I am legal to carry in this particular jurisdiction, she is not.

I am carrying a 9mm SIG-Sauer pistol on my dominant side hip, and a 38 Special snub-nose revolver in a pocket holster on my non-dominant side. She is perfectly competent with either. Should danger threaten, the common law principle as recognized by state law in this particular jurisdiction would allow me to arm her due to exigent circumstances. Thus, there would be two trained and equipped "threat managers" capable of dealing with the situation, instead of just one.

"You bloodthirsty gun people only carry weapons because you want a chance to hurt or kill someone!"

On the contrary, we carry guns so we will be *less* likely to have to kill or cripple someone. It's called "Peace Through Superior Firepower."

available weapon saved the life of a private citizen caught up in a gunfight. In three of those seven instances, the primary defensive handgun had been snatched away by a homicidal criminal, and the second gun saved the life of the law-abiding citizen, who in each case was able to deploy the backup weapon quickly and effectively. In each of the other four instances, the primary handgun had run dry while shooting it out with armed criminals, and because reloading the empty gun was impractical or even impossible under the circumstances, the ability to instantly transition to a second loaded handgun literally made the difference between life and death.

There is another area in which having a second weapon on one's person can make a huge difference to law-abiding armed citizens when deadly danger threatens. In the "concealed carry community," there are a great many people who only actually carry guns part of the time. The carrying of a back-up handgun allows one competent armed citizen to arm another citizen, who might be equally competent but, at the moment, unarmed in the face of suddenly breaking danger.

History has shown that the greatest power of the gun is its power to *deter*. Bear in mind that criminals, by definition, target only victims they believe they can overpower. When the intended victim draws a gun, the predator realizes that their erstwhile target has the ability to kill them instantly. This tends to modify their behavior immediately, without a shot being fired.

Remember the Lott study, referenced above, which showed in the 1990s that the overwhelming majority of times a citizen drew a gun to ward off a criminal, the incident ended with no blood being shed on either side of the encounter. The studies of famed criminologist Gary Kleck showed the same thing in the 1980s. A study by the California Attorney General's Office in the 1970s showed it, too.

Another way to see it is to simply take the gun out of the picture, and examine the remaining alternatives. When asked about self-protection, opponents of gun ownership rights will typically suggest pepper spray or an unarmed combat class. Let's look at how well that has worked on the street for police, who have the strongest pepper spray and some of the best unarmed combat training.

While pepper spray certainly has its place at the

...this 9mm SIG P239 is the likeliest of all to deter him with no bloodshed on either side, or at worst, stop him decisively before he reaches her with his knife?

Contrast this with a victim who draws a gun and is obviously prepared to immediately open fire. The difference in deterrent effect is literally night and day. In terms of body language, a shooting stance with a drawn firearm is the ultimate exclamation point.

Thus, we have an ironic reality. The person who is not armed with a deadly weapon will very likely have to kill or cripple a determined attacker to defeat the threat. By contrast, the person who is armed with a deadly weapon is *hugely* more likely to be able to end the threat with no physical injury on either side, due to the tremendous deterrent effect offered by their legally carried firearm.

> *"You don't have any right to carry guns anyway! The Second Amendment is about the National Guard, not personal protection!"*
>
> **The Bill of Rights was framed shortly after the American Revolution. A "National Guard" in the time of the revolution would have been Tories loyal to King George and duty-bound to crush the American patriots. Do you really think this was what the framers intended to empower and enable?**

lower levels of the force continuum, it has never been seriously put forth by police or other protection professionals as adequate for dealing with an armed antagonist. In fact, law enforcement history is rife with criminals so violent that pepper spray had no effect on them, and they did not stop their violent aggression after being sprayed until after officers had been forced to shoot them, or strike them with batons so many times that they had been permanently injured.

Attending any women's rape prevention class or basic self-defense class, one will be taught to attack the assailant's genitals, eyes, or throat, or to pick up some object and strike him repeatedly in the head. We are talking about crushed testicles, eyes gouged out, suffocation, and fractured skulls resulting in profound brain injuries. All these results fit in the category of life-threatening trauma and/or grave bodily harm: a deadly force level of injury. Deadly force is deadly force, whether delivered with bare hands, clubbed objects, *or* a deadly weapon per se.

The big difference is deterrent effect. It is greatly lacking with "lesser weapons." In one notorious case, a rapist murdered two women because, he said later, he became enraged when one of them sprayed him with a Mace-like substance. A violent aggressor is likely to do little more than laugh if an intended victim he perceives to be smaller or weaker than himself squares off in a martial arts stance.

The American Bill of Rights may be the most carefully crafted delineation of individual rights in the history of the human experience. It strains credibility to the breaking point to ask thinking people to believe that somehow, those who wrote it accidentally included a "state's rights" issue near the top of the list. The Bill of Rights was drawn largely from the constitutions of the existing colonies that preceded it, many of which are absolutely explicit about the right to bear arms being an individual right, not a collective one, and many of which expressly include personal and family protection among the reasons for ensuring that right. Anyone who doubts this has not done his homework. Even opponents of individual firearms ownership have admitted, after reviewing the vast body of Constitutional scholarship, that the Second Amendment was indeed originally intended to be an individual right.

The arguments will not be concluded within the lifetimes of anyone reading this. The debate has become too emotional and too polarized. Those persons who have accepted the responsibility for their safety and the safety of those who count on them can only stand prepared to defend, not only innocent lives, but the very practice of carrying weapons to fulfill those responsibilities.

Chapter 3

WHERE YOU CAN *(AND CAN'T)* CARRY

Article II

A well regulated Militia, being necessary to the security of a free State, the right of the people to keep and bear Arms, shall not be infringed.

When and where to carry a gun is a little like when and where to go nude. In either case, there will be times and places where you'll find it comfortable, and even times and places where others will be happy that you're in that condition. However, there are also times and places where it will be inappropriate, offensive, and even illegal.

Houses of Worship

I remember going to church one Sunday with my older sister when I was a little

Many like to believe that the *"bear arms"* portion of Second Amendment means that the Bill of Rights is all they need for concealed carry. Not in this world. If that sweet little Kahr Elite MK9 is to be carried concealed, you have to be within the law!

kid, and being shocked and even outraged when a state trooper who worked that area came in and sat in the pew in front of us, with his big 6 ½" barrel Smith & Wesson Model 27 357 Magnum swinging in plain view in its flapped swivel holster. How dare he bring a deadly weapon into a house of worship!

There has been a lot of water under the bridge since that Sunday, and I have totally changed my view on the topic.

A few years ago, a maniac walked into a religious service being held in a

In recent years, great advances have been made for concealed carry rights in Midwestern states, but the two worst states for CCW are in that region also. Pistol is the handy, effective 9mm EMP from Springfield Armory.

hotel conference room in Wisconsin. He opened fire, and committed mass murder before killing himself. He apparently assumed, correctly, that in a state which had no provision for private citizens to carry concealed handguns in public, no one could stop him from carrying out his monstrous plan. That was exactly how things turned out.

In Texas, not long after then-Governor George W. Bush signed shall-issue concealed carry into law, the law was modified to allow permit-holders to be armed in places of worship. A mass murderer entered a church in Fort Worth, scouted around until he found a prayer meeting peopled exclusively by teenagers, and opened fire there, exacting a terrible toll in human tragedy. He apparently knew that elsewhere in the church, there just might be armed, responsible adults who would shoot back and put him in jeopardy. He carefully selected the one sub-group of victims who, too young to have carry permits under Texas law, would be helpless.

On the West Coast, a rabid anti-Semite looked for Jews to murder. He later admitted that he thought about hitting a synagogue, but feared someone might be armed and shoot back. So, instead, he committed

mass murder in a Jewish day care center. This is typical of cowards: they seek unarmed, helpless victims.

All over the world, terrorists have learned that to strike terror literally into the souls of those they intend to intimidate, mass murder at a religious center can get the morbid attention they seek. Militant Islamists have murdered those of other belief systems at houses of worship from the Middle East to Pakistan, and a mad Israeli military reservist killed several innocent Muslims when he opened fire at a mosque. Clergyman Peter Hammond of South Africa lists the following series of terroristic mass murders at churches in his foreword to Charl van Wyk's book, *Shooting Back*. (Christian Liberty Books, Cape Town, South Africa, 2001.)

"When I saw the shocking carnage at St. James Church (in Kenilworth, South Africa), it immediately brought similar bloody scenes flooding back into my mind," wrote Hammond. "Over the last 19 years of missionary work I have personally come across scores of similar atrocities, in Angola, Mozambique, Rwanda and Sudan. In August 1983, Frelimo troops killed 5 pastors and burnt down all 5 churches in Maskito Village, Zambezia Province, Mozambique. In September 1983, Frelimo troops killed over 50

first the armed man knew about the attack, was when he woke up the next morning to find the base deserted. He later discovered the bodies of his fellow missionaries on the sports field. Gun-free is no guarantee."

The author of the book *Shooting Back: The Right and Duty of Self-Defence*, Charl van Wyk, was in the St. James church that terrible day when the terrorists opened fire. Here is his own account:

He wrote, "Grenades were exploding in flashes of light. Pews shattered under the blasts, sending splinters flying through the air. An automatic assault rifle was being fired and was fast ripping the pews – and whomever, whatever was in its trajectory – to pieces. We were being attacked!

"Instinctively, I knelt down behind the bench in front of me and pulled out my 38 Special snub-nosed revolver, which I always carried with me. I would have felt undressed without it. Many people could not understand why I would carry a firearm into a church service, but I argued that this was a particularly dangerous time in South Africa…

"…Well my moment of truth had arrived, I thought, as my hands steadied around the revolver. The congregation had thrown themselves down – in order to protect themselves as far as possible from the deluge of flying bullets and shrapnel. By God's grace, the view of the terrorists from my seat, fourth row from the back of the church, was perfect. The building was built like a cinema with the floor sloping towards the stage in front. So without any hesitation, I knelt and aimed, firing two shots at the attackers. This appeared ineffective, as my position was too far from my targets to take precise aim with a snub-nosed revolver. I had to get closer to the terrorists.

"So I started moving to the end of the pew on my haunches and leopard-crawled the rest of the way when I realized that my position was too high up. The only way I could make those heartless thugs stop their vicious attack was to try and move in behind them and then shoot them in the back at close range.

"I sprinted to the back door of the church, pushing a lady out of the way, so that I could kick the door open and not be hindered as I sought to get behind the gunmen to neutralize their attack. As I desperately rounded the corner of the building, outside in the parking area, I saw a man standing next to what was the 'getaway' car. Resting on his hip was his

Where the laws aren't right, work for change! Author leaves Wisconsin State House in Madison after testifying for shall-issue concealed carry. Bill passed Legislature, but when anti-gun governor vetoed it, gun owners' civil rights forces fell one vote short of over-ride.

Christians and burned a church in Pasura village. At Chilleso Evangelical Church, in Angola, Cuban troops shot 150 Christians during a church service. At New Adams Farm in Zimbabwe, 16 missionaries and their children were murdered in November 1987…On 23 June 1978, terrorists who supported Robert Mugabe murdered nine British missionaries and four young children, including a three-week old baby, at the Elim Mission Station."

Added Hammond, "It is worth noting that the only British missionary at the Elim Mission Station who had a firearm – he owned a 38 revolver – was also the only survivor! Being cowards, the terrorists left him alone, preferring defenceless victims. The

automatic rifle. He had it pointed up to the heavens as if in defiance of the Lordship of Jesus Christ!

"The man was looking in the direction of the door through which they had launched their attack. Was he waiting for people who would make easy targets to come running out, or maybe even for me? I stepped back behind the corner of the wall and prepared to blast the last of my firepower. I strode out in full view of the terrorist and shot my last three rounds. By this time, the others were already in the car. My target jumped into the vehicle and the driver sped away immediately, leaving behind the acrid stench of burning tyres and exhaust fumes..."

Elsewhere in this book, we discuss such factors as the selected carry gun's ammunition capacity, and the carrying of spare ammunition. In this case, van Wyk's five-shot revolver was now empty, but it is telling to examine his first thoughts in the immediate aftermath. Wrote van Wyk, "It's hard to express my feelings as I watched them drive away, but I remember thinking, 'Lord, why haven't I got more ammunition? Why? Why? Why?'"

It turned out that one of van Wyk's shots had wounded one of the terrorists, one Khaya Christopher Makoma, and his first two rounds of return fire had been enough to send the assassins fleeing with their AK47s. At least that was the assessment of the South African Police, never a pro-gun organization, when it issued van Wyk a commendation for his actions. The award read, "Mr. Charl Adriaan van Wyk is hereby commended for outstanding services rendered in that he: on 25 July 1993 endangered his own life in warding off the attack perpetrated on the St. James Congregation in Kenilworth. His action in pursuing the suspects on foot and returning fire prevented further loss of life. One of the suspects wounded in the incident was later arrested."

In some jurisdictions, a sign like this means the same as "CCW Illegal Here!"

It is generally accepted that it is illegal for a private citizen to wear a gun in a U.S. Post Office, irrespective of concealed carry permits.

Charl van Wyk, like many others, cites Biblical confirmation of his choice to be armed. **Proverbs 25:26:** "Like a muddied spring or a polluted well is a righteous man who gives way to the wicked." **Luke 22:36:** "If thou hast not a sword, sell thy cloak and buy one." (This particular quote was a favorite of my old friend Harlon Carter, the dynamic president of the National Rifle Association.) **Nehemiah 4:14:** "Don't be afraid of them. Remember the Lord who is great and awesome, and fight for your brothers, your sons and your daughters, your wives and your homes." **Exodus 22:2:** "If a thief is caught breaking in and is struck so that he dies, the defender is not guilty of bloodshed."

Remember that in the original Hebrew, the Sixth Commandment is not "Thou shalt not kill," but "Thou shalt not commit murder." That is, thou shalt not kill with evil intent.

I have trained many clergymen over the years, most of them the religious leaders of their particular parish or synagogue. One was a Bishop of the Catholic church. Most (not all, but most) of these particular

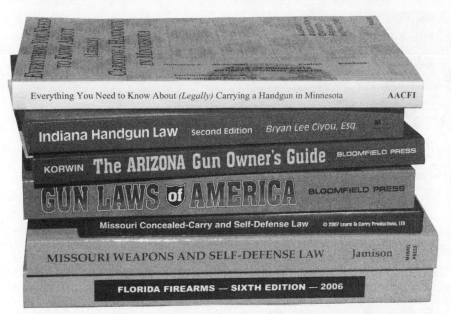

There are gun law compendia for many states, but remember that the laws are constantly changing. Review them, but update constantly!

of the educators' associations, who totally opposed the idea. No one, he scoffed, had ever heard of such a suggestion.

I then explained how the Israeli schools have had this system in place since the Maalot massacre of schoolchildren by terrorists in the mid-1970s, and had effectively put an end to such problems. The plainclothes bodyguards were volunteer parents and grandparents as well as teachers, all trained by the Israeli civil guard. When host Matt Lauer sarcastically asked if the plan would include assault weapons, I replied that the discreetly concealed 9mm semiautomatic pistols of the Israelis had worked just fine.

Similar concepts are in place in Peru, the Philippines, and elsewhere. We've also seen proof of the efficacy of an armed citizen response in school shootings in the United States. In Pearl, Mississippi a twisted teen named Luke Woodham stabbed his mother to death to get the key to his estranged father's gun cabinet, and the next morning showed up at school with a 30-30 deer rifle. He opened fire, with fatal results. As Woodham ran to

padres were scrupulous about making it clear to me that the utmost confidentiality was necessary in regard to their training. It was obvious why that was, but it was a Bishop who said it best. "If it was to get out that I carried a gun every day," said the Bishop, "I would end up as the parish priest in Flat Rock, Iowa."

In some jurisdictions, houses of worship are off-limits for legal concealed carry. In others, it may be OK to carry there in the eyes of the law, but forbidden by that particular church's policy. In some states, you can lose your permit for carrying in a place that is "posted" against the practice. In others, there is no penalty for ignoring a "no-guns" policy, but if your weapon is spotted, you can expect to be asked to leave. If you do not comply, you can then be arrested for "trespass after warning," and in addition to that particular offense, your permit to carry may now be in jeopardy.

Stay within the law, and use common sense. It ain't all about "praise the Lord and pass the ammunition."

Carrying in Schools

The series of mass murders in American schools in the last few years, particularly the atrocity at Columbine High School in Littleton, Colorado in 1999 and the one at Virginia Tech in 2007, have brought up the issue of whether teachers or other school personnel should be armed on campus. The issue has raised some heated discussions on both sides.

Shortly after the Columbine incident, I was called by the *Wall Street Journal* and asked to write a short essay for their op-ed page on the topic, in which I came out strongly for a policy that would allow for volunteer teachers and other staff to be specially trained and authorized to carry concealed handguns while at school. TV's *Today Show* got hold of it, and invited me to appear opposite a spokesman for one

"In the place/That has the steeple/They may not welcome/ Pistol-packin' people."

In most jurisdictions, concealed carry is illegal in courthouses. Check the laws in any jurisdiction where you carry.

the armed offender at gunpoint, at which time he instantly gave up.

The reality is as obvious as a corpse on display in a funeral home casket. Guns in the hands of good people stop armed bad people from committing mass murder. "Gun-free zones" literally become hunting preserves for the psychopaths who hunt humans.

Federal Buildings

As a general rule, Federal buildings are off-limits for private citizens with firearms, concealed carry permits notwithstanding. If you feel a compelling need to carry a gun in one of those places and don't want to take this advice, phone the office you wish to visit and ask them about their policy. In the unlikely event that they tell you "Sure, it's OK to carry here," get something in writing on Government letterhead with a signature from a responsible individual.

The place most folks with permits especially want to carry is, of course, the Post Office. It's the one office of the Federal government that the private citizen most frequently visits. There has been a great deal of controversy over this issue. Some people interpret the wording of the regulation that generally prohibits firearms from such places as exempting permit-holders. There are others who consider that interpretation to be wishful thinking.

I have occasion to enter Post Office branches all over this country, and there is generally a sign present (sometimes conspicuous, sometimes not) stating flatly that firearms are not permitted on these premises. Stating later in court that what you read on this or that electronic gun forum on the Internet saying you could carry in Post Offices, carried more weight in your mind than a sign posted by that Office flatly prohibiting carry there, is not going to put you in great shape if you are arrested by security there for illegal CCW.

My advice to private citizens is conservative, and simple: "Don't carry a gun inside the United States Post Office, or any other Federal building.

Courthouses

I don't personally know of any courthouses anymore where the private citizen can carry a gun around inside. In a handful of jurisdictions (check *carefully* to see if yours is one) it is legal for the

his car, assistant principal Joel Myrick ran to his, and retrieved a compact Colt Officers 45ACP automatic. He confronted the escaping Woodham, who crawled out of his car and cravenly surrendered. The young murderer had been heading in the direction of a nearby junior high school, still in possession of the death weapon and an ample supply of ammunition.

In Pennsylvania, another crazy punk kid opened fire with a small caliber pistol at an off-grounds school affair. The owner of the venue grabbed a shotgun from his office and took the vicious little punk at gunpoint. The latter, of course, surrendered, and a massacre was very likely averted. In Virginia, a mass shooting at a law school was aborted when two adult students drew their own handguns and took

Most jurisdictions forbid carry of concealed weapons at school sporting events.

A majority of jurisdictions forbid private carry of handguns at schools. Author would like to see this change to the proven-safer Israeli paradigm.

armed citizen to actually check his or her gun into a lockbox at Courthouse Security when they enter, and retrieve it when they leave. These, unfortunately, are few and far between. I have also seen court security personnel literally become hysterical when someone simply asked them about the legality of firearms in the courthouse. ("Oh, my God! A gun! Do you have a gun? *Do you have a gun?!?")*

When in doubt, call Security at the Courthouse in question, and get it sorted out clearly beforehand. Make sure they understand that you are a private citizen with a carry permit, and not a police officer.

Federal Courthouses in particular take guns very seriously. If you are carrying your gun when you walk through the front door and ask the guards at the metal detectors if you can check your gun, *you're already in violation because you're already inside the courthouse proper.*

Carrying a gun at church is no longer unthinkable, in jurisdictions where it is not expressly forbidden. In a case that happened as this book went to press, an armed citizen gunned down a heavily armed mass murderer at a religious center and saved countless lives.

Here's a question for the teacher: in jurisdictions where you're legal to have a gun in your glove box but can't carry one any place where alcoholic beverages are sold, where do you stand legally when you visit this drive-through beer store?

For all these reasons, the general rule of thumb is, "Don't bring a gun to the courthouse." If the gun is evidence, talk to the attorney who summoned you there, and he will go through the process of getting the gun brought in, turned over to Security, and brought to the courtroom and back out at the appropriate time.

Alcoholic Beverage Establishments

Gunpowder and alcohol can obviously be a pretty scary mixture. Different jurisdictions handle that in different ways. I used to enjoy visiting the Shortstop, a tavern on LA's Sunset Boulevard. It was the model for the bar Joe Wambaugh called The House of Misery in his novel, *The Black Marble*. It was a cop bar. Most times I was in there, there were probably only three or four people in the place that weren't carrying guns.

At this writing (2007), it is perfectly legal to carry your gun into a tavern in Massachusetts or New Hampshire, and have a drink or two, if you have a CCW permit. Obviously, if you get drunk and do something stupid with the gun, you can expect to go to prison. It's your responsibility to be, well, *responsible*.

In one case I was called in on recently, a Massachusetts CCW-holder dropped in at his favorite watering spot, and didn't even have time for one drink

In most jurisdictions, your carry permit allows you to be armed in a Wal-Mart...but not in New Mexico if that particular store sells alcoholic beverages.

Ending up here for a CCW error would be a very bad thing...

...but ending up here because you were helpless is an even worse outcome. Proper planning, mind-set, and knowing the right thing to do can keep you out of both places.

If jurisdiction's prevailing law says "no guns in county or municipal buildings," check to see where that leaves you when you visit the public library.

Not long ago, a New Hampshire man was having a quiet drink in a city bar, when a weirdo pulled out a gun with murder clearly on his mind. The citizen, licensed to carry his little Kel-Tec "rat gun," drew and shot him. The offender lived, but after being shot gave up his attempts to hurt innocent people and focused solely on surviving his gunshot injuries. To the best of my knowledge, at this writing, the armed citizen who shot him has not been criminally charged. He, too, had a permit and was perfectly legal to carry while drinking moderately and responsibly...*in that jurisdiction.*

In our nation's patchwork quilt of state-by-state laws, things change depending where you are. In North Carolina, you can't even carry your gun into a restaurant that has a liquor license, even if you're not drinking. The same is true in Virginia, with one exception: you can "open carry" a handgun in a restaurant with a liquor license, and even while consuming alcohol in a bar! Indeed, the VCDL (Virginia Citizens' Defense League) considers the "good restaurant access" factor to be one of the strongest pillars of their advocacy of open handgun carry. One night while teaching a lethal force class in Richmond, some VCDL members took me to the bar at an Outback to make a point. Most were conspicuously carrying handguns in unconcealed holsters. They were not hassled. I couldn't help but notice, though, that the customers at one table nervously summoned a waiter and pointed, with frightened expressions, at the Glock 21 45 automatic on the hip of one VCDL member. The waiter explained that it was legal, and he was sorry, but there was nothing he could do about it.

Then you have the state of Florida, where at this writing, you can suck up all the booze you want in a *restaurant* with a liquor license. However, if the *maitre 'd* says, "Your table will be ready in a few minutes; you can wait in the bar," the second you step over that threshold you're committing a Class IV Felony, and your automatic loss of your concealed carry privilege will be the least of your problems. In that state, even if you are not consuming alcohol, you are forbidden to have your gun in any premises that makes more than 50% of its income from serving alcohol by the drink.

In Texas, not only can't you pack in a bar or a restaurant with a liquor license, you can't even enter a liquor store with your gun on to purchase a bottle

before a man he well knew to be a viciously brutal bully began harassing a local woman. The armed citizen stepped in, and became the object of the bully's wrath. Bouncers intervened and kept the bully, who was known locally as "Killer," from attacking the permit holder.

They all left the bar separately, a few minutes apart, the armed citizen leaving last. He was carrying a Beretta 40 in a hip holster under his sweatshirt. As he drove away, he saw a man violently attacking a woman. Pulling over, he saw it was the bully and the woman from the bar, whom the bully had been strangling moments before. He jumped out of his car and ordered the man to let her go. The bully threw her to the ground, screamed "I'll kill you!" and lunged at the CCW holder, who by now had drawn his Beretta. He fired one shot. The assailant went down, mortally wounded, and the rescuer survived a more than three-year legal nightmare that culminated with his acquittal of all the charges (Murder, Manslaughter, and Aggravated Assault) that were lodged against him. If he had not been carrying his gun (legally, under that state's laws) both he and the woman he saved might have been killed or profoundly injured.

of wine to bring home, unopened, for dinner. The same is true in New Mexico. A few years ago in the Albuquerque area, a madman with a knife attacked a woman in a local Wal-Mart and nearly murdered her. He was plunging his knife into her as an armed citizen leaned over the counter with a licensed-to-carry semiautomatic pistol, and shot him dead. All including the victim, who survived, realized he had saved her life. Alas, anti-gun organizations pushed for his prosecution on the grounds that he was illegally carrying the gun, because Wal-Marts typically sell carry-out alcoholic beverages. What saved this heroic gentleman was the fact that he was in the one Wal-Mart in the area that *didn't* have a liquor license.

The lesson is clear. *Know the law regarding the carry of firearms in alcoholic beverage establishments, in the community you happen to be in at the moment.* There is no national standard.

The simplest and most logical course of action is to *stay the hell out of bars when you're carrying a gun.* Even simpler and more logical, *just stay the hell out of bars.*

One of my mentors was the late, great Lt. Frank McGee, the legendary NYPD man who turned that department's Firearms Training Unit into a Firearms *and Tactics* Unit, took an overall tactical approach to training that caused the rate of the officers' gunfight survival to skyrocket. During one short period in the 1970s, three police officers were shot and killed in gunfights that occurred while they were off-duty in New York drinking establishments. Under Frank's tutelage, the FTU literally instituted a bloc of "off duty bar-room survival" training.

When this guy pulls you over for a routine stop and you're legally carrying a gun, there are things you need to know beforehand.

Frank strongly urged his officers to stay out of bars for one simple reason: bars are full of unknown drunk idiots with guns. I can tell you that he lived what he taught, too. McGee was a man who liked to light up an L&M cigarette and sip a glass of good Scotch...but he liked to do it someplace where it was safe to relax.

One time back in the '80s, Frank and I were guest-teaching at an Instructors' Update class at Smith & Wesson Academy in Springfield, Massachusetts, and both had rooms at a hotel in nearby Chicopee. After class, I invited Frank to join me for a drink in the hotel bar. "The hell with that," growled Frank. "You know why I hate bars. Come on by my room and have some Scotch."

"Ah, c'mon," I teased. "Bars have atmosphere. It'll be fun." I finally cajoled him, against his better judgment, into joining me at the hotel bar. Damned if we weren't just starting our first drinks, when a stereotype butch lesbian started a raging fight with her more "femme" lover in the bar. Frank flashed a triumphant smile at me and said, "See? *See?*" And then, with the hard-learned people skills of a New York cop, he spoke softly to the couple with a charm that would have evaporated the morning dew from the Blarney Stone, and had the aggressor tearfully apologizing to her lover in minutes.

At which point, we left the bar, me shaking my dumbfounded head. Frank McGee had made the point. All I could mutter was, "How the hell did you *arrange* that?"

I still visit bars occasionally, but less and less as the years go by, and never any more in Florida, New Mexico, or other states with those rules. If I need to meet someone in a bar on business where it's not legal to carry my gun on my person, I secure the gun in the hotel room.

If you use alcohol, use it the way you use guns: responsibly.

And One Other Thing...

You can be driving along, minding your own business, perfectly legal to have your concealed weapon on ... and the blue, or red, or blue-and-red lights start flashing in your rear-view mirror. You are about to undergo a routine traffic stop while carrying a loaded gun. How exactly do you handle that?

If this book was larger, I could tell you enough stories for a *loooong* chapter on this topic alone. It isn't, so let's skip the war stories and cut to the bottom line, which is: it's situational. I say that because you'll find yourself in three different kinds of states. 1) Those that require a CCW holder to identify himself or herself immediately upon contact with police who are in the performance of their duties. 2) States that don't have that, but do cross reference their CCW files with the state department of motor vehicles, so when a cop runs your license tag he immediately comes up with the fact that the owner is licensed to carry. 3) States where neither of those things are in force.

In the first kind of state, the best way to ID yourself is to carry your CCW card right next to your driver's license, and hand the two to the officer, without saying a word about the CCW. They'll see it, and take it from there. (Many or even most will relax a little, knowing they're dealing with someone who was investigated and deemed a proper person to carry a loaded, concealed handgun in public.) You have not uttered that scary "G-word" that frightens passersby, and young rookie cops who might be riding along tonight.

In the second kind of state, do exactly the same thing. You're not required to by law, but the cop knows when he stops you that you're likely to be carrying, and if he has to ask to find out, he may well see it subconsciously as you practicing "deception by omission of information." Ergo, CCW along with driver's license, as in the previous case.

In the third kind of state, where I'm a sworn officer, neither of the above is the case, and frankly I don't care. If I've pulled you over and I'm worried about you being armed, I'll ask you, at which time I'll expect an honest answer. You blurting at first contact something about having a gun tells me you've got a lot of ego invested in it, and that makes me nervous.

But, that's just me. A lot of brother and sister officers in my and similar jurisdictions tell me that the driver handing over the CCW reassures them. So, go with the short form, which will work wherever you are legal to carry: just fork over the CCW with the DL. The officer performing the stop will take it from there.

If the officer asks you to step out of your vehicle, it means that either you fit the description of someone he's looking for who did A Bad Thing and you'll be patted down, or that you were driving carelessly enough to give him probable cause to believe you might be "under the influence," in which case there is about to be a roadside field sobriety test. While some of my brothers and sisters use the gaze nystagmus test for this, most of us still use the Rohmberg series, which will involve movements such as arms extending out to the sides, which can reveal your holstered weapon. In either case, you don't want finding the gun to come as a surprise. If I was instructed, "Please step out of the car," I would keep my hands in plain sight and motionless and reply, "Certainly, Officer. However, I'm licensed to carry, and I do have it on. Tell me what you want me to do." The statement begins and ends with respectful deference and lawful compliance, and avoids anything that sounds like "I've got a gun," which is generally interpreted as a threatening statement.

I've been on both sides of these stops. Some cops will ask to take custody your gun while the stop is underway. They have the legal right to do that. Don't argue or give them Second Amendment lectures: they'll see it as a dangerous person with a gun who is non-compliant with lawful commands, and your night will quickly go downhill and your carry permit may soon grow wings and leave you. I wouldn't reach for the gun if the officer wanted that. I would say, "Certainly, Officer/Deputy/Trooper. However, I don't want it to look to anyone else as if I'm pulling a gun on an officer. The pistol is in a holster on my right hip. You're welcome to take it. Tell me what you want me to do."

If the officer insists on you handing it over, do it *very* slowly and carefully, with the muzzle in a safe direction and finger clear of the trigger guard. If you can simply unfasten the holster and hand over the holstered weapon, that's even safer.

Would've been easier if you'd just followed the speed limit, huh?

The Bottom Line

The laws of the given jurisdiction in a nation that's a patchwork of gun laws, are the laws you have to follow. It's your responsibility to know the turf in that regard, wherever your travels as a free American take you.

> The laws of the given jurisdiction in a nation that's a patchwork of gun laws, are the laws you have to follow.

COMPENDIUM OF STATE LAWS GOVERNING FIREARMS

Since state laws are subject to frequent change, this chart is not to be considered legal advice or a restatement of the law. The following chart lists the main provisions of state firearms laws as of the date of publication. In addition to the state provisions, the purchase, sale, and, in certain circumstances, the possession and interstate transportation of firearms are regulated by the Federal Gun Control Act of 1968 as amended by the Firearms Owners' Protection Act of 1986. Also, cities and localities may have their own gun ordinances in addition to federal and state restrictions. Details may be obtained by contacting local law enforcement authorities or by consulting your state's firearms law digest compiled by the NRA Institute for Legislative Action. All fifty states have passed sportsmen's protection laws to halt harrassment.

Compiled by NRA Institute for Legislative Action; 11250 Waples Mill Road; Fairfax, Virginia 22030

State	Gun Ban	Exemptions to NICS2	State Waiting Period-Number of Days		License or Permit to Purchase or Other Prerequisite		Registration	
			Handguns	Longguns	Handguns	Longguns	Handguns	Longguns
Alabama	—	—	—	—	—	—	—	—
Alaska	—	RTC	—	—	—	—	—	—
Arizona	—	RTC	—	—	—	—	—	—
Arkansas	—	RTC[3]	—	—	—	—	—	—
California	X[1]	—	10[5]	10[5,6]	10,11	—	X	X[13]
Colorado	—	—	—	—	—	—	—	—
Connecticut	X[1]	—	14[5,6]	14[5,6]	X[9,11]	—	—	X[13]
Delaware	—	—	—	—	—	—	—	—
Florida	—	—	3[6]	—	—	—	—	—
Georgia	—	RTC	—	—	—	—	—	—
Hawaii	X[1]	L, RTC	—	—	X[9,11]	X[9]	X[12]	X[12]
Idaho	—	RTC	—	—	—	—	—	—
Illinois	7	—	3	2	X[9]	X[9]	X[14]	X[14]
Indiana	—	—	—	—	—	—	—	—
Iowa	—	L, RTC	—	—	X[9]	—	—	—
Kansas	—	—	7	—	7	—	7	—
Kentucky	—	—	—	—	—	—	—	—
Louisiana	—	—	—	—	—	—	—	—
Maine	—	—	—	—	—	—	—	—
Maryland	X[1]	—	7[5]	7[4,5]	X[10,11]	—	—	—
Massachusetts	X[1]	—	—	—	X[9]	X[9]	—	—
Michigan	—	L	—	—	X[9,11]	—	X	—
Minnesota	—	—	7[9]	X[9]	X[9]	X[9]	—	—
Mississippi	—	RTC3	—	—	—	—	—	—
Missouri	—	—	—	—	X[9]	—	—	—
Montana	—	RTC	—	—	—	—	—	—
Nebraska	—	L	—	—	X	—	—	—
Nevada	—	RTC	7	—	—	—	7	—
New Hampshire	—	—	—	—	—	—	—	—
New Jersey	X[1]	—	—	—	X[9]	X[9]	—	X[13]
New Mexico	—	—	—	—	—	—	—	—
New York	X[1]	L, RTC	—	—	X[9,11]	9	X	X[15]
North Carolina	—	L, RTC	—	—	X[9]	—	—	—
North Dakota	—	RTC	—	—	—	—	—	—
Ohio	7	—	7	—	7	—	7	—
Oklahoma	—	—	—	—	—	—	—	—
Oregon	—	—	—	—	—	—	—	—
Pennsylvania	—	—	—	—	—	—	—	—
Rhode Island	—	—	7[5]	7[5]	X[11]	—	—	—
South Carolina	—	RTC	—	—	—	—	—	—
South Dakota	—	—	2	—	—	—	—	—
Tennessee	—	—	—	—	—	—	—	—
Texas	—	RTC	—	—	—	—	—	—
Utah	—	RTC	—	—	—	—	—	—
Vermont	—	—	—	—	—	—	—	—
Virginia	X[1]	—	—	—	X[10]	—	—	—
Washington	—	—	5[8]	—	—	—	—	—
West Virginia	—	—	—	—	—	—	—	—
Wisconsin	—	—	2	—	—	—	—	—
Wyoming	—	RTC	—	—	—	—	—	—
District of Columbia	X[1]	L	—	—	X[9]	X[9]	X[9]	X

COMPENDIUM OF STATE LAWS GOVERNING FIREARMS

Since state laws are subject to frequent change, this chart is not to be considered legal advice or a restatement of the law.

All fifty states have passed sportsmen's protection laws to halt harrassment.

State	Record of Sale Reported to State or Local Govt.	State Provision for Right-to-Carry Concealed	Carrying Openly Prohibited	Owner ID Cards or Licensing	Firearm Rights Constitutional Provision	State Firearms Preemption Laws	Range Protection Law
Alabama	—	M	X[19]	—	X	X	X
Alaska	—	R[17]	—	—	X	X[24]	X
Arizona	—	R	—	—	X	X	X
Arkansas	—	R	X[20]	—	X	X	X
California	X	L	X[21]	—	—	X	X
Colorado	—	R	[22]	—	X	X[22]	X
Connecticut	X	M	X	—	X	X[25]	X
Delaware	—	L	—	—	X	X	X
Florida	—	R	X	—	X	X	X
Georgia	—	R	X	—	X	X	X
Hawaii	X	L	X	X	X	—	—
Idaho	—	R	—	—	X	X	X
Illinois	X	D	X	X	X	—	X
Indiana	—	R	X	—	X	X[26]	X
Iowa	—	M	X	—	—	X	X
Kansas	7	D	7	—	X	—	X
Kentucky	—	R	—	—	X	X	X
Louisiana	—	R	—	—	X	X	X
Maine	—	R	—	—	X	X	X
Maryland	X	L	X	—	—	X	X
Massachusetts	X	L	X	X	X	X[25]	X
Michigan	X	R	X[19]	—	X	X	X
Minnesota	—	R[18]	X	—	—	X	—
Mississippi	—	R	—	—	X	X	X
Missouri	X	R	—	—	X	X	X
Montana	—	R	—	—	X	X	X
Nebraska	—	D	—	—	X	—	—
Nevada	—	R	—	—	X	X	X
New Hampshire	—	R	—	—	X	X	X
New Jersey	X	L	X	X	—	X[25]	X
New Mexico	—	R	—	—	X	X	X
New York	X	L	X	X	—	X[27]	X
North Carolina	X	R	—	—	X	X	X
North Dakota	—	R	X[21]	—	X	X	X
Ohio	7	R	7	7	X	—	X
Oklahoma	—	R	X[21]	—	X	X	X
Oregon	X	R	—	—	X	X	X
Pennsylvania	X	R	X[19]	—	X	X	X
Rhode Island	X	L	X	—	X	X	X
South Carolina	X	R	X	—	X	X	X
South Dakota	X[16]	R	—	—	X	X	X
Tennessee	—	R	X[20]	—	X	X	X
Texas	—	R	X	—	X	X	X
Utah	—	R	X[21]	—	X	X	X
Vermont	—	R[17]	X[20]	—	X	X	X
Virginia	—	R	—	—	X	X	X
Washington	X	R	X[23]	—	X	X	—
West Virginia	—	R	—	—	X	X	X
Wisconsin	—	D	—	—	X	X	X
Wyoming	—	R	—	—	X	X	X
District of Columbia	X	D	X	X	NA	—	—

COMPENDIUM OF STATE LAWS GOVERNING FIREARMS

With over 20,000 "gun control" laws on the books in America, there are two challenges facing every gun owner. First, you owe it to yourself to become familiar with the federal laws on gun ownership. Only by knowing the laws can you avoid innocently breaking one.

Second, while federal legislation receives much more media attention, state legislatures and city councils make many more decisions regarding your right to own and carry firearms. NRA members and all gun owners must take extra care to be aware of anti-gun laws and ordinances at the state and local levels.

Notes:

1. "Assault weapons" are prohibited in **Connecticut, New Jersey** and **New York.** Some local jurisdictions in **Ohio** also ban "assault weapons." **Hawaii** prohibits "assault pistols." **California** bans "assault weapons", .50BMG caliber firearms, some .50 caliber ammunition and "unsafe handguns." **Illinois**: Chicago, Evanston, Oak Park, Morton Grove, Winnetka, Wilmette, and Highland Park prohibit handguns; some cities prohibit other kinds of firearms. **Maryland** prohibits "assault pistols"; the sale or manufacture of any handgun manufactured after Jan. 1, 1985, that does not appear on the Handgun Roster; and the sale of any handgun manufactured after January 1, 2003 that is not equipped with an "integrated mechanical safety device." **Massachusetts**: It is unlawful to sell, transfer or possess "any assault weapon or large capacity feeding device" [more than 10 rounds] that was not legally possessed on September 13, 1994 and the sale of handguns not on the Firearms Roster. The City of Boston has a separate "assault weapons" law. The **District of Columbia** prohibits new acquisition of handguns and any semi-automatic firearm capable of using a detachable ammunition magazine of more than 12 rounds capacity and any handgun not registered after February 5, 1977. **Virginia** prohibits "Street Sweeper" shotguns. (With respect to some of these laws and ordinances, individuals may retain prohibited firearms owned previously, with certain restrictions.) The sunset of the federal assault weapons ban does not affect the validity of state "assault weapons" bans.

2. **National Instant Check System (NICS) exemption codes**:
   RTC-Carry Permit Holders Exempt From NICS
   L-Holders of state licenses to possess or purchase or firearms ID cards exempt from NICS.

3. **NICS exemption notes: Arkansas**: Those issued on and after 4/1/99 qualify. **Mississippi**: Permits issued to security guards do not qualify.

4. **Maryland** subjects purchases of "assault weapons" to a 7-day waiting period.

5. Waiting period for all sales. **California**: 10 days; sales, transfers and loans of handguns can be made through a dealer or through a sheriff's office. **Maryland**: 7 days; purchasers of regulated firearms must undergo background checks performed by the State Police, either through a dealer or directly through the State Police. **Rhode Island**: 7 days; private sales can be made through a dealer or the seller must follow the same guidelines as a sale from a dealer.

6. The waiting period does not apply to a person holding a valid permit or license to carry a firearm. In **Connecticut**, a certificate of eligibility exempts the holder from the waiting period for handgun purchases; a hunting license exempts the holder for long gun purchasers. **California**: transfers of a long gun to a person's parent, child or grandparent are exempt from the waiting period.

7. In certain cities or counties.

8. May be extended by police to 30 days in some circumstances. An individual not holding a driver's license must wait 60 days.

9. **Connecticut**: A certificate of eligibility or a carry permit is required to obtain a handgun and a carry permit is required to transport a handgun outside your home. **District of Columbia**: No handgun may be possessed unless it was registered prior to Sept. 23, 1976 and re-registered by Feb. 5, 1977. A permit to purchase is required for a rifle or shotgun. **Hawaii**: Purchase permits are required for all firearms **Illinois**: A Firearm Owner's Identification Card (FOI) is required to possess or purchase a firearm, must be issued to qualified applicants within 30 days, and is valid for 5 years. **Iowa**: A purchase permit is required for handguns, and is valid for one year. **Massachusetts**: Firearms and feeding devices for firearms are divided into classes. Depending on the class, a firearm identification card (FID) or class A license or class B license is required to possess, purchase, or carry a firearm, ammunition thereof, or firearm feeding device, or "large capacity feeding device." **Michigan**: A handgun purchaser must obtain a license to purchase from local law enforcement, and within 10 days present the license and handgun to obtain a certificate of inspection. **Minnesota**: A handgun transfer or carrying permit, or a 7-day waiting period and handgun transfer report, is required to purchase handguns or "assault weapons" from a dealer. A permit is valid for one year, a transfer report for 30 days. **Missouri**: A purchase permit is required for a handgun, must be issued to qualified applicants within 7 days, and is valid for 30 days. **New Jersey**: Firearm owners must possess a FID, which must be issued to qualified applicants within 30 days. To purchase a handgun, a purchase permit, which must be issued within 30 days to qualified applicants and is valid for 90 days, is required. An FID is required to purchase long guns. **New York**: Purchase, possession and/or carrying of a handgun require a single license, which includes any restrictions made upon the bearer. New York City also requires a license for long guns. **North Carolina**: To purchase a handgun, a license or permit is required, which must be issued to qualified applicants within 30 days.

10. A permit is required to acquire another handgun before 30 days have elapsed following the acquisition of a handgun. In **Virginia**, those with a permit to carry a concealed weapon are exempt from this prohibition.

11. Requires proof of safety training for purchase. **California**: Must have Handgun Safety Certificate receipt, which is valid for five years. **Connecticut**: To receive certificate of eligibility, must complete a handgun safety course approved by the Commissioner of Public Safety. **Hawaii**: Must have completed an approved handgun safety course. **Maryland**: Must complete an approved handgun safety course. **Michigan**: A person must correctly answer 70% of the questions on a basic safety review questionnaire in order to obtain a license to purchase. **New York**: Some counties require a handgun safety training course to receive a license. **Rhode Island**: Must receive a state-issued handgun safety card.

12. Every person arriving in **Hawaii** is required to register any firearm(s) brought into the state within 3 days of arrival of the person or firearm(s), whichever occurs later. Handguns purchased from licensed dealers must be registered within 5 days.

13. "Assault weapon" registration. **California** had two dates by which assault weapons had to be registered or possession after such date would be considered a felony: March 31, 1992 for the named make and model firearms banned in the 1989 legislation and December 31, 2000 for the firearms meeting the definition of the "assault weapons in the 1999 legislation. In **Connecticut**, those firearms banned by specific make and model in the 1993 law had to be registered by October 1, 1994 or possession would be considered a felony. A recent law requires registration of additional guns by October 1, 2003. In **New Jersey**, any "assault weapon" not registered, licensed, or rendered inoperable pursuant to a state police certificate by May 1, 1991, is considered contraband.

14. Chicago only. No handgun not already registered may be possessed.

15. New York City only.

16. Purchasers of handguns who do not possess a permit to carry a pistol must file an application for purchase, which will be retained by the chief of police or sheriff for one year.

17. **Vermont** and **Alaska** law respect your right to carry without a permit. **Alaska** also has a permit to carry system to establish reciprocity with other states.

18. Provisions of this law are stayed pending an ongoing dispute in the courts.

19. Carrying a handgun openly in a motor vehicle requires a license.

20. **Arkansas** prohibits carrying a firearm "with a purpose to employ it as a weapon against a person." **Tennessee** prohibits carrying "with the intent to go armed." **Vermont** prohibits carrying a firearm "with the intent or purpose of injuring another."

21. Loaded.

22. Municipalities may prohibit open carry in government buildings if such prohibition is clearly posted.

23. Local jurisdictions may opt of the prohibition.

24. In the Right to Keep and Bear Arms Amendment of the **Alaska** Constitution.

25. Preemption through judicial ruling. Local regulation may be instituted in **Massachusetts** if ratified by the legislature.

26. Except Gary and East Chicago and local laws enacted before January 1994.

27. Preemption only applies to handguns.

Concealed carry codes:

R: Right-to-Carry "Shall issue" or less restrictive discretionary permit system (**Ala., Conn.**) (See also note #21.)

M: Reasonable May Issue; the state has a permissive may issue law, but the authorities recognize the right to keep and bear arms.

L: Right-to-Carry Limited by local authority's discretion over permit issuance.

D: Right-to-Carry Denied, no permit system exists; concealed carry is prohibited.

PREPARATION AND AFTERMATH

In the entertainment media, gunfights begin with the draw and end with the last shot. In the real world, you need to be prepared beforehand, and ready for the ordeal that is likely to follow.

No way out. The Lindsey incident took place in this boxed-in parking lot.

It's about sunset right now outside my hotel room in Denver, a chilly evening. December 7, 2006. Pearl Harbor is on our minds, of course, this being the anniversary of the sneak attack that changed the history of America and the world. But right now, I'm dealing with a case of a law-abiding gun owner who has suffered a sneak attack from fate.

The case closed today, and it went to

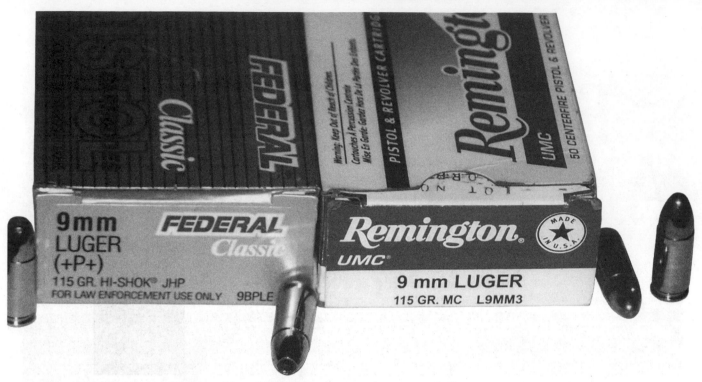

Be able to articulate why you chose the caliber and ammo that were used. Federal +P+ 115-grain JHP *(left)* is an excellent choice in 9mm, but full metal jacket, right, is not.

the jury about 45 minutes ago. Eleven months earlier, the client, 58, was driving to the Veteran's Administration hospital to pick up some medicine. His name is Larry Lindsey. Already asthmatic, he had just been diagnosed with diabetes, and overall was not in the best of health. He walked with a cane and a pronounced limp, the legacy of an accident on a city street a few years earlier when a careless motorist blasted through a red light and ran him down on a crosswalk.

On the Interstate that goes through Denver, a young-looking man in a Ford Taurus, racing zig-zag through the high speed traffic, cut into his lane. The smaller car nearly ran Larry's vehicle off the road. Acutely aware of the dangers posed by such driving – not only reminded constantly by his lingering injury, but by the fact that he had lost loved ones to drunk and reckless drivers in the past – Larry always made a point of calling in such dangerous motorists on his cell phone. But the Taurus had accelerated ahead so quickly, still cutting left and right through traffic, that he hadn't been able to get the license plate number.

He continued on his way. As he reached his exit, he saw a familiar car stopped at the edge of the exit ramp: the tan Taurus, with the same young man at the wheel. Larry instinctively slowed, and suddenly, the vehicle

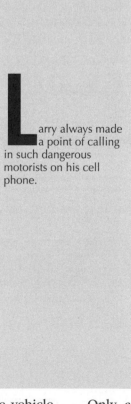

arry always made a point of calling in such dangerous motorists on his cell phone.

shot out directly in front of him, nearly colliding. Larry swerved and hit the brakes, and barely missed plowing into the concrete wall on the right side of the exit ramp. As he brought his vehicle back on path, Larry saw the Taurus' driver mouth a curse at him and raise his middle finger in contempt ... and then blast through a red light, turning right, in flagrant violation of a big sign that read, "NO RIGHT TURN ON RED."

This, Larry decided, was just too blatant to ignore. When traffic allowed, he too turned right, following the tan Taurus that was now a considerable distance ahead of him. He decided he was going to write down the license number and phone it in. As he drove he dialed 9-1-1 on his cell phone, and was put on "hold." Ahead of him, he saw the car take a right, then a left. He followed in time to see it pull quickly into the parking lot on his left.

He slowed, turned into the lot – and stopped dead in the narrow mouth of the parking lot. Instead of going to the right where the main parking spaces were, the tan Taurus had pulled into the third slot on the immediate left of the exit, a short row of Handicapped spaces. The vehicle had come to its sudden stop in front of a large HANDICAPPED sign.

Only a few steps away from the vehicle, Larry

Trials can be scary. Law enforcement personnel barricade the streets for a block in each direction around the courthouse because of death threats against the defendant in one case the author worked.

figured he'd jot down the license number and be out of there. 9-1-1 Dispatch had not yet taken him off "hold."

But other things weren't "holding" at all.

The driver boiled out of the car, coming toward Larry, screaming obscenities. Fifteen or twenty paces ahead of Larry's car, a very tall and strong-looking young man emerged immediately from the apartment house entryway and proceeded toward him at a fast walk. Then another came out behind him.

Five feet eight, pushing sixty, a little overweight, and crippled and sick, Larry wasn't sure he would be a match for one athletic young man, let alone three. The third one seemed to drift away, but the tall one was approaching straight at him and the driver of the Taurus was almost at his left door, screaming "I'll kick your ass! I'll kill you!"

In his younger days, Larry Lindsey had spent eight years in the United States Marine Corps, much of it in Vietnam, where his MOS was Combat Photographer. His issue weapon had been a 1911 45 automatic back then. A gun guy all his life, he had grown to like the issue pistol, and had chosen as his personal defense gun a stainless steel Kimber Custom Shop Gold 1911 45. He kept it in his

In his younger days, Larry Lindsey had spent eight years in the United States Marine Corps, much of it in Vietnam, where his MOS was Combat Photographer.

console with pretty much the same load-out to which the USMC had accustomed him: in a holster with loaded magazine and empty chamber, backed up by two more loaded mags in a leather pouch.

Larry flipped open the console and took out the holstered pistol, holding it in plain sight where he hoped they could see it. The man on his left screamed another F-word curse…and his right hand dove under his jacket toward his back, as if going for a pistol.

Larry ripped the holster off the Kimber, jacked a 230-grain Federal Hydra-Shok into the chamber, and brought up the pistol.

Suddenly, the two men were moving back, and Larry wasn't in danger anymore. His cell phone was still in his lap where he had dropped it when he went for his pistol. Glancing behind him, Larry saw an opening in the traffic and he backed out into the street, then drove to the nearest corner and pulled into a parking lot there. He dialed 9-1-1 again, and this time, he got through. He told the dispatcher what happened.

Unfortunately, the tall man who had menaced him had whipped out his own cell phone before Larry was out of the parking lot. His call went in to Dispatch at 3:02 PM, and Larry's did not get in until 3:03. The first responding officer arrived at the scene at 3:10, a respectable eight-minute response time.

That officer would testify that he never received any radio notification that Larry had called in his complaint. He seemed surprised when he was shown the facts on the 9-1-1 call log, in court, by defense attorney Paul Grant.

The same officer would testify that he had decided almost immediately upon his arrival to arrest Larry Lindsey, who was now in the grip of a full-blown asthma attack. After all, two witnesses had identified the crazy man in a state of road rage who had waved a silver-colored pistol at them, and the man had admitted drawing the gun on the pair the officer now considered victims.

Larry Lindsey was arrested at the scene. He was charged with two counts of Felony Menacing, and later released on $50,000 bail.

The trial began on December 6. Jury selection was done by morning, with the prosecution removing almost every gun owner. This is par for the course. Neither side wants someone on the jury who might identify with the people on the other side of the case. Among the twelve jurors and one alternate finally selected there was but a single one who owned firearms. He had two, which he kept empty, fitted with trigger locks, inside a gun safe. A loaded gun, he said during the jury selection process called *voir dire*, was just too dangerous to keep around. This, apparently, was enough to satisfy the prosecutor.

Reloaded ammo is great for practice, hunting, and competition, says author, but he strongly recommends against it for defense use.

The state took the rest of the day to establish its case. A story emerged of a nice twenty-something kid, an immigrant from the Middle East with no record, who accidentally cut in front of a motorist who must have been one of those Angry White Males. The driver had boiled up in road rage, followed him for several blocks, pulled in behind him and pulled out a big silver pistol, with which he threatened to "blow his brains out" along with those of his equally innocent twenty-something friend, an immigrant from Eastern Europe, who had done nothing but come out of his apartment building.

The cops took the stand. Yes, said the arresting officer, he had been called to the scene of a crime of threatening to shoot someone without reason… found two complainants willing to testify…found the defendant who admitted having a gun just like the one the complainants had described…and determined immediately that he was guilty and placed him under arrest. Much emphasis was placed on the large caliber of the weapon. The prosecutor elicited from the officer that the hollow-point bullets, 230-grain Federal Hydra-Shok, were designed to expand and tear "larger wounds." And, oh my God, there were *two spare magazines!* Enough bullets to kill two dozen people!

On the morning of December 7, the assistant district attorney would announce that her case was closed. Attorney Paul Grant had chosen to call only two witnesses: the defendant, and me. The ADA strenuously objected to my presence, so an informal hearing was held on the record in chambers.

It seems that when Grant had sent the routine list of witnesses he intended to call to the prosecutor who'd had the case previously, the fax had not gone through. He hadn't known that. When he mentioned to the new prosecutor on the case the week before that he would be calling an expert to testify, she went through the roof.

The judge was not happy about the glitch. However, he was diligent in his duties and he recognized that the defendant had certain rights. The prosecutor's questioning of the arresting officer the day before had elicited testimony that made the pistol seem an avatar of malice because of its caliber, its spare magazines, its hollowpoint ammunition; Grant, who had seen that before, argued that he had a right to rebut those arguments. Incredibly, the prosecutor argued that since it came through a material witness instead of an expert, that material could not be rebutted by an expert. Grant responded, successfully, with a logical argument: *whoever* had said it, the poison was in the water, and he had the right to administer an antidote of his choice. The judge agreed.

Grant wanted me to testify also as to the standards of care for private citizens in such things, the rules of engagement as it were. The prosecutor adamantly objected. I was, she said, going to tell the jury that the defendant's use of the gun was justified, and that issue was something only the jury could determine. The judge asked me what my take was on that.

I explained that I had no intention of going to "the ultimate issue," the guilt or innocence of the defendant, and that I agreed this was a question that only the triers of the facts could answer. However, I added, I believed the defense attorney's job was to show the jury that a reasonable, prudent person, in the same situation and knowing what his client knew, would have done the same thing. The element of "knowing what the defendant knew" required him to show the jury how such decisions are made by lawfully armed citizens, and what the rules of engagement are understood to be. It was to establish those parameters that he had brought me in.

And, of course, the judge agreed.

I went on the stand first thing after court convened. The prosecutor stipulated to my credentials and expertise, a professional move by any advocate against an adverse expert witness because it limits how much of his qualifications and background the jury will hear in the opening moments of testimony.

Defense attorney Grant asked the right questions, and I laid out those "rules of engagement," which will follow shortly in this chapter. We explained the "furtive movement" element: that when someone such as the young Iranian immigrant made a move consistent with going for a gun, and not reasonably consistent with anything else under the circumstances, it would reasonable and prudent of someone such as the defendant to immediately draw his own gun and take him proactively at gunpoint.

One by one, we cut down the shibboleths that had built up around the defendant's choice of gun and ammunition during the prosecution's case. The

The trial began on December 6. Jury selection was done by morning, with the prosecution removing almost every gun owner. This is par for the course.

45-caliber pistol was quite common in America, very popular in law enforcement, in fact approved for the Denver Police Department and carried by a great many of its officers. The type of gun the defendant had employed was adopted by the United States Military in 1911, had been standard with our armed forces until the mid-1980s, and was still used by our military among pistol teams, the Army's Delta Force, and the Marine Corps' Recon unit, which in fact had recently purchased a quantity of Kimbers functionally identical to the Kimber 45 in evidence.

I explained that generations of American service personnel had returned to civilian life after completing their terms of service, and had decided that if the 1911 45 pistol was good enough to be issued to them by Uncle Sam to protect their country, it was good enough for them to purchase to protect their home and hearth and loved ones. In turn, countless Americans who had never joined the military had been taught by their parents to use those same 45s, and bought one or more when they in turn grew up and made the lawful decision to have a gun to protect themselves and their loved ones. This was why the 1911 was so very popular and common among armed citizens, and also the fact that its design features made it ideal for many forms of pistol matches, which the defendant would testify he had competed in regularly until becoming too physically debilitated to do so.

The two spare magazines that augmented the loaded pistol? I explained that this was a typical "load-out" for those who carried a gun. Since before any of us was born, the standard law enforcement rule was a loaded gun plus enough spare ammunition for two full reloads. I told the jury that they would see uniformed officers in the courthouse during their breaks, and that they would notice each had a double pouch on their duty belts to carry two spare magazines to complement their fully loaded weapon. Since many of them had high-capacity pistols, some would be carrying as many as 54 duty cartridges on their person, i.e., a fully loaded Glock 17 with 18 9mm rounds in it and two spare 17-round magazines in the pouches. The military load-out, since the 45's adoption in 1911, had been loaded gun in holster plus two magazines in pouches. I pointed out that testimony would show that the defendant had served for some eight years as a USMC combat photographer in Vietnam (where he had been wounded in action) and that every day there he carried what the Government issued him: a 1911 45 auto with an empty chamber and full magazine, and two spare fully loaded magazines, in the holster and double mag pouch he was issued. This was exactly what he'd had in the car with him on the day in question, albeit with eight-round competition magazines instead of seven-round GI mags.

As a competitor for many years, the defendant needed at least two magazines to shoot even prosaic NRA bullseye matches, and three to shoot a stage in IDPA. If he just stopped at the public outdoor range for some shooting – which, records would show, he had done just a couple of days before the incident – there would be a finite amount of actual shooting time in between stand-downs to examine and change targets. During those stand-downs, there would be time to refill the magazines. Then, when it came time to shoot, the guy who came to shoot could spend his shooting time doing more shooting, just as the guy who came to a golf course to play golf would rather play eighteen holes than nine. I could see some of the jurors nodding their heads in affirmation. And of course, should a defensive pistol have to be used for serious purposes, more ammo could be required, or a spare magazine might be necessary to clear a malfunction. They "got it." They realized a person for whom pistol shooting was a sport might want to have multiple loaded magazines for purposes other than mass murder.

The hollowpoints? I explained that virtually every law enforcement agency in the country had adopted such ammunition, including the Denver PD which last I knew had Speer Gold Dot as standard issue for every approved caliber. (Detroit, Michigan is clutched so tightly in the iron fist of political correctness that "hollowpoints" are anathema there, so Detroit coppers are issued Federal Expanding Full Metal Jacket ammunition, in which the operative term is "expanding.") I then went on to point out the reasons for that, which are listed elsewhere in this book but, briefly, include reduced likelihood of ricochet that could endanger bystanders, reduced likelihood of over-penetration that could jeopardize the same innocents, etc. The Federal Hydra-Shok in particular had at one point been the "gold standard" among American police before the coming of higher-tech JHPs from that maker and others, and remains in wide law enforcement use.

Paul Grant closed the direct examination by asking me if I told my students that they might be wise to avoid following dangerous people to report them to police. I told him that was true, and explained why: that folks who came in late and didn't see what you saw could mistake you as the aggressive pursuer chasing a hapless victim, and the result could be a "false positive" that made the good guy look like the bad guy and vice versa. It was a good note on which to end the direct.

Cross-examination was interesting. The seasoned prosecutor was well-spoken and utterly professional. If you drew a gun because you thought the other man was going to draw one, but he turned out to be unarmed, wouldn't that be a mistake? No, I answered,

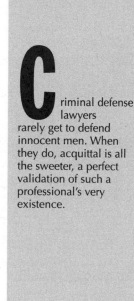

Criminal defense lawyers rarely get to defend innocent men. When they do, acquittal is all the sweeter, a perfect validation of such a professional's very existence.

not if the totality of the other man's words and actions were reasonably construable to any prudent person as indicating that he *did* have a gun. Besides, two strong young men threatening to beat up and kill a physically disabled man in his late fifties constituted disparity of force twice over. I had already explained to the jury on direct that disparity of force meant that even ostensibly unarmed men were so likely to kill or cripple you under these violent circumstances that this likelihood constituted the equivalent of one or both of them being armed with a *per se* deadly weapon.

And so it went for almost two and a half hours, until I was done. I headed back to the hotel to wait in case I was called back. Out of hearing of the jury, the prosecutor informed the judge and the defense lawyer that she might call a rebuttal witness, whose purpose would be to refute my testimony. Therefore, I had to stick around for sur-rebuttal, which would involve my taking the stand once again to shoot down the rebuttal testimony.

Which brings us to late afternoon of December 7. I learn after court has adjourned for the day that the prosecutor has given up on rebuttal, the defendant has told his story, and both advocates have given their closing arguments. There's nothing more I can do here. I pick up the phone and make arrangements to fly out early the next morning.

December 8, 2006: I'm in the Atlanta airport waiting to board my connecting flight for the final leg of my journey home when my Treo rings. It's Paul Grant. The jury has come in with the verdict.

Not Guilty on all counts.

Criminal defense lawyers rarely get to defend innocent men. When they do, acquittal is all the sweeter, a perfect validation of such a professional's very existence. A relieved Paul Grant reminds the judge that there is the small matter of some of his client's property, which at this moment has ceased to be evidence in the custody of the Court, which should be returned to his client.

The prosecutor jumps to her feet and says, "Your Honor, the state is preparing a motion for the gun to be destroyed."

The judge looks at her in something close to disbelief and asks, "On what grounds?"

"There's a statute," she blurts.

Patiently, the judge asks, "*What* statute?"

The prosecutor replies that she doesn't know, exactly, but she intends to find it.

Some people just *hate* to lose.

Lessons

A week later, I received an email from the defendant. "This is the first chance since the trial that I have had

She's 5'0", and they're about 6'4". How many elements of "disparity of force" could be present here?

here in a 'civilized' environment could have so many similarities to an engagement in active combat. There was the same tendency to focus solely on the threat at hand, excluding almost everything else, and the same auditory exclusion and time distortion. The stress of the situation also made it very difficult to remember the chronological order of things.

"It is a very strange sensation to have your mind racing at such speeds as to make the moment seem as if it is taking place in agonizingly slow motion. It's almost impossible to keep tabs on everything at once…assessing the danger, keeping an eye on two or more aggressors (who happen to be in different locations), trying to safely retrieve and handle your handgun, while simultaneously trying to watch the traffic behind you so that you can safely back out of the parking lot. The whole time I was praying that I didn't have to shoot this idiot, but I also realized that pulling the pistol was my only way out of a deadly situation. Thankfully, it did what I intended for it to do. It defused the situation immediately and I was able to extract myself and wait for the police.

"I used my pistol in self defense, knowing full well what the aftermath would most likely be. I knew that Denver almost always prosecutes an individual if he has used a firearm to defend himself, but I also believed that I had no other choice in the matter."

He concluded, "After the trial, a juror asked me if this had changed my mind about carrying a firearm

to actually sit down and compose a letter to properly thank you," he wrote. "The whole ordeal of the trial, coupled with the emotional and financial drain of the previous eleven months had taken such a toll on my wife and myself that we just took a few days off to spend some time with each other. It is amazing just how much better I feel now.

"I can't tell you how much we appreciated your presence in the courtroom, and your testimony. Because of you and Paul, Natasha and I will be spending Christmas together again this year. We both agree that this is our best Christmas ever. We hope that you and your family have a very Merry Christmas, and a Happy New Year!

"The one thing that I never could have anticipated was that the elements of a confrontation with bad guys

for self defense. Since she claimed to be one of my defenders early on in deliberation, I'm sure that what she meant was that if I had not had my handgun with me that I would not have had to defend myself, yet a second time, in court. Even after the trial and my acquittal of all charges, she still could not see the whole picture, and failed to consider the likely outcome had I been unarmed. I explained to her that the experience had only reinforced my belief that we live in perilous times, and that I should always carry a firearm to defend myself."

Whew! Where do we begin? Let's start with the obvious.

I can't overemphasize that "false positive effect" that I spoke of in court. This whole thing went the way it did after the gun was put away because the defendant didn't get his story in to the authorities before his antagonists did. The entire criminal justice system is geared on the assumption that whoever calls in first is the complainant, the *victim*. The good guy now, by default, becomes the bad guy: the *suspect*. The *perpetrator*.

In situations like these, you're a contestant in what I've come to call "the race to the telephone." The winner gets to be the good guy, and the loser automatically becomes the bad guy.

I know what you're thinking: that's not how it should be, and it isn't fair. You're right. It isn't fair, and it isn't how it should be. But, ya know, I don't think you paid the price of this book to find out how I think things should be. I think you paid it to find out how things *are,* and, well, this *is* how they are.

Please don't think that the criminal justice system always goes after the wrong guy. That's actually fairly rare. Most of the time, the system works. But that's partly because, most of the time things "go as usual."

By that I mean, what happens most of the time is that the person who calls in *is* the innocent victim as well as the complainant. Most of the time, the person complained about *is* the perpetrator. After you do criminal justice for a living for a while, it becomes business as usual to accept things as such. Complainant equals victim, complained about equals suspected perpetrator. Soon everyone from the dispatcher who takes the call, to the cop on the beat who responds, to the prosecutor who takes the case to court, accepts this as a matter of course.

That's why, when testifying in this particular case, I used the term "false positive" to the jury. I wasn't there to blame the arresting officer. He worked with what he had to work with. Call says, "Man with gun threatens people." A BadThing. Gets to scene. Complainants confirm, "Yup, threatened us with gun!" Hmmm. Suspect says, "Sure, I pulled the gun – it's right there – and warned that I would shoot, but –"

Well, you and I might also say, "Save it for the judge, buddy, you're under arrest." Probable cause now exists to make the arrest. Sorting out the excuses and alibis? That's largely for the courtroom.

At one point in that trial, I was asked in front of the jury if I was prejudiced against cops. Hardly, I replied; I had *been* a sworn police officer for 33 years, and still was one, albeit on a part time basis. If the assistant district attorney had asked me on cross if I was prejudiced against prosecutors, I would have said much the same: Hardly, because I've spent more than seventeen years as a police prosecutor. (In the state where I serve, selected police officers are sent to a two-week course at the state law enforcement academy after which, if we can pass the stringent final exam, we are declared "police prosecutors."

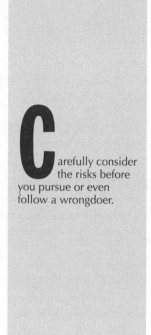

C arefully consider the risks before you pursue or even follow a wrongdoer.

We can prosecute violations and misdemeanors all the way through on our own, and can go as far as arraignment with felonies and second seat for the rest of the trial with a "real" prosecutor if he or she wants us to. "Second seat," called "second chair" in some jurisdictions, mean that you're acting as co-pilot to the designated prosecutor who is the pilot. Only a few states have this system, but it works amazingly well.)

Just as I respect cops and prosecutors, I respect physicians and other medical professionals. They rarely make mistakes…but they're human, and they *can* make mistakes. They work daily with reliable systems and protocols that let them diagnose and treat problems. Most of the time, those things perform as intended. But, every now and then, an unforeseen aberration occurs in the way things normally work, and a test registers "positive" when in fact it should register "negative." Professional history, logic, the momentum of routine, and a little thing called "business as usual" now come together, and because the test indicated "positive," the patient is treated as if he had the disease. Hopefully, the wrong treatment is discovered in time to rectify the situation, give the proper treatment, and heal the patient.

The criminal justice system works exactly the same way.

When the guy who started the problem calls in first, and says the good guy is the bad guy, we have the "false positive" result. In the medical example, the symptoms have mimicked those of the given disease, and treatment for that disease is prescribed. In the legal example, actions mimic those of a given crime, so the "patient" is treated as if he had committed the crime. In the medical environment, continued monitoring of the patient's condition will hopefully determine that the wrong treatment was prescribed because of the false positive, and the matter will be rectified. In the legal environment, that usually doesn't happen until you get to court, as was the case for this unfortunate defendant.

So, to make a long story short, the lesson is, *be the complainant! Win that "race to the telephone" in the aftermath of the incident.*

Another lesson, discussed in both direct and cross and worthy of reiteration here, is: *carefully consider the risks before you pursue or even follow a wrongdoer.* As I said on the stand that day in Denver, a private citizen chasing a suspect is a little like a dog chasing a car: he has no idea what he's going to do with his quarry if he catches it, but he will feel an almost irresistible urge to chase it.

Our society sends a very mixed message on this. Somewhere in America almost every day, some brave citizen will chase a thief or follow a bank robber or trail a road-raging driver as Larry did in this case.

Author, right, observes as lighting experts determine ambient light at a crime scene. This could be a critical element for the jury to weigh.

Often, there is a successful conclusion. Thanks to that concerned citizen's diligence and willingness to "get involved," the person who did the bad act is captured by the police and the public is made safer. Sometimes, it's even the citizen who captures the bad guy, and then the newspapers lionize that good citizen as a hero.

Well, I think that's a good thing, in the moral sense. Back when the English Common Law was formed, it included an element called "hue and cry." A formal police department would not be established in England until long after, under the great Sir Robert Peel for whom British "bobbies" are nicknamed. In those long ago times, it was understood that citizens had to do their own policing. Thus, it was a public duty to "raise a hue and cry" when one saw a crime committed: to shout "Stop, Thief!" and give chase, hopefully soon joined by a like-minded crowd of good citizens, and lay hands upon the malefactor and hold him until the traveling magistrate could be brought to the village to supervise the imposition of the King's justice. It is from this heritage that we have today's laws creating something called "citizen's arrest" in virtually all of our United States, where the English Common Law remains the model of our system of justice.

However, when the newspaper and TV news stories appear applauding the heroic citizen who led the police to the bad guy or even captured him by his lonesome, please notice that there's almost always a quote from a police spokesman who says, "We appreciate this citizen's heroism, but we have to urge the public not to go after people they see commit crimes. It can be very dangerous."

They ain't just blowing politically correct smoke. The bad guy may just turn on you, just as the car the dog is chasing can suddenly go in reverse and run over the puppy. What are *you* going to do if the bad guy screams at *you*, "I'll blow your f—kin' head off!" as he reaches as if for a pistol?

Well, if you can't get a gun on him as quickly as Larry got a 45 on this guy, you could be on the fast track for your body heat going from 98.6 degrees Fahrenheit to room temperature. And if you *are* as fast as Larry, you can find yourself going through the same terrible ordeal in court that he did.

Maybe you're *faster* than Larry. Let's say you're in the exact same circumstances, and you put a 230-grain Hydra-Shok into the man's center chest, heart into spine, before he can get his gun he reached for first, out of its hiding place. He's what some folks would call DRT: Dead Right There.

The first responding officers will approach the body. IF they find a pistol in his hand, you *may* be home free. But IF they DON'T, you're in deep trouble. You've just shot an unarmed man.

Go back to the way the prosecutor cross-examined me in this case. She was trying to get me to say that if you pull a gun on a man you have reason to believe is going to criminally shoot you with a gun of his own, and he turns out to be unarmed, it's wrong. Well, as I explained, that's plain and simple BS. The law has never demanded that the bad guy actually have a gun, or that the gun be real instead of fake, loaded instead of empty, operable instead of broken and useless. All the law has ever demanded, insofar as the attacker being armed, is that his manifest intent – his obvious intent, as manifested by his words and/or his actions – be such that any prudent person would be reasonable to conclude that he was indeed capable of killing you.

Alas, over the years, a huge number of prosecutors have failed to see that. In law school, deadly force law is a tiny drop in a great sea of tort law, contract law, and general legal principles. I've talked to attorneys who spent more time in law school studying maritime law than deadly force or self-defense law. This forces the prosecutor, absent special training, to fall back on legal formulae.

The formula says that the key ingredients of Manslaughter are recklessness or negligence, coupled of course with the death of the alleged victim. Some perceive bad judgment to be the equivalent of recklessness and/or negligence. "Hmmm…you thought he had a gun, but he didn't. Your judgment was obviously wrong. You killed him. Let's see what my law school notes say…bad judgment, plus death, equals…Manslaughter! Yes, that seems to be an appropriate charge." And there you are, in court with your future on the line.

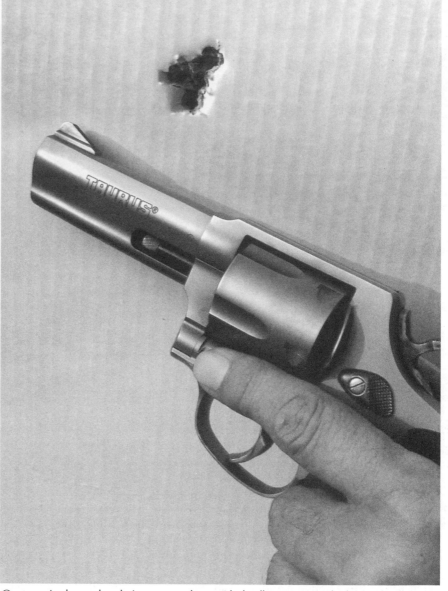

Once you've learned to do it, you can shoot with deadly accuracy at high speed with a good double-action revolver like this Taurus Tracker. There's no good reason to rely on a defense gun with a "hair trigger," opines the author.

Even if the other guy *did* turn out to have a gun, remember that I only said you *may* be home free. Way back in 1984, I was hired by two famous criminal defense lawyers, Roy Black and Mark Seiden, to speak in the defense of Officer Luis Alvarez. Luis was a Miami street cop who, along with his young rookie partner, was arresting a man for illegal possession of a concealed handgun in a crowded video arcade. The man went for his gun, a stolen RG-14 revolver loaded with hyper-velocity Stinger 22 Long Rifle hollowpoints, and Alvarez shot him dead.

It was a cross-racial shooting, and it triggered a race riot. The city needed a scapegoat, and Alvarez was the chosen sacrifice. He was charged with Manslaughter. Now, at the time the suspect made the drawing movement that led to his death, Alvarez already *knew* this man was armed with a handgun. He had approached him, put a hand on the bulge under the suspect's sweater, and instantly realized that his hand was on a revolver. The cop asked him, "What's that?" The suspect replied – with what would turn out to be his last words on Earth – "It's a gun."

The prosecution, to get a conviction, needed to show that Alvarez had acted recklessly. Their position was that Alvarez should have waited to actually see the man draw the gun. They put forth an expert as a witness who testified, "He shouldn't have fired until he saw the gun." Asked about that when my turn came on the witness stand, my reply was, "If you wait to see the gun, you're going to see what comes out of it." I then did a demonstration and showed the jury how quickly a gun could be drawn from a waistband when carried as it was found on the dying suspect's body. There was a whole lot more to the eight grueling weeks Black and Seiden put in on that trial, from jury selection to verdict, but it ended in an acquittal. Which triggered *another* riot, but that's another story.

Now, let's get back to the Lindsey case, the one in Denver. You will recall the discussion of actions leading up to the final encounter, and how it is important that the jury know and assess how each of the players was acting in the short period of time leading up to the encounter. If you have a case like Lindsey's that's "he said/she said," in this case two complainants versus one defendant and no impartial, objective eyewitnesses, it's going to come down to taking one man's words over those of another, or those of a couple more.

The number of people testifying on one side can be convincing, but is not necessarily the best evidence. (By that standard, if a victim was gang-raped and all the perpetrators solidly denied it, the victim would never get justice.) When it goes to "he said/she said," the relative credibility of each witness's testimony must be weighed separately. This will include other factors in what the court calls "the totality of the circumstances." Therefore, each individual's actions in the short time frame leading up to the encounter can be used by the jury to determine who seemed most likely to have committed a reckless act that disregarded the value of human life.

Let's look at the Larry Lindsey case again with that in mind. Lindsey was a sick man en route to the Veteran's Administration hospital to get much-needed medication, yet he diverted from his own needs to get the license number so he could report the offending vehicle to the authorities before the reckless driver could kill someone. This, I submit, would be seen as a selfless and highly responsible action by a private citizen who had no legal duty to do that, though of course he had the right.

Now, let's look at the chief witness against Larry. How many reckless acts, connotative of irresponsible action and therefore corroborative of Larry's account of the incident, did *this* guy commit? At least five are evident.

(1) He initially cuts Larry off on the Interstate, nearly running him off the road.

(2) He suddenly darts onto the exit ramp and cuts Larry off *again,* nearly forcing his vehicle into a concrete wall this time. (The driver will later admit to this particular offense, but will say that he didn't mean to do it.)

(3) The other driver flipped Larry off. Now, obviously, that's not a "shooting offense," but it shows you that you're dealing with someone who has some hostility going and perhaps an anger management thing. After all, we would all tell our kids that giving the bird to a stranger you've cut off in traffic is provocative at the very least, and therefore, not a responsible thing to do.

(4) Larry saw him blast through a "no right turn on red" light. Another dangerous act that's construable as showing disregard for the safety of oneself and others: more irresponsibility.

(5) In the penultimate moment before the confrontation, the driver who became the complainant *whipped* his car into a handicapped space, with no apparent need for that sort of speed. Again, while obviously not an offense that warrants gunpoint, it's something that shows you an agitated man in a hurry, a man who does not care much about the needs of others…and an irresponsible man.

If you are the juror who has to determine which of these men was most likely to act irresponsibly in the moments that followed, what do their actions in the moments leading up to the confrontation tell us? This is what the courts and the law are looking for when they demand that actions be considered "within the totality of the circumstanccs."

Hardware Lessons

Be able to explain your choice of gun and ammunition, and even accessories. There are some who will be your adversaries in court who will make it appear that your having a gun with you at all was paranoid. Be able to articulate why you did choose to arm your home, your shop, or your person. Be able to explain why carrying sufficient ammunition is a practice recommended by responsible firearms professionals for very good reasons, and has nothing to do with any plan to massacre shoppers at the mall.

At this writing, I'm consulting on an *amicus* brief for an appellate case in the Northeast, *Commonwealth v. Pepicelli. Amicus curae* are "friend of the court" briefs, which explain in depth a certain issue in the case at bar. At his original trial, the armed citizen defendant was convicted of criminal homicide after fighting off men who had come after him and endangered others at a family cookout. Aware of a previous pattern of threats, Pepicelli was armed with a Glock pistol and carrying a spare magazine when the incident went down. The prosecution argued that only a man who intended to shoot someone would bring a loaded pistol to a family barbecue…that only a man who intended to shoot many people would carry a spare magazine…and that carrying a high-capacity semiautomatic pistol such as the Glock was somehow nefarious to begin with.

And they got away with that. The reason is, their argument went unchallenged by a defense lawyer who apparently was not well versed in these particular areas. Pepicelli was convicted and sentenced to prison. His appeal is now underway, under the able direction of Lisa Steele, one of the nation's top appellate lawyers. The original trial lawyer had been wise enough to seek out an expert witness, and he chose Tom Aveni, who is a highly qualified instructor and researcher in the field, and very capable. Unfortunately, the judge refused to allow any testimony in the above areas.

It is the exclusion of that testimony that is being challenged in the appeal, and in the various *amicus* briefs that are being submitted.

Ammunition can also be an issue. I have seen many cases where the prosecutors and plaintiff's lawyers have argued that the use of hollow points constitutes malice. Their arguments generally come almost word for word from an article published some thirty years ago in the liberal magazine *The Nation*. This article was titled "The Vietnamization of Main Street." The focus of its attack was the sweeping adoption of hollowpoint ammunition by America's police. The thing reeks of BS and total misconception. It includes phrases such as "bullets shaped like the nacelles of jet engines" and "The bullet doesn't explode, *you* do."

There are several ways to defuse this attack. One that has worked well for me for some years is to advise defense counsel to ask every police officer who testifies during the state's case an important question on cross-examination: "What sort of ammunition do you carry on duty, Officer?" Almost certainly it will prove to be some sort of hollowpoint, though the counselor will want to confirm this well beforehand, prior to asking the question. It's a foolish or too-adventurous attorney who asks a question to which he or she does not already know the answer.

It's still good to have an expert witness for your own side whose training and experience encompasses this area. This guarantees bringing in the testimony that the HPs are less likely to dangerously over-penetrate or ricochet. Such an expert should also bring out the point that since hollowpoints have come into use, most shootings with them end with fewer gunshots inflicted than in the old days, when cops with impotent 158-grain round-nose lead bullets had to empty their revolvers into the bad guys to put them down, and sometimes didn't even stop the fight with *that*.

The more gunshot wounds a man sustains, the more likely he is to die, all other things being equal. The HP round's history of improved "stopping power" means the bad guy has to be shot fewer times to make him cease hostilities. Moreover, because it was designed to stay in the body, the hollowpoint slug will be less likely to punch a second open hole in the body as it exits. This reduces tension pneumothorax, the "sucking chest wound," and some believe it also somewhat reduces hemorrhage. The deeper penetrating "regular bullet" will by definition be capable of piercing more bone structures, blood vessels, organs, etc. Thus, with all these factors taken into consideration in The Big Picture, a solid argument can be made that the hollow-point bullet is *less lethal* and therefore even safer for the perpetrator who forces you to shoot him!

Some authorities recommend that the armed citizen carry the same round as that used by local law enforcement, on the theory that the prosecutor can't accuse you of using "extra-deadly malicious bullets" if that accusation is likely to tarnish local police who carry the same load. Some folks have attributed this advice to me. This is incorrect. I have mentioned that some experts suggest this, but I wasn't the one who came up with the idea. Is it smart? Well, it is *if* the department in question uses the right ammo! In 1998, if you lived in New York City and wanted to pack the same stuff as the local police department, that would have been 115-grain full metal jacket round nose 9mm "ball," one of the poorest choices for self-defense *or* law enforcement.

One argument against this has been, "Carrying the same load as the local cops might allow opposing counsel to suggest, *Your Honor, the defendant is a wanna-be Rambo! Why, he even loaded his deadly weapon with the same ammunition as our police carry, as if he was impersonating an officer.*

I have to tell you that I don't worry a whole lot about that particular attack. I haven't seen it happen yet. But, of course, someone not seeing it happen yet doesn't mean it hasn't happened yet, or that it won't happen in the future. That being the case, it wouldn't hurt to have an answer to the challenging question, "Is it not true that you loaded with police ammo because you fancy yourself to be a cop, even though you aren't one?"

The best answer is, "No, sir. The police are experts in protection against the kind of criminals who attack citizens. I thought if the ammunition was good enough for the police to use to protect my family, it was good enough for *me* to use to protect my family."

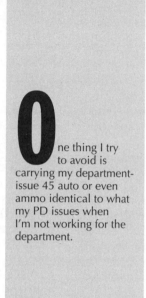

One thing I try to avoid is carrying my department-issue 45 auto or even ammo identical to what my PD issues when I'm not working for the department.

One thing I try to avoid is carrying my department-issue 45 auto or even ammo identical to what my PD issues when I'm not working for the department. The reason is that I don't want the department getting tied into a suit that might evolve from something I had to do to protect myself from death. The lawsuit won't do either entity, me or the department, any good. Each officer on my department is issued a permit to carry a concealed handgun, just like a citizen in our jurisdiction might possess. No, a sworn officer doesn't need a permit to carry a gun off duty, but I like them having the option.

Here's why, and it's kinda complicated, so please follow along. Remember, the lawsuit doesn't seek justice so much as it seeks money. Therefore, the plaintiff will go for the deep pockets. When House Resolution 218 was at long last signed into law by President George W. Bush and became LEOSA, the Law Enforcement Officers' Safety Act, sworn police and honorably retired cops around the country became eligible to carry guns nationwide, on their own time, irrespective

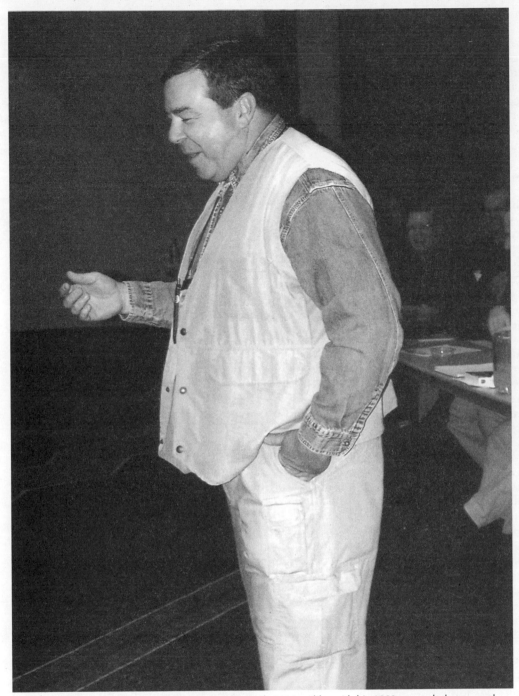

Dennis Tueller did a great service for cops and armed citizens alike with his 1983 research that proved the average man could close 7 yards from a standing start and deliver a fatal knife thrust in 1.5 seconds. Here, he explains his research at a deadly force symposium convened by the author at an ASLET seminar, 2006. In the background are noted authorities Brian Stover, Harvey Hedden, and John Holschen.

there to stop the carnage, and it didn't matter if they had the power to arrest the malefactor in that jurisdiction or not. Police chiefs in cities from New York to Chicago have dragged their feet and gotten in the way of other cops carrying there, or their cops carrying elsewhere, but once that is sorted out we'll start seeing "saves" from LEOSA that will prove the obvious legislative intent to be justified. Now, it will be a much shorter step to expanding the privilege to private citizens who can show the same trustworthiness and competency as those cops carrying nationwide.

If I'm outside my jurisdiction and have to shoot someone in self-defense while I'm carrying on LEOSA, my police department is effectively immune from lawsuit. I was not acting under "color of law" on duty; I was merely exercising a privilege granted by the Federal government to me and many others.

If, however, I'm outside my jurisdiction and shoot someone in self-defense *with the company hardware*, the agency can be sued. After all, they *gave me the ammunition and what is now "the death weapon."*

The lawsuit seeks big bucks. I don't have big bucks, and ain't worth suing by my lonesome. But the community any law enforcement agency serves has a tax base that plaintiffs' lawyers do see as representing big bucks. If there's no money there, there is less likely to be a lawsuit at all. Keep the blood out of the water, and you don't attract the sharks.

Avoid the "Hair Trigger Trap." I call it a trap for two reasons. First, cops and civilians and security professionals alike are much more likely to have to take people at gunpoint than to shoot them. If the finger goes to the trigger, as studies show it often

of arrest powers in a given jurisdiction. I personally think that, in time, this will be the precedent that could get a nationwide concealed carry privilege for armed private citizens who are provably both competent and law-abiding. It establishes a key ingredient called "obvious legislative intent." When LEOSA became law, the obvious intent of the Representatives and Senators who voted for it was to recognize that when bad people attempted to murder good people, it was a good idea to have more armed good guys and gals who might be does unconsciously, even when the person holding the gun is highly trained, the stage is set for accidental discharge due to several causes first identified by famed physiologist Roger Enoka. These include startle response, postural disturbance, interlimb response, etc. The lighter the trigger pull, the more prone the gun is to such unintentional discharges, often automatically considered "negligent discharges" by firearms professionals.

But there is a much more subtle trap. It has become a cottage industry in shooting-related lawsuits, and to a lesser extent in criminal prosecutions, for opposing counsel to present a false case of accidental discharge when in fact the shooting was intentional. This is because experienced lawyers know that self-defense to a charge of an intentional shooting is what's known in trial tactics parlance as "a perfect defense," but it's much harder for a defendant to prove that he didn't cock the gun and recklessly set the stage for an unintentional hair-trigger discharge.

The best way to avoid that bogus attack is to have a gun whose trigger weight is within factory specifications for police duty as opposed to target shooting. This is an argument against any gun that can be cocked to create a very light pull, unless the single-action pull is at least four pounds or more in weight. This is one reason so many police departments have gone with double-action-only handguns. One reason for the Glock pistol's enormous popularity, particularly among cops, is that BATFE has ruled it to be a double-action-only design. Just don't install the 3.5-pound connector, creating a light pull that the factory says should be used ONLY on competition pistols, and you should be fine.

The handload trap. Use all the reloads you want for practice, or match shooting, or handgun hunting. Heck, I do. But for a home defense gun, concealed carry handgun, or police duty weapon, factory ammo is the way to go. In most cases, the factory round will have better quality control and more reliability than a reloaded cartridge. If you don't believe me, ask anyone with experience as a range officer in any form of handgun competition, "Which is more likely to misfeed or misfire, a factory load or a handload?" Moreover, every factory defense round recommended in this book has a proven track record as a man-stopper in actual gunfights. No home-brewed ammo has that; actual shootings with reloads are very few and far between. (You could assemble a handload that duplicates a given factory load, and save some money, but now you're literally defending your family with a cheap imitation. That's the kind of clone ammo to use for practice, not for street carry.)

Two real problems come up in court with handloads. In *New Jersey v. Daniel Bias,* whether the death of a young woman was suicide or murder at the hands of her husband came down to forensic evidence testing, to wit, the determination of how far the gun muzzle was from her head before the fatal wound was inflicted. However, the death weapon was a Smith & Wesson Model 586 revolver charged with very light reloads in 38 Special +P cases. The police

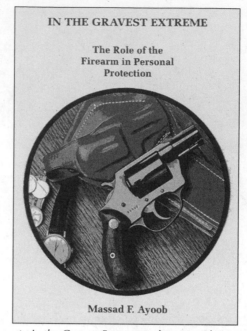

Ayoob wrote *In the Gravest Extreme* to show armed citizens the rules of engagement in deadly force encounters. It is available through Police Bookshelf, PO Box 122, Concord, NH 03302, www.ayoob.com.

insisted on doing their gunshot residue (GSR) testing with actual +P, which leaves GSR for a considerable distance, and there was none found on her head or hair. Defense experts tested reloads duplicating what the husband said he had made up and put in the gun, and could have shown that these wouldn't have left residue at the distance the gun was when the defense believe it discharged in the victim's own hand.

However, to make a long story short, that evidence never got in. It would have required the court to take the defendant's word for the handload "recipe." Even your reloading records, meticulous as they may be, won't help. You see, *the evidence was manufactured by the defendant,* and that goes for the records as well as the ammo. You can't prove it wasn't some BS you came up with afterward to get away with murder. I have challenged many Internet advocates of defensive handloads to find a case where the defendant's records or testimony as to load was accepted as GSR evidence. None has ever come up with a case.

Some scoff that GSR is unlikely to be an issue. They're wrong. Look at a few random issues of *American Rifleman* magazine's "Armed Citizen" column, and see at what close ranges most of those shootings take place. It's critical for you to be able to prove that the opponent was close enough to kill you with his knife, and he or his advocates in court are likely to tell the jury that he was too far away to present any danger to you. Gunshot residue testing may save you…*if* we can get it in. We regularly introduce GSR testing with factory ammo; I've never seen that *fail* to get in.

How likely is it that GSR will be an issue? Well, let's take a look at my own caseload at the moment. With the Lindsey case finished by a just acquittal, I'm down to ten on the current schedule, a nice round number that's easy to work with. One of those cases involves a citizen who drew a knife to protect himself, and another focuses on a cop who defended himself with blunt force. Neither, obviously, have anything to do with gunshot residue since no guns came into play at all. Of the remaining eight, GSR is an issue in *four* of them, and in one, it is a compelling issue. That's 40 percent of the cases overall, and *half* of the ten cases in this example. Does that sound as if GSR is "unlikely" to be an issue when *your* shooting comes?

Another thing to worry about with handloads is the argument, "This man was so intent in causing horrible, deadly wounds that regular bullets weren't deadly enough, so he made his own *extra-deadly* bullets!" That was the BS pulled by the prosecution in *State of NH v. Sgt. James Kennedy*. That argument was shot down by Jim Cirillo as expert witness for the defense. However, every courtroom argument is like a gunfight: it's better to avoid it than to have to fight it, and every now and then, the other side can get lucky and win.

By the way, remember those two cases the next time you hear on the Internet, "There has never been a case of anyone getting in trouble for using handloads." The *Kennedy* case ended with an acquittal, and that was justice. However, the *Bias* case went through three trials before the third jury found the kid guilty of Manslaughter and sent him to prison. Both his lawyers told me they felt that if he'd had factory ammo in the gun, they don't think he would have been convicted.

The Rules of Engagement

Every encounter will be different from every other: sometimes hugely, sometimes subtly. The only way to make sure you're right is to follow a formula when you make the decision whether or not to use lethal force. The formulae I'm about to show you are rock-solid, engraved in the stone of the law and what the court calls "common custom and practice" alike.

Deadly force is only permissible in a situation of *immediate, otherwise unavoidable danger of death or great bodily harm to oneself or another innocent person one has the right to protect*. The presence of that situation is determined by the *simultaneous* presence of three criteria: ability, opportunity, and jeopardy.

Ability means the attacker has the power to cause death or great bodily harm: that is, to kill or cause crippling injury. This usually takes the form of a *per se* weapon such as a gun or knife or club, but as noted above, can also manifest itself as *disparity of force*. Force of numbers, a hugely larger and stronger attacker, an able-bodied person attacking the disabled, high skill at unarmed combat *that is known to the shooter*, an adult violently attacking a child, even a male violently attacking a female are examples of

disparity of force. Even though they are ostensibly unarmed, their greater size, strength, etc. is so likely to kill or cripple that it becomes the equivalent of a deadly weapon. As noted earlier in this chapter as related to *Colorado v. Larry Lindsey*, a furtive movement that is consistent with going for a weapon (and consistent with nothing else) also suffices to create the ability factor.

Opportunity means the attacker is capable of immediately employing that power. In 1983, Dennis Tueller did the ground-breaking research that proved the average adult male can close a gap of seven yards from a standing start and inflict a fatal stab wound in 1.5 seconds on the average. From 100 yards away, it would take him longer, and shooting a man with a knife from the other end of a football field would probably not be seen as justifiable in most courts today. Within seven or even ten paces, though, the man with the knife has satisfied the opportunity factor.

Jeopardy is the final factor. The opponent must be acting in such a manner that any reasonable, prudent person in your situation would conclude that his intent was to kill or cripple you or the innocent person you deploy your gun to protect. As noted earlier, we're talking about *manifest intent*: an intent expressed in words and/or actions.

To be justifiable, deadly force must always be a last resort.

There is also an element that must be considered that has become known as *preclusion*. To be justifiable, deadly force must always be a last resort. Preclusion means, was there any way of avoiding this? Not just escape at the scene, but prevention: did *you* do anything to start the fight or "keep the ball rolling"? If you did, it impairs what the courts call "the mantle of innocence."

Some instructors teach preclusion as part of the same formula as ability/opportunity/jeopardy. I disagree, and separate it out in the training I give at Lethal Force Institute and elsewhere. There are two big reasons for this. First, Ability/Opportunity/Jeopardy (AOJ, for short) speaks to the assailant and the threat he presents to you. Preclusion speaks to *you*, and *your* exact situation, and *your* options in a given moment and place. It's "apples and oranges." Both elements need to be considered, but they need to be considered separately.

Second, AOJ is written in stone, but preclusion is fungible. Are you a cop, acting in the line of duty? If so, you have no duty to retreat, and indeed, under certain circumstances your retreat might be construable as cowardice or misfeasance of public office. Were you an armed citizen attacked in public in Florida in the year 2004? If so, the state law said you had a duty to retreat before using lethal force in self-defense. But today, the new (and, I like to think, improved) Florida law allows you to stand your ground without attempting to retreat if you are attacked in any place where you have a right to be. New York and many other states still have "retreat requirements" for public attack.

However, in any jurisdiction, you are allowed to stand your ground without resorting to retreat if you are in your home. It is called the "castle doctrine" because it stems from the ancient English Common Law that held "a man's home is his castle," and attacked there, he need not retreat.

Remember, however, that in any jurisdiction that has a "retreat requirement," retreat is *never* demanded unless it can be accomplished *in complete safety to oneself and other innocent persons.* In other words, you aren't expected to turn your back on a mugger's gun and attempt to outrun a bullet. You aren't expected to run away and leave your children behind, helpless against the attacker, like throwing the babies from the sleigh to placate the pursuing wolves. (Interestingly enough, I've been in cases against ruthless lawyers and prostitute expert witnesses who tried to convince juries that you *were* supposed to stoop to such levels. They did not win their cases.)

If this has been a long chapter, it's because it's a very involved corner of concealed carry, and we've barely scratched the surface here. My book

Power and responsibility are commensurate.

In the Gravest Extreme: the Role of the Firearm in Personal Protection is devoted to this topic, and has stood the test of time and the courts for more than a quarter of a century. Deadly force law being one of the more mature bodies of law, nothing terribly significant has changed in "the rules of engagement" since it was written. It is available through Police Bookshelf, PO Box 122, Concord, NH 03302, 1-800-624-9049, www.ayoob.com. At the same website you'll find a link for the classes I teach through Lethal Force Institute. The course I'd recommend would be the 40-hour LFI-I, which encompasses the legal/ethical/tactical elements plus several hundred rounds of hands-on combat shooting. If you already feel you're sufficiently competent with the "how" and want more about the "when," consider the weekend (two-day intensive lecture setting) Judicious Use of Deadly Force program.

The how and the when can't do it by themselves, though. You need both. Power and responsibility are commensurate. With great power, obviously, comes great responsibility, because power unchecked by responsibility becomes bullying among individuals and terrorism and tyranny in the collective.

At the same time, responsibility without the power to fulfill it may be the ultimate hopelessness.

Chapter 5

"GENTLEMEN (AND LADIES), CHOOSE YOUR WEAPONS"

Three approaches to snag-free carry revolvers.

(L) S&W Bodyguard (M/649) with shrouded hammer, DA/SA. (Center) factory bobbed hammer on DAO Ruger SP101. (R) "hammerless" configuration of DAO S&W Centennial (M/40-1).

One can't carry a concealed weapon without having a concealable weapon. Some are suitable for the concealed carry task, and some are not.

We can't cover every possible choice here. A swing through the Krause catalog will show you whole books on the 1911, the Glock, the SIG-Sauer, the Beretta, the Smith & Wesson series, etc. al. Other good choices from Paladin include *Living with 1911s* and *Living with Glocks* by Robert Boatman, and the outstanding *The Snubby Revolver* by Ed Lovette. I think Lovette's book should be read by anyone

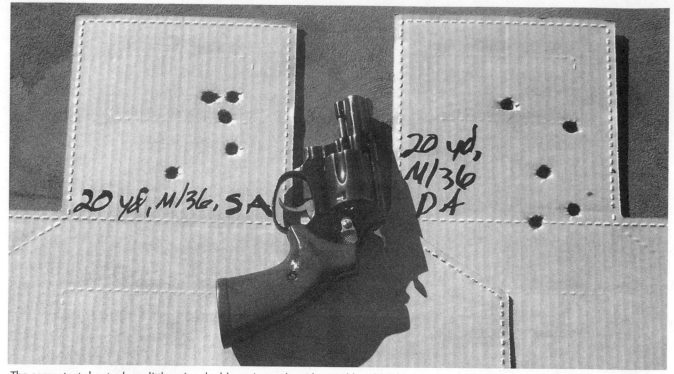

The competent shooter loses little going double-action-only with a snubby. This old M/36 Chief Special with Herrett stocks made 5 out of 5 head shots at 20 yards single action *(left)* and double action *(right)*.

Cocked to single action as shown, this S&W 649 can be a problem waiting to happen in a tactical situation. Author prefers double-action-only (DAO) S&Ws.

A bit larger than J-frames, and heavier, Taurus Tracker 45 *(top)* and Ruger SP101 357 *(below)*, are very "shootable" and substantially more powerful than 38s.

who owns or is thinking of owning a "snub-nose." It puts the whole *genre* in perspective.

As noted earlier, it's more convenient to have a "wardrobe" of concealable handguns, but it's not entirely necessary. Generations of young cops have learned that it's cheaper to buy a concealment holster for their full-size department-issue service handgun than to purchase a whole new gun and leather set for off-duty carry. Similarly, many armed citizens have learned that the full-size handgun they bought for home protection is concealable if they set their mind to it.

Cops have picked up on this, too. In 1967, Ordnance Sgt Louis Seman of the Illinois State Police convinced the ISP to become the first large department in the nation to adopt the Smith & Wesson Model 39 9mm

Today's new paradigm: polymer-framed, striker-fired autos. From top: Glock 22 in 40, S&W M&P in 9mm, Springfield XD Tactical in 45 GAP, 45 ACP Kahr P45, 40 cal. Taurus 24/7, and 9mm Ruger SR9.

semiautomatic pistol as a duty weapon. The reason was not firepower. At the time, troopers were required to be armed off duty. They carried 4- to 6-inch barrel Colt and Smith & Wesson service revolvers in uniform, and generally wore 2-inch barrel small frame 38 versions of the same guns on their own time. At qualification, the "snubby" scores were dismally inferior to those with the larger revolvers. Seman reasoned, correctly, that the Model 39 auto pistol would be light and flat enough for concealed carry, but would do fine for uniform wear as well. He was proven right: scores skyrocketed, and the troopers became comfortable wearing the slim Smith 9mms on their off-time. More recently, when NYPD went with 16-shot 9mm pistols and gave their officers the choice of the SIG P226 DAO, the heavy S&W Model 5946, or the polymer-frame Glock 19, the overwhelming majority chose the latter. This was partly because the Glock 19 was cheaper (NYPD officers buy their own guns through the department), but also because it was much lighter and the only one of the three options that was truly a "compact." The G19 was easier to carry all the time off duty, or when transferring to a plainclothes assignment.

Just as hunters and sportsmen have historically modeled their rifle choices on the nation's military small arms, America's armed citizens have historically followed the police establishment in choosing defensive handguns. When most of America's cops carried 38 Special revolvers to work, that same type and caliber was the most popular choice of home defense and concealed carry gun. Though private gun enthusiasts embraced auto pistols before American law enforcement in general, they did not switch to autoloaders *en masse* until the police did the same. Today, the snub-nose "detective special" genre remains extremely popular among cops for backup and off-duty wear, and the same style gun is very popular among armed citizens, but both tend toward the autoloader as a rule for full size "heavy duty" handguns.

Let's take just a cursory look at available choices today. In each weapon type, various sizes and calibers are available. This allows armed citizen and cop alike to have a deep concealment gun, a larger handgun that's concealable under heavier clothing, and perhaps

Many prefer a mix of modern and traditional. These are modern polymer-frame autos with hammer-fired mechanisms. From top: 9mm SIG P250 DAO, 45 ACP Heckler & Koch USP45, and 45 ACP Ruger P345.

Secrets of experience: moderately long-barrel guns with short grips deliver great shooting performance, and may be easier to carry at the waist than "snubbies." From top: Kahr Covert P40 in 40 S&W; S&W Model 64 38 Special with 4-inch barrel and Craig Spegel Boot Grips; and Colt CCO with 4 1/4-inch barrel of Commander mounted on short Officers frame, in 45 ACP, wearing Barnhart Burner stocks.

a still larger one for home defense or target practice, *all with the same fire controls and general "feel" for commonality of training and habituation,* so that skills developed with the one will transfer to the other. With some (but not all) combinations, one can also use the larger gun's speedloaders or higher capacity magazines for efficient spare ammo recharging with the smaller gun.

The New Paradigm "Automatics"

The proper term is considered to be "semiautomatic," but for my generation "automatic" was an acceptable descriptor of autoloading pistols which only fired one shot per pull of the trigger, so forgive me if I use it in this book for convenience. We all know what we're talking about.

The most popular *genre* of automatics today are striker-fired pistols with no "hammers" *per se,* and with polymer frames. Pioneered by Heckler and Koch

with the VP70Z and HKP9 series pistols of the 1970s and '80s – but *popularized* more than 20 years ago by the market-leading Glock brand – the polymer frame reduces weight, reduces cost, and is impervious to corrosion. The latter is an important point with guns carried concealed and often exposed to salty, rust-creating human sweat. Most of these pistols will have a trigger pull that's the same from first to last shot, which makes them easier to learn to shoot well. These include the Glock, of course, and also the Springfield Armory XD, the Kahr, Smith & Wesson's successful Military & Police series and cost-effective Sigma line, and the slim, reliable Ruger SR9 among others. The Glock line is far and away the most popular in American police service at this writing, but the S&W M&P is coming on strong in that sector and so, to a lesser degree, is the XD.

Double-action semiautomatics can be had with polymer frames (Beretta Ninety-Two and Px4, the current HK series, SIG P-250 and SIG-Pro, Ruger P95 9mm and P345 45, for example). These require a long, heavy (read "deliberate") pull of the trigger for the first shot, and are considered by some to be less prone to stress-induced accidental discharges for that

Two approaches to making 1911's butt less protuberant in concealment. Top: shortened Officer's frame on Colt CCO. Center: "Bobtail" configuration developed by Ed Brown, shown on his Executive model pistol. Below: standard size 1911 frame for reference, here a Smith SW1911. All 3 are 45 ACP.

S&W lightweight Centennials have been the choice of experts for deep concealment for more than half a century. Top: Original Centennial Airweight, circa 1953. Center, Model 442, early '90s, with Eagle grips. Below, Model 340 M&P, with factory-furnished Hogue grips, introduced 2007.

reason. They can be ordered DAO (double-action-only, with that same heavy pull for every shot, such as the popular Kel-Tec series), or TDA (traditional double action) in which the pistol cocks itself to an easy, light pull for every shot after the first. The latter will be fitted with a decocking lever to safely lower the hammer when the shooting is done. Of course, the same companies – plus Smith & Wesson and many more – offer double-action autos with steel or aluminum frame construction, too.

A classic favorite among American shooters is the single action semiautomatic, typified by the 1911 pistol that has been popular since the eponymous year of its introduction. To be ready for immediate, reactive self-defense, the 1911 type handgun has to be carried cocked and locked (hammer back, thumb safety in the "safe" position) with a live round in the chamber. This alarms some people not in tune with the tradition, and there is no shame for those people to simply go to a double action or striker-fired handgun instead. The 1911 was popular for concealed carry from the beginning because it is extremely *thin* for a gun of its power level, and is therefore very comfortable to wear inside the waistband or even in a shoulder holster. The most popular chambering is the one this gun was designed around, the 45 ACP (**A**utomatic **C**olt **P**istol), but enthusiasts have bought them in 38 Super, 9mm, 10mm, and other chamberings. The 1911 was designed by firearms genius John Moses Browning, who before his death did the initial design work on another famous weapon that bears his name, the Browning Hi-Power. Even slimmer, and capable of holding 14 rounds of 9mm Parabellum, this high quality weapon has something of a cult following in the CCW world.

Revolvers have earned a reputation for good reliability and have been around since the year 1836. A swing-out cylinder double action design is the easiest handgun for new shooters because of its simple "administrative handling," the routine loading and unloading, checking, and cleaning

Model 642 Airweight 38 Spl. may be today's "best buy" in a carry snub, opines author.

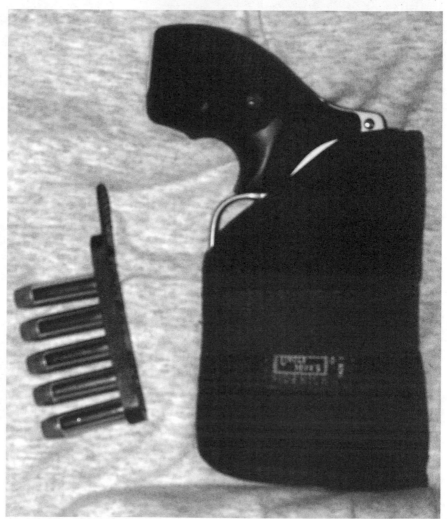

642 with Uncle Mike's grips and pocket holster, backed by Speed Strip, and loaded with 135-grain Gold Dot 38 Spl. +P is an excellent everyday carry snubby set-up.

Crimson Trace Lasergrips make an excellent addition to hard-to-shoot snubby revolvers.

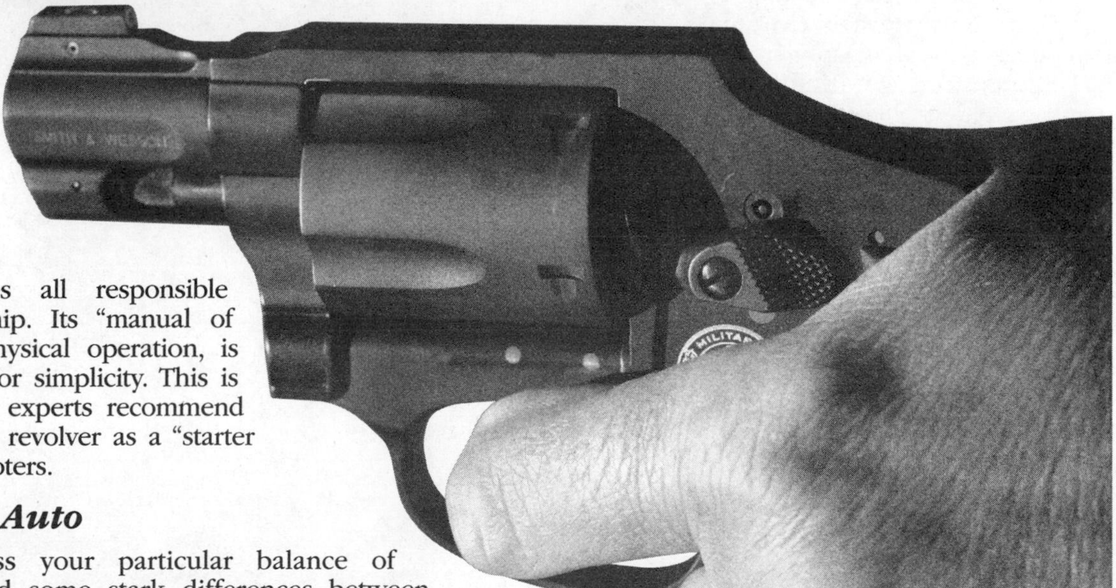

that accompanies all responsible firearms ownership. Its "manual of arms," i.e., its physical operation, is without parallel for simplicity. This is one reason most experts recommend the double-action revolver as a "starter gun" for new shooters.

Revolver or Auto

As you assess your particular balance of needs, you'll find some stark differences between the attributes of the double action revolver and the semiautomatic pistol. Let's go for a quick overview.

All autoloading pistols have long bearing surfaces between slide and frame, making them sensitive to proper lubrication. They are also depended on clean, pristine magazines with unfatigued springs. Thus, auto pistols are more maintenance intensive than revolvers, which can be left unlubricated and at rest literally for decades with no degradation in function.

Seen here with 340 M&P, Centennial's design lets the hand get higher on the backstrap for superior recoil recovery in rapid combat fire.

firepower's what you want, a semiautomatic is what you need.

Most semiautomatics can jam if pressed against an assailant's body before firing, as can happen in a belly-to-belly fight to the death or rape attempt. The pressure will push most autos' slides out of battery, or firing alignment of the parts, preventing even one shot from being fired. If the first shot discharges, viscous blood, fat, and brain matter may be back-blasted from a shot against bare flesh into the barrel bushing area of the autoloader as it cycles, preventing the slide from closing into battery for a subsequent shot. With a revolver, however, this is not a consideration. If your likeliest threat profile is a contact-distance mugging, rape, or murder attempt, the revolver will give you an advantage. Muzzle contact shots are particularly devastating since the violently expanding gases of the muzzle blast are directed into the opponent's body, causing massive additional damage.

Revolver shooters have tended historically to practice with light loads, using mild wadcutters

Ayoob says "Friends don't let friends carry mouse guns." Compared to S&W 40-1 38 *(top)*, the NAA 22 Magnum *(center)* and 22 Short *(bottom)* mini-revolvers should be seen as enjoyable recreational guns, not fighting weapons, he feels.

Military spec auto pistols such as the Glock, Beretta, SIG, etc. have large tolerances between the moving parts, allowing them to function when sand or dirt get in the mechanism; the more finely fitted revolvers may choke if dropped in a sand pile or immersed in mud. Thus, while the revolver is more forgiving of lack of routine maintenance, the automatic is more forgiving of field abuse.

In the serious defense calibers (38 Special and up) revolvers have only five shots in the small frame models, six in the standard frame, and occasionally seven or eight in the larger, progressively harder to conceal sizes. The smallest 9mm autos start at seven rounds on board, quickly progress to ten or eleven, and if you can carry a light polymer-frame, full size 9mm auto, you're up to 18 rounds or so, twenty if you don't mind a small magazine extension protruding from the butt. With quick-interchanging magazines, the autos are also much faster to reload. By any measure, if

There is such a thing as "too big" in defensive revolvers, such as the 460 Smith & Wesson. Author whimsically holds 8 3/8-inch version, left, and short barrel "emergency" model, right.

or feeble 130-grain generic 38 Special range loads for training, and then loading monster Elmer Keith Memorial Magnum loads of 357 persuasion for the street. Cops got away from that long ago, because they realized that light loads didn't prepare the officer to hit with a hard-kicking gun at the moment of truth. Too many private citizens still delude themselves this way. An advantage of the auto pistol is that it won't *run* with light loads, forcing the shooter into relevant practice.

Shorter, more efficient auto pistol loads tend to produce less muzzle flash at night than revolver ammo of equivalent power levels, i.e., 38 Special versus 9mm, 357 Magnum versus 357 SIG, or 45 Colt versus 45 ACP or 45 GAP (**G**lock **A**uto **P**istol). The less muzzle flash, the less the shooter is blinded by his or her own weapon, another advantage to the auto.

Autos tend to have squared-off "handles" that press tightly against the body, particularly in pocket, ankle, belly-band, or other deep concealment carry modes. This means the fingers of the drawing hand may have to fight a little to get between the flesh and the gun to gain a drawing grasp. The rounded profile of the small frame revolver allows a much faster grasp, hence a much faster draw. Score a point for the revolver here, particularly in pocket, ankle, or belly-band carry.

Revolvers tend, overall, to be somewhat more reliable than auto pistols, which can jam from being held with a limp wrist, from using too short or too long a cartridge, or from lack of lubrication or magazine damage. Particularly for non-experienced shooters and those who don't routinely lubricate their guns, this gives the "wheelgun" a reliability edge. (Auto shooters, remember to lubricate your carry gun monthly, even if you don't shoot it. Lubricant is liquid; it drains and evaporates.) If you carry in an ankle holster, grit builds up on the gun quickly. Only a few "military-spec" small autos seem to survive this buildup without jamming: the Kel-Tec P11 and P3AT, the baby Glocks, and the Kahrs, for example. Revolvers tolerate this grit buildup in ankle holsters much better.

One thing we've seen more and more since autoloaders became predominant in police work is that if they are carried with a manual safety locked in the "safe" position, they offer an element of proprietary nature to the user if a criminal gains control of the weapon. This feature is generally the province of auto pistols instead of revolvers. However, the K-frame (38-size frame) or larger S&W revolver can be converted to Magna-Trigger configuration by Rick Devoid. Such a

Kel-Tec P3AT (below J-frame S&W shown for comparison) is extremely flat and easy to carry, but author does not trust its 380 cartridge as much as he does 38 Spl. +P.

P3AT by Kel-Tec is reliable in current production, says author, and certainly light and flat.

today seem to prefer autoloaders, but most experts recommend revolvers for beginners and for that class of gun owners that expert Mark Moritz defined as NDPs, or non-dedicated personnel. It also explains why the revolver is so popular as a hideout/backup gun among even highly trained gun people.

When in doubt, do what I do. With a service-grade automatic on my hip and a light, snub-nosed revolver in my pocket, I figure I'm covered whether St. Peter turns out to be a Bill Jordan/revolver fan or a Jeff Cooper auto fan when I meet him on Judgment Day…

Concealed Carry Gun Features

Whatever your choice, there are some features that are particularly suitable for concealed carry. You want a carry gun that is **snag-free.** No sharp edges. Nothing to hook on clothing and reveal the pistol, or wear holes in the garments, or catch on fabric and fatally stall a defensive draw. If you just have to have a sharp-edged, non-ramped front sight, make sure your holster has a "sight channel" that will prevent "catching." Some shooters really do have a need for adjustable rear sights – they're carrying a hunting handgun or match handgun that needs to be precisely zeroed, and may need the sights adjusted to take advantage of different ammunition power levels – the edges of those sights should be rounded, even if a custom gunsmith has to do it.

The carry gun of your choice will probably be available in a variety of size formats. Here are the four currently produced 9mm Glocks. From top, target size G34; service size G17; compact G19; subcompact G26.

conversion can only be fired by someone wearing a magnetic ring. When my little ones were not yet at an age of responsibility, my "house gun" (and often my carry gun) was a 4-inch barrel Smith & Wesson 357, MagnaTriggered. It will come out of retirement now that I've got grandkids. I gave a 2 1/2-inch barrel MagnaTrigger Combat Magnum to my youngest when she became a mom – Devoid tuned the action, too – while her older sister was comfortable with her pet S&W Model 3913 9mm automatic in this regard, since it is equipped with both manual safety and magazine disconnector safety. Devoid (www.tarnhelm.com) can also fit a Cominolli thumb safety for all Glock pistols but the Model 36, offering proprietary nature to the user to Glock fans.

There are other factors to consider, but these are the key points. They help to explain why serious shooters

The old revolver paradigm, seen with S&W 38 Specials. From top: 6-inch K38 for pistol team use, 4-inch Combat Masterpiece for uniform wear, and 2-inch Chiefs Special for concealment needs.

Your model of choice may be available in various lengths. These are single-action-only SIG P220 45s. From top: 5-inch barrel target model, 4 1/4-inch service model, and 3.9-inch "Carry" model.

Make sure the grip and grip-frame area give the hand enough traction if wet with sweat or blood or rain. The defensive handgun, remember, is an emergency tool. Smooth metal frames coupled with pearl or even ivory "handles," if the latter don't have finger grooves, might as well be coated with wet soap. Some secure grip surfaces can be *too* tacky for concealed carry. Depending on the garments, "rubber" grips have been known to catch inner clothing surfaces and hike up the garment to reveal the handgun. Skateboard-like grips that lock the gun solidly into the hand can abrade coat linings. I find I can wear them next to bare skin, but a lot of my colleagues find them agonizing. On the other hand, some of those folks can wear cocobolo grips next to their skin, but in my case they cause an angry red rash. There are a lot of individualistic little tastes that you develop over years of concealed carry, and they tend to be highly subjective.

Night sights are a good idea. Most armed encounters occur in dim light, and Tritium sights can help.

When you wake up in pitch darkness in a strange motel room, those glowing sight dots guide your hand to the bedside defense sidearm like airstrip landing lights. Laser sights, particularly the convenient designs such as LaserMax (replacing the recoil spring under

Commonality of training and ammo, duality of purpose. Top, Glock 31 with Scott Warren night sights and InSight M3X white light unit, for police patrol and home defense. Below, Glock 33 with Trijicon night sights for backup and concealed carry. Both fire the powerful 357 SIG cartridge, and smaller gun will work with larger gun's magazines.

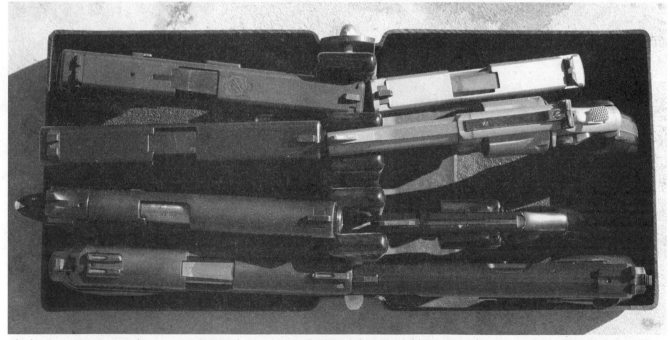

Thickness is an important dimension in CCW selection. Top to bottom, left: Springfield XD, Glock 22, Kimber 1911, SIG P226. From top at right: Kahr P40, S&W K-frame, S&W J-frame, and Browning Hi-Power. Note slimness of 1911 and Hi-Power formats, a reason for their popularity among CCW professionals.

the barrel in popular autos), and the Crimson Trace LaserGrip (bolt-on, for popular revolvers and autos) can enhance your hit potential in the dark. They're a Godsend for those with vision problems that allow them to identify a threat, but don't let them focus on gunsights that are at arm's length. The deterrent effect of the red laser dot on a suspect at gunpoint may have been over-rated by manufacturers and advertisers, but if there's a chance of that working, it's a chance you want on your side. Laser sights are also a tremendous training aid in dry fire and even live fire, allowing the shooter to better become accustomed to holding the gun as steady as possible as the index finger smoo-oothly rolls the trigger back until the shot.

White light attachments make great sense for home defense, and it is logical to purchase as an all-around defense pistol an autoloader that has integral frame rails that allow slide-on/slide-off units by SureFire, InSight, Streamlight, Blackhawk, and so on. Police are going to larger holsters made to carry light-mounted guns, and a few manufacturers (Blade-Tech, for one) produce concealable holsters that carry light-mounted automatics. As the light units become smaller, this practice will become more practical for concealed carry.

Size and Shape Factors

Bulges under the clothing are the key enemy of effective concealment, and the "handle" area of the gun tends to be the biggest offender here. The long grip-frame of a full-size duty pistol is best concealed by carrying it on the strong-side hip, tilted sharply forward until the backstrap of the grip is pointed almost at the armpit. This may require a slight crouch to effect the draw, but that's something most people do in a high-stress danger situation anyway.

Nonetheless, smaller gun butts are a plus for concealment. One of the lesser recognized concealment

"Fluffy the pet revolver," author's S&W 357 fitted with Magna-Trigger conversion. Gun can only be fired by someone wearing magnetic ring, provided. This concept has many tactical uses for homes with small children, prisoner transport, etc.

Size is not necessarily relative to power. From top: Colt Pocket Nine in 9mm Luger; Colt Pony 380; NAA Guardian 32, and Beretta 25/22 Short.

Carry gun of author's oldest daughter is this Sokol-tuned S&W Model 39. It holds nine rounds of 9mm and is a perfect carry size. SIG's analogous pistol, the P239, was advertised as "Personal Size," for good reason.

secrets is that a medium-length barrel coupled with a minimized grip frame can give the carrier the best of both worlds. Three good examples would be the K-frame Smith & Wesson revolver with a 4-inch barrel and stocks cut level with the metal butt; my favorite concealed carry Colt 45 auto among the extensive line the company has offered since 1911, the CCO with 4 1/4-inch Commander barrel and commensurate length slide mounted on the short-butt Lightweight Officers frame; and the popular Kahr Covert series, in which the barrel/slide of their standard-length guns (compact by most other makers' standards) is mated with the stubby frame of their Micro models. With autos, this generally reduces cartridge capacity by a round or two due to the necessarily shorter magazine, but that's a reasonable price to pay for a gun that conceals like a snubby

This hammer-shrouded Colt Detective Special picked up this much lint and dirt carried in an ankle holster between cop-owner's range qualifications. It still worked, one reason author likes revolvers for pocket and ankle wear.

White light attachment rail on dust cover of modern pistols is a useful feature, converting them to higher-capability home defense weapons when the light is in place. This is the SIG P250c in 9mm Luger.

but shoots like a service pistol. My old friend Marty Hayes, the master shooter and instructor who directs Firearms Academy of Seattle, once created a Glock 40 perfect for concealed carry that I called the Glock 22-1/2. He took the standard service-size sixteen-shot Glock 22 and shortened its butt to take the 13-round Glock 23 magazine. This gave maximum concealment, still offered an excellent grasp, and a total of fourteen versus sixteen rounds was not deemed to be an unfair price to pay for the improved concealment.

Rounded butts work well. Ed Brown came up with a "bobtail" lower rear end for his own line of factory custom 1911 automatics, which he has licensed to the Dan Wesson company for their brand and which is available for custom gunsmithing as well. With any handgun (revolvers are particularly suitable) rounding the edges of the grips at the bottom will improve concealability.

Additional Safety Factors

The trigger pull should be *smooth* on a defensive handgun, but *not particularly light.* One factor that occurs to human beings under stress is vasoconstriction. Blood flow is redirected away from the extremities and into the internal organs and major muscle groups, as if to "fuel the furnace" for the superhuman effort

Author has carried this Browning Hi-Power, tuned by Cylinder & Slide Shop, coast to coast in the U.S.A. and from Europe to Africa. Great feel and "shootability" combine with thinness to make it more concealable than it looks in profile. Worldwide availability of Browning parts and 9mm Luger ammo doesn't hurt, either.

about to come. This is why frightened Caucasians become deathly pale, and it is why people in life-threatening stress situations become grossly clumsy. A light trigger pull can now much more easily discharge prematurely and unintentionally.

There are two problems with this. One is the potential for unintentional discharge itself. (Yeah, I know, it's trendy to call it "negligent discharge" unless there was a mechanical defect. I've worked in the criminal justice system since 1972, and I still believe in the "innocent until proven guilty" part. The automatic assumption of negligence if the discharge was not caused by mechanical failure seems to have arisen from firearms academies sponsored by liability conscious firearms manufacturers. I'm still comfortable with the term "accidental discharge" (AD) until negligence has been clearly and convincingly proven.)

Accidental discharges, sometimes with tragic and fatal results, *have* been clearly and convincingly related to very light trigger pulls over the years by countless police departments. Decades ago, the police departments of Los Angeles and New York City went to double-action-only revolvers, because so many bad things had happened with revolvers cocked to single action. NYPD now mandates a nearly twelve-pound

Ed Lovette, who wrote the book *The Snubby Revolver*, a must-read for CCW practitioners in author's opinion.

Gun expert Dean Speir pronounced the Glock 30 the ideal concealed carry pistol. Match-accurate and totally reliable with duty loads, it carries 11 rounds of 45 ACP.

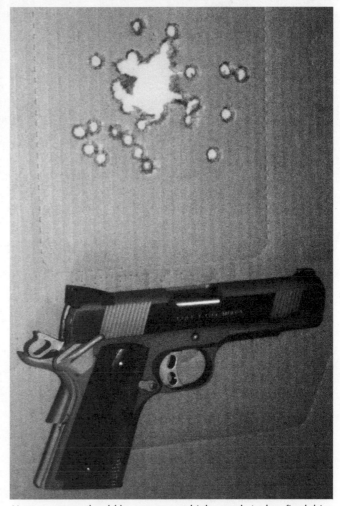

Your carry gun should be accurate at high speed. Author fired this 60-shot, perfect score qualification target with one of his Colt 45 CCO pistols, shown.

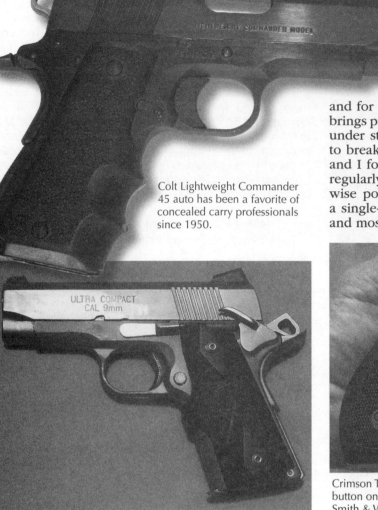

Colt Lightweight Commander 45 auto has been a favorite of concealed carry professionals since 1950.

(NY2, or "New York Plus") trigger module in all Glock pistols carried by members of their service. The New York State Police, for the exact same reason, pioneered the original "New York trigger" (NY1) for the Glock 17 9mms they adopted in the 1980s, and for the Glock 37 45 GAPs they carry today. This brings pull weight up to 7.75-8.0 pounds. It works well under stress for accurate hits; it's actually less likely to break than the standard trigger spring it replaces; and I for one have it in each of the several Glocks I regularly carry concealed. In a 1911 pistol, no street-wise police instructor or gunsmith will recommend a single-action pull weight of less than four pounds, and most suggest something closer to five.

Crimson Trace LaserGrip activates when middle finger depresses button on front of grip in normal firing grasp. It's shown here on a Smith & Wesson Titanium Model 342 38 Special.

Subcompact 1911s are popular among professionals. Famed instructor Gila Hayes carries hers, an Ultra Compact 9mm Springfield Armory, as shown with modified safety, sights, and LaserGrips added.

Laser sights are useful, especially in poor light. Here author centers a target after dusk with Ruger SP101 revolver equipped with Crimson Trace LaserGrips.

Precision shots are needed in self-defense more often than folks think. Late model S&W M/40-1 (right), has better sights than such J-frame S&Ws used to have, but even better are those on Model 340 PD (left). Big AO Express night sight in front is easy to pick up in close, fast shooting, and the eye settles it into generous U-notch rear sight if precision shot is needed.

The second problem with the light trigger pull is the false allegation of an accidental discharge. Here's the situation I've seen play out over and over again in both civil and criminal cases over the years. Good guy shoots bad guy. Publicity-hungry prosecutor or money-hungry plaintiff's lawyer needs a scapegoat to grab political or financial profit. This attorney fabricates a case of accidental discharge due to recklessly cocking hammer and creating hair trigger (or carrying pistol that would always fire with "hair trigger"). This BS allegation is dignified in court as the accuser's "theory of the case." Without this frail hook on which to hang the bogus case, it probably would have gone away. Instead, the shooter who fired in self-defense goes through a nightmarish (and nightmarishly expensive) ordeal. See the "Aftermath" chapter.

Camera catches recoil and muzzle flash as author fires Ruger SP101, the most controllable of the "baby Magnums" in his opinion, with full power 125-grain 357 loads at dusk. These weapons are controllable at speed, but only with the right techniques and enough shooting experience. Notice slight jolt to head and upper body.

Three modifications stand out on this Glock 17. Heinie Straight-8 sight...Cominolli thumb safety fitted by Rick Devoid at Tarnhelm...and oversize magazine release from GlockWorks. Not every shooter needs every available modification.

Good lights are essential to self-defense in poor light. FL/GA Regional Champion with Enhanced Service Revolver, Jon Strayer, demonstrates the very useful Liberator flashlight by First Light, Inc. at 2007 national championships. Affixing quickly to the back of the hand, it leaves both hands free. Revolver is Mulkerin Custom S&W 45.

One is wisest to avoid it entirely. The revolvers I carry for personal defense will fire double action only. Some came that way from the factory and some were modified. My carry autos are either double action (with heavier-than-target-grade trigger pulls even on single action), my XDs have 6 to 7 pound trigger pulls, none of my carry 1911s are lighter than 4 pounds, and as noted my carry Glocks have New York triggers in the 7-8 pound pull range. Anyone who tells you it's impossible to shoot well with these guns, doesn't know how to shoot. I've won IDPA matches with Glock and XD pistols in the above pull weights, and for three years running won the NH Police Association annual state shoot with a Glock 22 that had a New York trigger, shooting against some who had put 3.5 pound pulls in their guns before the match.

Selecting the Gun Wardrobe

In a clothing store, it's hard to go wrong with "the basics": "basic black," gray pinstripe, and all of that. In the world of CCW, the first of "the basics" is a small revolver.

S&W's J-frame series is the odds-on choice of professionals. High quality, smart engineering, and a wide range to choose from: 22, 32 H&R Magnum (off and on), 38 Special, and 357 Magnum. My advice would be to go with the 38 Special, though the little 22 Kit Guns make great "understudies" for cheap practice. An all-steel 2-inch (actually 1 7/8-inch barrel in most cases) will run about 20 ounces. The aluminum frame Airweights go about 15 ounces, a profound difference when the gun is carried in a pocket or on the ankle, but much less noticeable in a belt holster. The AirLites are available in various mixes of Titanium and Scandium, and are proportionally expensive due to the rare materials used in their construction, but they can get down to the eleven and twelve ounce weight range. There's no excuse *not* to carry when adequately powerful handguns come this light.

Of course, the lighter the gun, the harder it kicks with the same ammunition. The all-steel small frames aren't too bad, even with 38 Special +P ammo. The Airweights are downright unpleasant, and after I've finished a 50-shot qualification I'm glad it's over. The AirLites, however, are downright painful, and with Magnum loads they're torture devices. I find them

Modern paradigm handguns are widely considered inferior to the classic 1911 45, but that's not necessarily so. In the single-action 45 division, CDP, the top three places at the 2007 IDPA National Championships went in order to David Olhasso with Springfield Armory XD45 *(top)*, David Sevigny with Glock 21SF *(center)*, and Ernest Langdon with S&W M&P *(below)*, all in 45 ACP.

more painful to shoot than the mighty Smith & Wesson 500 Magnum hunting revolver, by far. If you get them in 357, load them with 38s and do yourself a favor.

It's a myth, by the way, that it's OK to practice with mild loads but carry monster Magnums because somehow, fight or flight reflex will make up for the kick in an actual defensive shooting. True, the dump of nor-epinephrine and endorphins that accompanies high level body alarm reaction may block the pain of the recoil, but that won't keep a too-powerful gun from twisting in your hand and preventing you from getting fast, accurate follow-up shots. You don't need me to tell you that a hit with a 38 Special beats a miss with a 357 Magnum.

The J-frame – a 32-size frame with a cylinder bored out for five 38 rounds instead of six 32s – can be had in three styles, all dating back to the period between 1949 and 1955. The original Chiefs Special series is the "conventional style" double-action revolver, with exposed hammer that allows thumb-cocking to single action. The Bodyguard style is that gun with a built-in "hammer shroud" patterned after the bolt-on Colt shroud introduced shortly before, which keeps the hammer spur from snagging on clothing or pocket

This late model S&W has current style cylinder latch, designed not to ding the thumb upon recoil, and above it the Internal Locking System, which purists despise and new shooters seem to like.

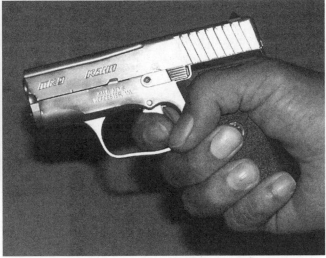

Subcompact carry guns can be "too small for your hand," necessitating technique changes. Trigger reach is so short on this Kahr that author's trigger finger is blocked by thumb in traditional grasp; thumb will need to come up. Little finger is tucked under short butt since there's no room for it on the frame...

Introduced in 2007, this Model 40-1 Classic was the first S&W in years to appear without the internal lock. It has the old "lemon-squeezer" grip safety, and traditional square latch that purists associate with the S&W breed.

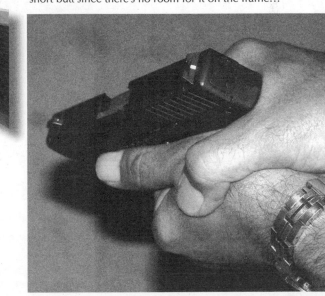

...author's two-hand grasp on the Kahr puts firing thumb on support hand out of the way of trigger finger, and support hand thumb well forward to avoid the sharp edge on the Kahr's slide release lever.

linings during a fast draw. A small button-size portion of the hammer is exposed to allow thumb-cocking for light-pull single-action shots. The third variation is the Centennial series, known colloquially as a "hammerless" but actually having a hammer that is totally enclosed inside its streamlined frame.

It is generally accepted that for fast defensive shooting, double action is the way to go. With this in mind, the Centennial is clearly the best bet, followed by the Bodyguard, followed by the Chiefs. The reason is found by analyzing shooter ergonomics in live fire, not theory born in dry fire.

When a revolver recoils, it wants to torque its muzzle up and to the side. With the conventional-hammer Chiefs series, the butt can roll up into the web of the hand, getting after one to three shots to a position where that web of the hand blocks the hammer and prevents subsequent shots from being fired until the gun is re-gripped. That won't happen with the Bodyguard, whose hammer is shielded within its slot, and whose shroud is shaped in a way that catches at the web of the hand and prevents "roll-up." The Centennial is even better, because not only can't the gun roll up, but in addition the shape of the rear frame allows the shooter's hand to grasp the gun higher. This lowers the bore axis *vis-à-vis* the gun hand and arm, keeping the muzzle down,

Carry gun choice involves a balance of "heavier gun easier to shoot, lighter gun easier to carry." Author weighs choice between 14 oz. Kahr PM9 (left, all black) and 22 ounce Kahr MK9 (stainless, right). Each is a 7-shot 9mm of identical overall dimensions.

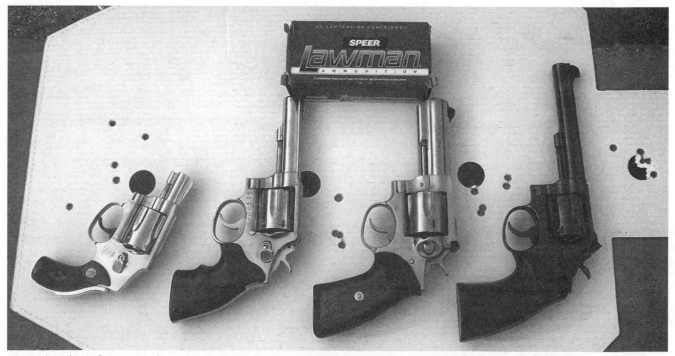

Longer barrel equals easier to shoot accurately, harder to carry. Left to right: 2" barrel S&W J-frame Centennial has produced a roughly 4" group. S&W Model 64 and Ruger GP100 with 4" barrels have shot much tighter. Best group of all came with 6" barrel S&W K-38, far right. All fired at 25 yards with Speer Lawman 158-grain +P .38 Special ammo.

S&W M&P 11-shot 45 ACP has optional thumb safety, comes with rails to hold this Streamlight white light attachment. Somewhere out there is a handgun with exactly the features you want.

and maximally enhancing the shooter's recoil recovery rate for the most accurate possible rapid fire.

Because the Centennial can *only* be fired double action, it also prevents cocked gun accidents and possible false accusations of same. All these reasons have combined to make the Centennial series not only the most popular of the J-frames overall, but in most years of late the best seller among J-frames overall.

Factoring in cost, shootability, and portability, the S&W Model 642 Airweight is my personal choice among all those available, most of which I own or have owned and all of which I've shot. It's the one I'd personally recommend. Taurus has a line of similar revolvers in all three hammer styles which are acceptable alternatives, trading less fancy finish for a lower price tag.

Going up a notch, there are slightly larger revolvers that are more powerful. The two I could most strongly recommend are the snub-nosed Ruger SP101 357 Magnum and the 2-inch barrel Taurus Tracker in 45 ACP. The latter takes the rimless auto pistol cartridges in a fast-loading "moon clip," and mine shoots to point of aim at 25 yards with groups like a service revolver's. The SP also has target-grade accuracy. Each has extra-cushiony trips to bring their recoil down to manageable levels. In the 25-ounce weight range,

these are too heavy for my taste for pocket or ankle carry, but for the person who wants a small, powerful snubby in a belt holster, they're great.

Next on the "concealed handgun wardrobe necessities list" is a compact semiautomatic pistol, if you're comfortable with that type of handgun. Glocks in compact (G19 9mm, G23 .40, G32 .357 SIG, G30 .45 ACP, and G38 .45 GAP) are all good choices. So are the many other compact (i.e., medium size) modern autos you'll find in the *Gun Digest,* where there's more space to pore over the various models and size/weight specifications than here. In the 1911, Commander and Officers size work well. For many, something more *sub*-compact fits the body better. These would include the "baby Glocks" in the same calibers, the Micro-series Kahrs, and the smallest of the 1911s by their many makers.

Finally, a full-size gun makes particular sense under cold-weather wardrobes, which can amply conceal them. In cold weather, with gloved or cold-numbed hands, a pistol with a longer grip-frame may be easier to handle. I like something with a large trigger guard, and whose trigger won't rebound so far forward that it can snag on or be blocked by thick glove material, which could make it fail to re-set. A TDA auto pistol will generally fill that bill, as will the Glock or XD. I get leery of single-action pistols when cold or gloves have further reduced a vasoconstricted hand's ability to feel the trigger, and the glove-blocking factor leaves most revolvers out entirely.

The bottom line of "concealed handgun wardrobe selection" is this: the gun's size and shape must fit hand, body, and clothing selection alike. You probably don't dress the same every day. When you "dress to kill" (forgive me, I couldn't resist) you also need to vary that particular "wardrobe" to better suit your daily needs.

Final advice: In the immortal words of author and big game hunter Robert Ruark, "Use Enough Gun." Small-caliber weapons simply don't have the "oomph" to stop a violent human being. I coined the phrase "Friends don't let friends carry mouse-guns," and I'll stick by that. The cessation of homicidal human threat is the *raison d'etre* of CCW. If the Weapon you're Carrying Concealed isn't powerful enough to do that job, you've undercut the whole purpose of the mission. I personally draw the line above the marginal 380 ACP and consider the minimums to be 38 Special +P in a revolver and 9mm Luger in a semiautomatic pistol. On the top end, only master shooters can handle the violent recoil of 41 and 44 Magnums. For most people, the best bet is in a caliber range that encompasses 38 Special, 357 Magnum, 9mm Luger, 40 Smith & Wesson, 10mm Auto, 45 ACP, and 45 GAP. There are other rarely-carried rounds within that range, but any of those – with proper high-tech hollow-point defensive ammunition – can be reasonably counted on to get you through the night.

For more on gun and ammo selection, I'd refer you to my *Gun Digest Book of Combat Handgunnery, Sixth Edition,* available from Krause. The bottom line is, it's not about "what gun did you have" so much as it's about "did you have a gun?" Modern ultra-compact, ultra-light 38 Special and 9mm Luger handguns give you adequate power in extremely small and light packages. You just don't have to settle for anything

Even gun color is a debatable issue. Some like matte black, as in the Kahr PM9 above, because it doesn't call attention to the gun. Others *want* the bad guy to realize he's at gunpoint, and like the conspicuous silver color of stainless MK9, below, by the same maker.

less, when innocent lives – including your life and the lives of those you most love – will likely be at stake if and when the shooting starts.

Chapter 6

DEFENSE LOADS OF CHOICE:
The Word From The Street

Sterile lab testing in ballistic gelatin is great, but the ultimate laboratory is the street, the author maintains. Here are the loads that seem to be doing best there, input written in blood from gunfights police departments have experienced with this ammunition.

Premium lines from four big makers, covering four popular calibers. This, for the most part, is the type of round the author recommends.

Defensive ammunition choice is about picking what works best to neutralize armed and dangerous human beings before they can maim or murder. Scientific testing of ammo in ballistic gelatin can help predict bullet performance in the field, but at the end of the day, it is the performance and not the prediction that will matter.

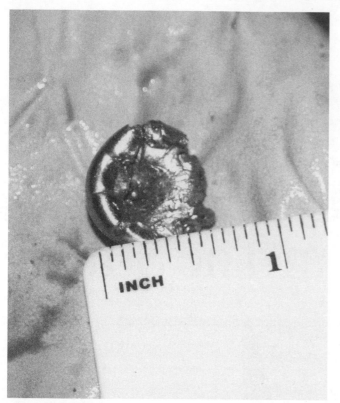

This 230-grain standard velocity Gold Dot 45 ACP bullet expanded to some 60-caliber after striking bone, kept on going to deliver massive wound track. Expansion was not textbook, but neither are living things. Gold Dot has done very well in officer-involved shootings.

Thirty-four years of carrying a sworn police officer's badge, 20 years as chair of the firearms committee of the American Society of Law Enforcement trainers, and several years now on the advisory board of the International Law Enforcement Educators and Trainers Association have combined with several trips to major seminars of groups like the International Law Enforcement Firearms Instructors Association and the International Homicide Investigators Seminars to give me a solid base of cops who've investigated a lot of shootings for their departments. These aren't "war stories," they are full investigations of shootings including evidence recovery, complete autopsy and forensic ballistic testing protocols, and intensive debriefings of the shooters and the witnesses. From that collective pool of knowledge emerges a profile of which duty cartridges perform the best.

OBVIOUSLY, POLICE ISSUE AMMUNITION IS USED IN A SIGNIFICANT MAJORITY OF THESE SHOOTINGS. That's why police duty calibers and loads have the strongest "data bases" to learn from.

Fortunately for armed citizens, they and the police tend to choose the same calibers. Picking a load that has proven itself on duty with the police gives the armed citizen added confidence in what their chosen gun/cartridge combination can deliver. As many have noted, using ammunition that is widely issued to police is a strong defense against unmeritorious courtroom allegations such as, "He used evil hollow point bullets that rend and tear, and that shows he had malice in his heart!"

HST is Federal's current top defense load. These two bullets expanded differently because they met different resistance. The one on left went through a hog's heavy skull before utterly destroying the brain; the one on the right entered the shoulder and tore a large wound through the chest. Both animals were stopped instantly. +P 230-grain 45 round was doing better than 950 fps from 5-inch barrel.

Let's look at what the "street feedback" is indicating is working best in the "ultimate laboratory" these days.

38 Special

Concealed carry permit instructors tell me that the 38 Special revolver, usually in compact short-barrel form, is one of the most common guns brought to their classes by students, and often the single gun that their graduates most commonly carry on the street. For most of the 20th Century, this caliber revolver was also by far the most popular in law enforcement, with plainclothes and off duty officers generally carrying "snubbies," and uniformed personnel generally carrying larger framed, longer barrel models.

At this writing, there are still thousands of senior cops carrying "grandfathered" 38 revolvers on duty in New York City and Chicago, and many more who carry them as backup or off-duty guns. In fact, the snub-nose 38 seems to be the most popular police backup handgun to this day, and is still widely used for off duty carry.

Only two cartridges really stand out as head and shoulders above the large pack of available 38 Special rounds. These are the "FBI load" and the "New York load."

The FBI load gets its sobriquet from the fact that this round was adopted by the Federal Bureau of Investigation circa 1972, right after Winchester introduced it. It was also adopted by the Chicago PD,

Base-on view of expanded 45 ACP Federal HST 230-grain +P bullet that instantly dropped a man-size hog with a chest shot. Bullet destroyed both lungs and top of heart, expanded to approximately 90-caliber.

Seen from bottom, this Winchester Ranger 127-grain +P+ 9mm round expanded to slightly over 60-caliber, and at 1250 foot seconds impact velocity did massive and instantly fatal damage to a man-size hog.

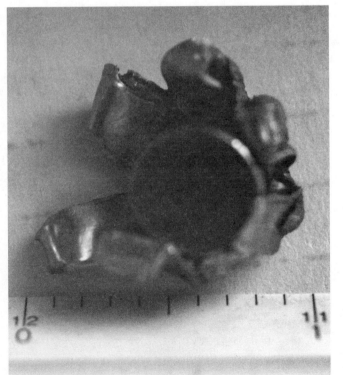

Base-on view of still-bloody HST 230/45 +P recovered from hog shot in skull and killed instantly. Expanded diameter is a hair under an inch at widest point. Irregular expansion was due to striking heavy bone on slight angle, which did not deviate bullet from its trajectory. Penetration depth was optimal.

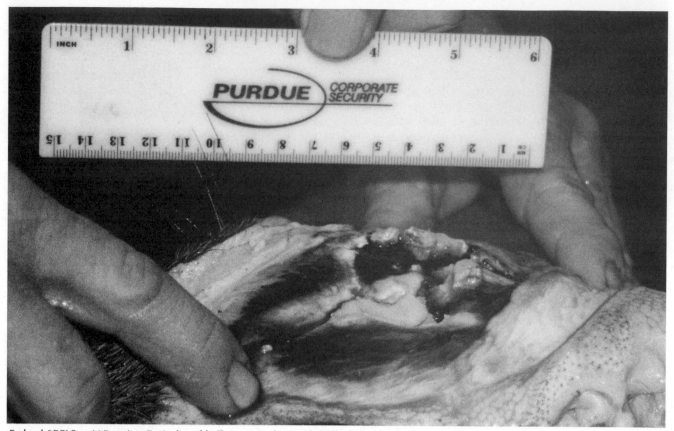

Federal 9BPLE, a 115-grain +P+ jacketed hollowpoint, shattered skull of hog at entry point for a more than 2-inch area, went on to virtually liquefy brain and lodge in base of skull. Truly massive damage, optimum penetration.

and remains the 38 Special load of issue there to this day. Metro-Dade (now Miami-Dade) police likewise found it to perform superbly, as did cops throughout the U.S.A., and it continues to be known by some locally as the "Chicago load" or "Metro load." This cartridge comprises an all-lead, semi-wadcutter shaped hollowpoint bullet at +P velocity.

It works particularly well out of a 4-inch barrel, but cops quickly discovered that the projectile generally upset and expanded at least to some degree – even out of short barrels that reduced velocity. The reason was that with no tough copper jacket to peel back, the soft lead expanded more easily in flesh.

Winchester and Remington both produce this 158-grain LSWCHP +P round. The Remington seems to have the softer lead of the two, and therefore, opens a bit more dramatically. This is a good thing.

A few years ago, NYPD realized it still had some three thousand officers carrying 38 Special service revolvers as primary handguns, and that the overwhelming majority of their plus/minus 35,000 sworn personnel carried snub-38s as backup and off-duty guns. They approached Speer to create a load that would optimize 38 Special terminal ballistics when fired

The 9mm Luger (aka 9X19, 9mm Parabellum, 9mm NATO) is one of the most popular among armed citizens, and also still widely used by the nation's police.

from a revolver with a barrel measuring 1-7/8 inches. Ernest Durham at Speer led the project, and the result has now become known colloquially as the NYPD load. It comprises a wide-mouthed 135-grain Gold Dot bonded, jacketed hollowpoint at +P velocity.

In numerous shootings with both snubs and 4-inch service revolvers, NYPD officials tell me that they are more than satisfied. Because of the lighter bullet, it kicks less than the FBI load, and because of the modern Gold Dot technology, it expands widely and reliably. They have found it to be a good man-stopper.

Either will work well. In a snubby, I prefer the Gold Dot for two reasons. First, the lighter recoil is helpful in fast, accurate shooting. Second, the all-lead FBI load is more lightly crimped than the Gold Dot, and when fired in a super-light snubby in the ten or eleven ounce weight range, such as the Titanium or Scandium S&W AirLites, recoil is so severe that after a shot or two, the projectiles can start pulling loose from the case mouths. They "prairie dog" up out of the chamber at the front of the cylinder, where they can strike the forcing cone of the barrel and lock the gun up solid. While this can happen with any make of the all-lead +P FBI load, it does not occur with the Speer NYPD load.

Remington Golden Saber 124-grain +P from 4-inch barrel Glock 19 killed man-size hog cleanly and instantly with one shot, penetrated deeply, and expanded to roughly 50-caliber.

9mm Luger

The 9mm Luger (aka 9X19, 9mm Parabellum, 9mm NATO) is one of the most popular among armed citizens, and also still widely used by the nation's police. As a result, we have a huge amount of street experience to tap into as to what works well and what doesn't in this caliber.

In the late 1980s through most of the 1990s, 147-grain hollowpoints of conventional copper jacketed construction were the trendy issue rounds. They worked spottily – sometimes they expanded, and sometimes they just punched narrow little through and through wounds like ball ammo – and as a result, most departments that used this stuff either switched to more powerful calibers, or went to 9mm ammo that was going faster, with lighter bullets.

For many years, the "Illinois State Police load" – a 115-grain standard JHP launched at some 1300 fps – proved itself to be the most decisive man-stopper available. It still works great. Federal's version of this load, the 9BPLE, is standard issue for the DeKalb County lawmen, on the tough turf that surrounds and encompasses Atlanta, Georgia. These guys get into so many firefights that they've drawn political heat for

> For many years, the "Illinois State Police load" – a 115-grain standard JHP launched at some 1300 fps – proved itself to be the most decisive man-stopper available.

"shooting too many people." They have proven that when they shoot people with a 115-grain JHP doing 1300 foot seconds out of their issue Beretta service pistols, the bad guys go down and stop trying to kill them. This is A Good Thing.

Other loadings have emerged that have the same decisive stopping power in 9mm. They include Winchester's 127-grain Ranger series +P+ at 1250 foot-seconds, and Speer's Gold Dot 124-grain +P at the same velocity. Chicago PD switched to the 124-grain +P after multiple dismal stopping failures with 147-grain subsonic, and NYPD has used this round with great effect for some fifteen years. Both are delighted with it. Orlando cops are issued P226 SIGs and 127-grain +P+ Winchester, and many shootings since, they've found it to be as effective as any handgun caliber could be.

Personally, I carry the 9BPLE in one particular Beretta that shoots it better than any other carry load, and Winchester Ranger 127 grain +P+ in virtually all my other 9mm pistols, long or short barrel.

Some folks have bought into the theory that the 147-grain subsonic has been so widely recommended by authority figures, it *must* be good. The fact is, there's

Winchester Ranger SXT is an example of *modern* 147-grain 9mm subsonic hollowpoints that have proven themselves suitable to police and citizen self-defense use. Earlier versions of this cartridge expanded erratically and often over-penetrated.

a new generation of 147-grain subsonic that *is* pretty darn good. It utilizes new-generation high-tech expanding bullet technology expressly engineered to make the bullets open up at velocity below the speed of sound. These include the CCI Speer Gold Dot, the Federal HST, and the Winchester Ranger.

Amarillo, Texas Police report excellent results with their issue load for those officers who choose 9mm pistols, the 147-grain Gold Dot. A major department in the Pacific Northwest is now issuing Federal HST 147-grain subsonic, and reports excellent results in numerous shootings. LAPD and LA County Sheriff's Department find that fewer officers and deputies are opting for larger caliber guns bought out of their own pockets, because they are reassured by how well Winchester Ranger 147-grain 9mm has worked for their brothers and sisters in numerous line of duty shootings.

Still, the faster bullets seem to be the way to go. There is much more corollary tissue damage around the wound channels with the faster 9mms, with medical examiners documenting "macerated" flesh, that is, tissue chopped up like burrito filling. You don't see that with subsonic rounds, even though a high-tech modern 147 grain may actually expand

Developed for the snub-nose revolvers of NYPD, Speer Gold Dot 135-grain +P is author's load of choice in 38 Specials today. The bullets will not "pull" from recoil in super-light revolvers like 11-ounce S&W 342, left, as happens with 158-grain lead +Ps.

very slightly more than a lighter 9mm bullet, simply because it has "more lead to spread."

357 Magnum

One cartridge stands above all others in this caliber in the history of American law enforcement: the 125-grain semi-jacketed hollowpoint loaded to a velocity in the 1400 foot-second range (from a 4-inch barrel). Some experts argue whether the wide-

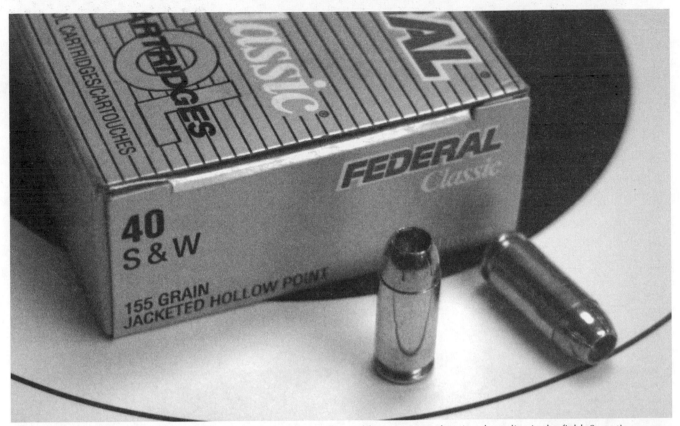

Affordably priced Classic line Federal 155-grain JHP has performed superbly in 40 S&W shootings by police in the field. Sometimes you don't need premium-price ammo to "carry with confidence."

mouthed Federal version of this load, or the scallop-jacket Remington version that originally popularized the 125-grain 357 among cops, is the single best of the breed. It seems to be an argument akin to how many angels can dance on the head of a pin. The Winchester 125-grain Magnum load does not have either of those features, but worked every bit as well for such departments as the Maine State Police when they carried 357 revolvers.

This round tends to create a wound channel that is nine to eleven inches deep, but very wide, with tremendous damage around the radius of the wound track. It also has a nasty muzzle blast and pretty sharp recoil. The great combat shooting trainer and combat pistol champion Ray Chapman used to say that the 125-grain Magnum load's almost magical stopping power was the only reason to load 357 instead of 38 Special +P ammunition into a fighting revolver chambered for the Magnum round. I tend to agree.

When departments such as City of Indianapolis Police Department, and the state troopers of Kentucky and Indiana issued that load, there were literally tons of bad guys shot with 125-grain Magnums, and they tended to go down "right now." Texas Department of Public Safety personnel were known to refer to this round's "lightning bolt effect," and I knew Kentucky troopers who called it "the magic bullet." Even though velocity dropped considerably from the 2.5-inch barrels of Indiana State Police detectives' Combat Magnums, or from the 3-inch Military & Police 357s of Indianapolis plainclothesmen, the bad guys seem

Check your carry ammunition carefully before loading. Even the best manufacturers can make mistakes. This visibly defective 9mm ball cartridge came out of a factory box.

to go down just as fast. The 125 grain 357 Magnum semi-jacketed hollow point earned its title, bestowed by expert Ed Sanow, as "King of the Street," and this remains the Magnum load of choice today. I have no personal preference between the Federal, Remington, and Winchester brands.

This 140-grain 40 S&W Cor-Bon DPX, using all-copper Barnes X bullet, did a satisfactory job of quickly killing a large hog.

This Speer Gold Dot 124 grain +P 9mm round from 4-inch Glock 19 instantly killed a large hog, did massive internal damage, and had expanded impressively by the time it stopped at optimum penetration depth. This load has worked famously well for NYPD for several years in many shootings.

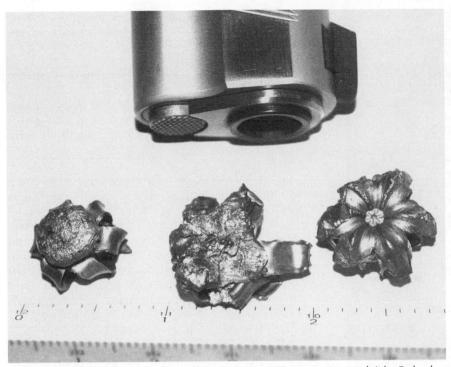

Relative bullet expansion. Left, Winchester 127-grain SXT 9mm; center and right, Federal HST +P 45 bullets, each 230-grains. Larger bullets have "more lead to spread," but lighter bullets can be run to higher velocities. Each creates massive wounds.

357 SIG

In the early '90s, spurred by Texas troopers and rangers who loved the SIG 45 pistol but missed that "lightning bolt" stopping power effect of their old 357 Magnum revolvers, SIG worked with Federal Cartridge to create the 357 SIG round. It resembles a 40 S&W necked down to 9mm, though the actual construction is somewhat more complicated than that. Different companies load to different velocities, and depending on pistol and barrel, factory 125-grain JHPs are delivering 1325 to over 1400 fps.

High-tech bullets that open rapidly but stay together seem to work best in this caliber. The most widely proven is the Gold Dot. From Texas to Virginia, it has been kicking butt with no horror stories of stopping failures. New Mexico State Troopers fell in love with the 357 SIG a few years ago, and stayed with that cartridge when they ordered their new S&W M&P auto pistols. North Carolina Highway Patrol gave up its beloved Beretta pistols after more than twenty years to adopt the SIG-Sauer, because they could get it chambered for 357 SIG.

Gunfights indicate that this cartridge is particularly good for shooting through auto sheet metal and window glass, yet does not deliver on the street the dangerous over-penetration that some gelatin tests had indicated might happen. The spent, expanded bullets are normally recovered from the far side of the criminal's body, or from his clothing, or from the ground within a few feet behind where he was located when shot.

Winchester Ranger in 125-grain 357 SIG has worked well in actual shootings. Remington Bonded Golden Saber in 125-grain 357 SIG is deliciously accurate, and performs superbly in FBI protocol gelatin testing, though I haven't run across any actual shootings with it yet. The overwhelming majority of 357 SIG shootings by police have occurred with the 125-grain Speer Gold Dot, and it has worked so well it is unquestionably the most "street proven" load in this caliber.

40 Smith & Wesson

Introduced in 1990 by S&W and Winchester, this 9mm Luger-length 10mm cartridge was designed to split the difference between the 9mm's higher round count in the gun, and the 45 auto's larger caliber. It succeeded hugely at that in police work, being chosen by more law enforcement agencies today than any other. It has become popular among armed citizens for that exact same compromise factor.

First generation ammo, a 180-grain subsonic with a conventional JHP bullet, did better than expected, but still wasn't spectacular. It pretty much duplicates the ballistics of the old 38/40 blackpowder handgun load of the 19th century frontier. I've run across a lot of shoot-throughs with 180-grain standard JHP, more than would be desirable for home defense. Those who like the 180-grain subsonic's ballistics want to go with high tech hollowpoints that open more aggressively, penetrate a little less, and seem to produce a more decisive stopping effect. The 180-grain Gold Dot has earned a good reputation in cities such as Boston and Milwaukee. The 180-grain Federal HST has produced some truly impressive one-shot stops in the Pacific Northwest. The 180-grain Winchester Ranger, particularly in its latest iteration, also works distinctly better than a conventional copper-jacketed bullet of this weight and velocity.

It appears that the medium-weight bullets at higher velocities are providing the best combination of penetration depth, expansion, and overall decisiveness of ending encounters. Not the 165-grain subsonic .40 – the so-called "minus-P" – but 165-grain JHPs traveling at 1140 or so feet per second, and 155-grainers at about 1200 fps. The latter has worked very well for the U.S. Border Patrol, which

The 180-grain Federal HST has produced some truly impressive one-shot stops in the Pacific Northwest.

Why carry spare ammo? Something could muck up the magazine in your gun. If this muddy 1911 9mm mag was not properly cleaned, it would be a jam waiting to happen the next time it was put in a defensive firearm.

seems to have used mostly the Remington brand. Other non-high-tech .40 caliber JHPs in this weight range that have delivered impressive performance are the Federal Classic and the Winchester Silvertip, both 155-grainers. These are also less expensive than the top-line premium lines.

High-tech bullets still do well in this weight range, though. The 165-grain Winchester Ranger and Speer Gold Dot seem to lead the pack by a narrow margin.

45 ACP

A standard pressure 230-grain 45 ACP with conventional JHP bullet pretty much duplicates the recoil and trajectory of GI hardball in the same weight, allowing cost-effective training once the user is certain the given pistol will feed the hollowpoint of choice. The 45's big bullet and well-earned reputation for stopping power make it more forgiving of less-than-optimum ammo choices, though you still want to stay away from full metal jacket because of its tendency to grossly over-penetrate, and to ricochet.

In a low-priced round, generic Winchester 230-grain JHP "white box" is a street-proven choice. It used to be sold in boxes marked "For Law Enforcement Only," if that tells you anything. For maximum effect, though, a premium bullet is the way to go. Federal's Hydra-Shok is a well-proven man-stopper, long the "gold standard," and still a good choice today,

With one 17-round magazine in place, two more in the belt, and one more round topped off in the chamber, this Glock 17 puts 52 shots at the wearer's immediate disposal.

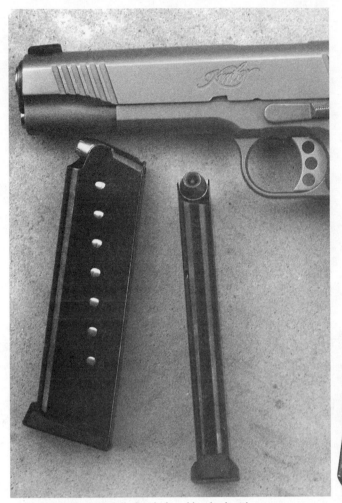

Kimber stainless 45, fully loaded and backed with two more eight-round ACT magazines of Federal 230-grain Hydra-Shok, gives the wearer a 22-round load-out. Elsewhere in the book, read the story of the man who got in trouble for carrying just such an outfit, but was acquitted once rationale for spare ammo was explained to jury.

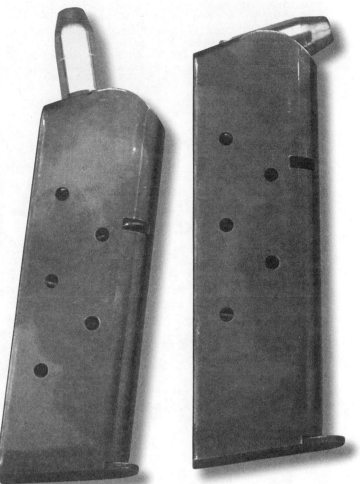

Another reason to carry spare ammo. Topmost round position on each of these 1911 magazines has been compromised by clearing extraction failure/double feed malfunction. A fresh magazine ready to grab and reload can be a lifesaver in such circumstances.

but expansion characteristics (especially through intervening substances) are enhanced in the new HST line from the same maker. CCI Gold Dot has worked well for numerous departments in both 200- and 230-grain weights; Remington 230-grain Golden Saber has worked quite well in the hands of certain units during the War on Terror; and one state police agency I'm aware of has experienced a string of one-shot stops with the Winchester SXT/Ranger 230 grain. These are all standard pressure loads.

Short barrel 45 ACPs are extremely popular among armed citizens today. CCI offers a Gold Dot Short Barrel 45 load, especially designed to open to full effect at lower velocities. I haven't run across any actual shootings with it yet, but gel testing indicates that it has met its design parameters.

The +P 45 ACP has worked well in 185-, 200-, and 230-grain loadings. The 185-grain +P has earned a good "stopping power" rep in its conventional JHP loading from Remington and is also available in Hydra-Shok and HST formats from Federal, and in Remington's own high-tech Golden Saber line. As a rule of thumb,

the 185-grain +P round will shoot pretty much to point of aim/point of impact out to roughly 100 yards in a pistol sighted in for 230-grain standard pressure 45 ACP at 25 yards. That makes it of special purpose interest to those in rural areas who can anticipate unusually long shots with their pistols.

The 45 GAP, or Glock Auto Pistol, is a shortened and strengthened 45 ACP round at standard pressure. Guns for it have been produced by Glock, ParaOrdnance, and Springfield Armory. The state troopers of Georgia, New York, and Pennsylvania have adopted the Glock in 45 GAP as standard, and shootings with it using 200-grain Speer Gold Dot and 230-grain Winchester Ranger have thus far proven it to be the absolute equal of the 45 ACP with the same bullets. Look for this round to gain in popularity in years to come.

That concludes the feedback from the street, with the calibers most used by cops and, therefore, most thoroughly evaluated in the wake of intensive investigation of officer-involved shootings.

At the time of this writing, it's the best this writer has to offer.

Cops have long understood that hollow point ammo is safer for all concerned. This is "FBI load," 158-grain +P lead semi-wadcutter hollow point, in a 4-inch Model 15 S&W service revolver. This was the bullet that "made" the 38 Special into a fighting handgun in the early 1970s, and is still a good choice except in ultra-light snubbies.

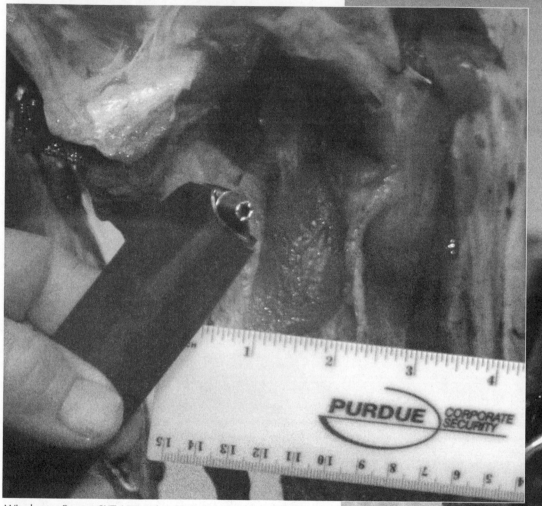

Winchester Ranger SXT 127-grain +P+ ammo in Glock magazine, compared to hole through muscle tissue made by such a bullet on hog. Remember this the next time someone tells you the bullet can only destroy what it physically touches.

Full metal jacket 9mm ammo like this has been known to be an impotent man-stopper for a century, and it horrendously over-penetrates in living tissue. After many innocent over-penetration casualties with it, NYPD dropped this ammo for hollowpoint, and solved the problem.

THE DANGERS OF OVERPENETRATING BULLETS

One critical rule of firearms safety is that the bullet must stay in its intended backstop. No responsible shooter would go to one of the older indoor shooting ranges that have a warning poster saying "LEAD BULLETS ONLY, JACKETED BULLETS CAN PIERCE BACKSTOP" and then proceed to pump hard-jacketed bullets into that frail backing.

On the street, the only safe backstop for the defensive handgun's bullets is the body of the offender. Therefore, it is not exactly responsible to be firing bullets that are likely to shoot through and through the assailant. This is one of the main reasons law enforcement in its virtual entirety has gone to

expanding bullet handgun ammunition in this country. It was a lesson written in blood.

Seven Cases Highlight the Reality

In 1999, New York City became almost the last major police department to adopt hollow point ammunition. They did so in the face of huge, long-term opposition based on political correctness and the erroneous perception of hollowpoints as wicked "dum-dum bullets." One reason they were able to pass it was that the city fathers had been made to realize how much danger the supposedly "humane, Geneva Convention-approved" ammunition previously used presented to innocent bystanders and police officers when the duty weapons were fired in self-defense or defense of others by the officers.

From the early '90s adoption of 16-shot 9mm pistols (Glock 19, SIG-SAUER P226 DAO, and Smith & Wesson Model 5946) through 1999, NYPD issued a full metal jacket "hardball" round, comprising a round-nose 115 grain bullet in the mid-1100 fps velocity range. *The New York Times* exposed the following facts in its startling report on the matter:

"According to statistics released by the department, 15 innocent bystanders were struck by police officers using full metal jacket bullets during 1995 and 1996, the police said. Eight were hit directly, five were hit by bullets that had passed through other people and two were hit by bullets that had passed through objects," stated the *Times*.

In other words, in rough numbers, 53 percent of these tragic occurrences were apparently missed shots,

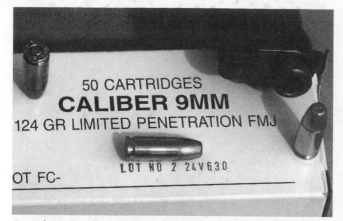

Even the U.S. military is looking at switching from ball ammo to expanding bullets. This is Federal's "Limited Penetration FMJ" ...

...and causing bullet to expand to 50-caliber or better.

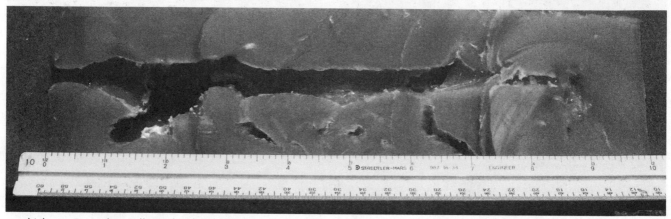

...which uses Expanding Full Metal Jacket technology developed by Tom Burczynski to deliver a more effective wound channel in ballistic wax by Ballistic Technologies' Bullet Test Tube...

while 33 percent were "shoot-throughs" of violent felony suspects. Counting bullets that went through objects to hit presumably unseen innocent victims (13 percent), that tells us that roughly 46 percent of these innocent bystanders were shot by over-penetrating bullets that "pierced their backstops." Let's call those victims **Cases One Through Seven.**

17 Officers Shot Due to Over-Penetration

The *Times* continued, "In that same period, 44 police officers were struck by gunfire using the old ammunition: 21 were hit directly, 2 were struck by bullets that ricocheted and 17 were struck by bullets that passed through other people." In round numbers, 52 percent of those "friendly fire" casualties were hit by bullets that apparently missed their intended targets. 42 percent passed through the bodies of the intended targets after the bullets struck the people they were aimed at. Let's tally *those* victims of over-penetration as **Cases Eight through Twenty-Four.**

Why would officers hit more of their own brethren than "civilian" bystanders in this fashion? For the simple reason that while victims and potential innocent bystanders tend to flee danger scenes, the cops are conditioned to "ride to the sound of the guns." In a close-quarters situation where a violent criminal is

attempting to harm or even murder another officer, cops try to grab him or stop him or even maneuver into a position from which to shoot him. All these actions can put them in the line of fire of brother officers.

Tunnel vision occurs in a majority of life-threatening encounters. This is the perceptual phenomenon of being able to see only the threat and being unable to cognitively recognize other people or objects that might be in the line of fire. Moreover, *the body of the offender may simply block the shooter's view of the brother officer who is trying to apprehend or restrain the attacker from behind.* In these situations, a "shoot-through" is highly likely to kill or cripple one of the Good Guys and Gals.

What does this have to do with private citizens' use of CCW handguns? Only this: *Where the cops jump in to protect their brother and sister officers, brave citizens may step in to protect their **actual** brothers and sisters, husbands and wives, sons and daughters, or fathers and mothers. Now it is your loved ones who are behind the offender – unseen by you – when you discharge your CCW weapon.*

Those 115-grain jacketed ball 9mm rounds will pierce more than two feet of muscle tissue simulating ballistic gelatin. So will 230-grain full metal jacket 45 hardball. By contrast, the depth of the average adult male thorax is probably no more than ten inches,

Ball ammo, like the excellent American Eagle at left, should be used strictly for practice in author's opinion. 147-grain JHP Subsonic as pioneered by Winchester *(right)* was better, but still erratic and unpredictable in its performance. Today there are much better ammo choices than either of these antique rounds for "street" use.

Federal 158-grain lead hollowpoint +P, fired from 2-inch S&W into chest of hog. The bullet killed quickly, expanded to approximately 50-caliber.

from front of chest to back. Nor is it solid muscle: the spongy tissue and large air volume of the human lung offer little resistance to a bullet. It's not just about New York City and 9mms. In Arizona some years ago, a peace officer fired his 45 service automatic at a large male offender rushing him with a knife. He couldn't see that a brother officer was running up behind the offender to grab and restrain him. His gunfire dropped the offender…and passed through his body with enough force to deeply pierce the abdomen of the second cop, who had been trying to rescue the one who fired. That wounded officer almost died from those injuries, inflicted unintentionally by shoot-

through with 230-grain full metal jacket 45 ACP. Call that incident **Case Twenty-Five.**

Many years ago in Los Angeles, an Aryan Brotherhood thug took several people hostage in an office. He demanded an escape vehicle and threatened to start shooting hostages if he didn't get one. A vehicle was provided, and he got into the car with the victims. At this point, the LAPD SWAT team launched smoke, and two members of the team whom I happened to know moved forward through the gray cloud, their issue Colt 45 automatics up and ready. When the perpetrator reached for his pistol, the cops opened fire, using department-issue 230-grain hardball. They fired four

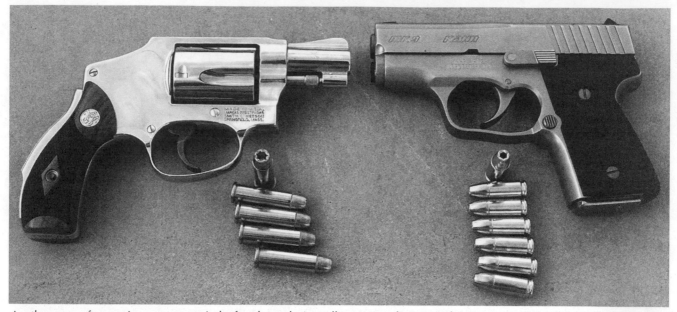

Another reason for carrying spare ammo is the fact that today's small carry guns don't carry that many rounds "on board." S&W J-frame, left, holds 5 38 Special cartridges, and Kahr MK9 at right holds 7 9mms.

shots between them, and killed the offender before he could launch a single bullet of his own. Autopsy showed any of the four hits would have been quickly fatal. However, only one of those bullets stayed in the offender's body. One of the three exiting slugs struck one of the hostages. Fortunately, the wound was not in a life-threatening location. LAPD quickly switched to hollowpoints, which is what they use today. Lesson learned. Call it **Case Twenty-Six.**

Ball Stops Poorly

Particularly in the small calibers, ball ammunition is infamous for its poor stopping power. When the Illinois State Police issued ball for their 9mm S&W pistols from 1967 through the early 1970s, their Ordnance Section told me, they never had a single one-shot stop on an armed felon unless he was hit in the brain or spinal cord. This led the ISP on an odyssey in search of more effective ammo, which culminated in the famously effective "Illinois State Police load," a 115-grain jacketed 9mm hollowpoint at +P+ pressure and 1300 fps velocity. Today, Illinois troopers carry 180-grain high-tech hollowpoint in 40 S&W caliber service pistols.

In **Case Twenty-Seven,** NYPD's last high-profile shooting incident with 9mm ball ammo, four plainclothes officers engaged a young man named Amadou Diallo when he turned on them pulling an object that appeared, in the poor light, to be a small automatic pistol. All four opened fire, and some five seconds later they had fired some 41 shots. Nineteen of those bullets struck Diallo before he went down and dropped the object he was holding, which turned out to be a black nylon wallet. Sixteen of the nineteen bullets had over-penetrated. Diallo died of his wounds. After a long and arduous trial, all four officers were acquitted. Had these officers been issued the department's new 124-grain Speer Gold Dot +P

hollowpoints in time, there is an excellent chance that he would have gone down much sooner, perhaps with as little as one gunshot wound, giving Diallo a far better chance of survival. No such horror stories have happened on NYPD since the hollowpoint ammo has been general issue.

Forensic Concerns

When a bullet goes through and through a human body, it is not always possible to correctly determine entry from exit, particularly if the gunshot victim lives long enough for the healing process to begin. Consider **Case Twenty-Eight,** in which the O.J. Simpson lawyers defending him against charges of murdering his wife and her young male acquaintance laid plans to impeach one of the state's medical examiners by bringing up a previous case in which he had mistakenly diagnosed a through and through gunshot wound, confusing back-to-front and front-to-back.

In late 2007, this writer was involved in a murder case in Massachusetts where it was alleged that the defendant had shot his opponent in the back of the neck, with the bullet exiting his face, implying that he was in no danger and therefore could not have acted in self-defense. The death weapon was a Beretta Model 96F pistol, and the death bullet was a 180-grain round of full metal jacket UMC 40-caliber practice ammunition. In fact, the bullet had entered the face of the attacking man, and coursed rearward and downward before exiting the neck. However, the assailant lived for a week before he succumbed. During that time, he was lying supine in a hospital bed with his body weight pressing the exit hole down against dressings and bed clothes as his body worked to heal the injury. This gave the wound a puckered appearance consistent with an entry wound. At the same time, doctors and nurses were treating the open

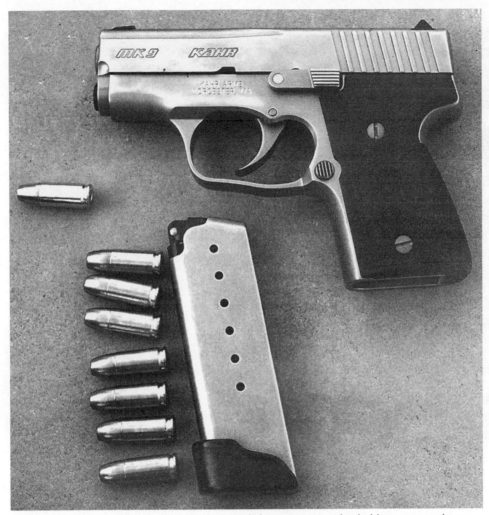

Micro Kahr 9mm comes with spare magazine with finger extension that holds seven rounds, not counting eighth in chamber. With this kind of cartridge capacity, carrying spare ammo is all the more important.

Colt Lawman 357 Magnum revolver loaded with 158-grain semi-jacketed Magnum hollow points, which have a history of frequently over-penetrating. At very close range, the high velocity bullet caused a large, "explosive wound of entry" in the soft tissues of the throat, and being largely spent when it exited the back of the neck, left a smaller wound at that point. Once again, the suspect lived for many days, lying supine and undergoing treatment. After he died, the state's pathologist concluded that the small wound in the back of the neck must have been the entry, and the larger one in front must have been the exit, leading to the theory that he had been "shot in the back of the neck in a police execution." Fortunately, the pathologist had the presence of mind to section out the wound track and preserve the flesh in Formalin, and it was sent to the Southwest Institute of Pathology for deeper examination. There, gunshot residue embedded in the throat area of the wound track conclusively proved the bullet had come in from the front, exonerating the

wound in the face, debriding it to prevent necrosis, so by the time he finally died, *that* wound had been cratered outward and mimicked an exit instead of an entry. The medical examiner had, apparently for these reasons, determined after death that entry was in the back and exit was in the front. Not until trial, after a three-year ordeal, did treating physicians familiar with gunshot wounds testify that when the "victim" came in, they diagnosed the wound as front entry/rear exit. Defense experts concurred, and the jury acquitted, as they should have. But **Case Twenty-Nine** probably wouldn't have gone to trial at all if the defendant had loaded his gun with proper hollow points, which almost certainly would have left the mushroomed bullet embedded inside the back of the neck and shown beyond a shadow of a doubt that the attacker was in fact shot from the front.

Years before, in the Tampa area, I had been involved in a similar case that showed even the wrong hollowpoint can over-penetrate and cause the same confusion. In **Case Thirty,** a young undercover narc became involved in a struggle with an armed dope dealer who tried to kill him. The cop was able to turn the suspect's own gun on him, a snub-nosed

wrongfully accused young officer. But if the distance had been another couple of feet apart at the time the shot was fired, that critical exculpatory evidence would not have been there. This is another reason why it's best to use a bullet designed to stay inside the human body.

Irresponsible Attitudes

Some people either just don't get it, or have a totally irresponsible attitude. A popular Internet gun forum recently had a thread in its Caliber Corner section titled, "Why is over-penetration bad?" Most of those who posted had a pretty good grasp on the issue. One or two responsible, gun-wise participants even posted a link to the *New York Times* story and statistics above.

Yet, even after that was posted, one participant wrote (the caps are his): "I have NEVER read ANY article or report addressing IDENTIFIED and actually occurring secondary victims." Now, you can put that down to simple ignorance, or haste in posting an opinion in a discussion he had not read and brought himself up to speed with. But how would you explain the following?

The practice of carrying spare ammunition is a long-standing one. This 1960s vintage Colt Agent six-shot 38 revolver was carried for decades by now-retired Chicago cop James Moore. Bianchi "spill pouch" with six spare rounds of 38 Special was common practice to carry even off duty by Chicago coppers of the day.

One fellow posted in the same discussion thread, "…and should over-penetration occur, oh well. The chances of it hitting someone else is practically non-existent."

Well, let's do the math. 46 percent of wounded innocent bystanders being hit by bullets that went through offenders' bodies or through objects that hopefully should have acted as backstops, is not "practically non-existent" by any stretch of the imagination. 42 percent of cops shot by friendly fire taking bullets that passed through the felony suspect first are not "practically non-existent." On the contrary, they are hugely significant.

In that same thread, one poster callously said, "It's too bad about the bystanders. I call it gene pool cleansing."

I don't think any comment is necessary on that one.

Never forget that we live in a time when police detectives are smart enough to get a warrant to seize the computers of those they investigate. Technology originally developed to track pornographers, child molesters, and white collar criminals will be applied to determine what Internet boards you may have posted to. When statements like "It's too bad about the bystanders. I call it gene pool cleansing," are

discovered and tracked to the suspect, his conviction for something from attempted murder upward is almost a slam-dunk.

Ignorance won't save you. You've heard and read people say that over-penetration is irrelevant because missed shots are a more likely danger. First, a defense that says in essence, "You must forgive me *this* mistake because I figured I'd probably make a much *worse* mistake" is a frail reed that will not withstand the gale-force winds of cross-examination. Second, 53 percent misses versus 46 percent shoot-throughs in the unintentional bystander shootings in New York hardly makes the latter "irrelevant." 52% misses versus 42 percent shoot-throughs in the friendly fire shootings of cops in the same study obviously shows that the over-penetrating bullet is not an "irrelevant" danger.

The next time some Internet ninja advises you to load ball ammo for home or public defense, think of the above thirty cases. They are documented reality. And they are not the only such cases.

Collective reality has given us a message, and it is this: Save the over-penetrating "hardball" for range practice. Load your concealed carry or home defense handgun with ammunition designed, and proven to be likely, to stay inside the body of the offender who forces you to shoot him. It's the responsible thing to do.

HIP HOLSTERS

Safariland 567-83 Model hip holster rides low, carries Glock 17 in this example.

The strong-side hip – i.e., the gun hand-side hip – is the odds-on choice for weapon placement for most of those who carry concealed handguns today. It is also the standard location for law enforcement officers in uniform. This is probably not coincidental.

Many ranges, police academies, and shooting schools will allow *only* strong-side holsters. The theory behind this is that cross draw (including shoulder and fanny pack carries) will cause the gun muzzles to cross other shooters and range officers when weapons are drawn or holstered. Some also worry about the safety of pocket draw and ankle draw. There are action shooting sports – PPC and IDPA, to name two – where anything but a strong-side belt holster is expressly forbidden. Once again, safety is the cited reason.

Quality concealed-carry hip holsters aren't new. This one, carrying a period S&W Model 39 9mm…

…was made circa 1974 by Seventrees, the innovative company led by the late Paris Theodore.

It is worthwhile to look at other such sports where cross draw holsters *are* allowed…but are seldom seen. In the early days of IPSC, cross draws actually dominated the winner's circle for a while. Ray Chapman wore one when he captured the first world championship of the sport. Today, however, even though it's still allowed, the cross draw has all but disappeared from that sport. A little history is in order. In the mid-1970s, a common IPSC start position was standing with hands clasped at centerline of the torso. With a front cross draw, this allowed the gun hand to be positioned barely above the pistol grip at the moment the start signal went off. IPSC started to go more toward hands-shoulder-high start positions (to give everyone a more level playing field, and to better allow range officers to see if a hand went prematurely to the gun), and the last such match I shot used mostly start positions with hands relaxed at the sides. These positions favored a gun on the same side as the dominant hand. In any case, a strong-side holster brings the gun on target faster because, standing properly, the weapon is already in line with the mark and does not have to be swept across the target.

We saw the same in NRA Action Shooting. Mickey Fowler for many years had a monopoly on the Bianchi Cup, using a front cross draw, specifically an ISI Competition Rig he and his colleague Mike Dalton had designed with Ted Blocker. However, in later years, the Cup has always been won with a straight-draw hip holster.

Because they begin at the academy with handguns on their dominant hand side, cops tend to stay with the same location for plainclothes wear. Habituation is a powerful thing. Master holster maker and historian John Bianchi invokes Bianchi's Law: the same gun,

A classic from one of the great holster authorities of all time, this left-handed IWB holster carries a Dan Wesson clone of the Browning Hi-Power…

…and was made by the great Chic Gaylord, whose timeless designs are now reproduced by Bell Charter Oak.

Bianchi Black Widow has either-side belt loops for tight carry of this Ruger GP100 357 against body, and fast thumb-break safety strap. It rides on a mated Bianchi dress gun belt. Holster and belt are more than 20 years old and in excellent condition, a tribute to Bianchi quality.

in the same place, all the time. It makes the reactive draw second nature.

We saw this in action in the IPSC world in the late Seventies. The second American to become IPSC world champion was the great Ross Seyfried. Ross shot a Pachmayr Custom Colt Government Model 45 from a high-riding Milt Sparks #1AT holster that rode at an FBI tilt behind his right hip. He was a working cattleman in Colorado and a disciple of both Elmer Keith and Jeff Cooper. It was a time when the serious competitors mostly either went cross draw, or wore elaborate speed rigs low on the hip. One who chose the latter was a multimillionaire for whom IPSC was purely sport. Frustrated that Ross had beaten him at the national championships in Denver, this fellow hired a sports physiologist to explain to him how

Seyfried had managed to beat him. "I don't understand it," the frustrated professional told the wealthy sportsman in essence after viewing tapes of Seyfried. "Your way is faster than his. The way this Seyfried fellow carries his gun is mechanically slower."

What physiologist and rich guy alike had missed was one simple fact: the multi-millionaire only strapped on his fancy quick-draw holster on match day and at practice sessions. Ross Seyfried wore a #1AT Milt Sparks holster behind his hip every day of his life, though in the saddle on the ranch he carried a 4-inch Smith & Wesson Model 29 44 Magnum. Ross and that holster had developed a symbiotic relationship. Reaching to that spot had become second nature, and made him faster from there than a part-time pistol packer with a more sophisticated, more expensive "speed rig."

Strong-Side Hip Advantages

If the navel is 12 o'clock, a properly worn concealment hip holster puts a right-handed man's gun at 3:30. In this position, just behind the ileac crest of the pelvis, clothing comes down in a natural drape from the latissimus dorsi to cover the gun without bulge. On a guy of average build, the holstered gun finds itself nestled in a natural hollow below the kidney area. With the jacket opened in the front, the gun is usually invisible from the front. Being just behind the hip, a holstered gun in this location does not seem to get in the way of bucket seats nor most furniture, and doesn't press into the body when the wearer leans back against a chair surface.

Because of its proximity to the gun hand, and because the gun can come directly up on target from the holster, the strong-side draw is naturally

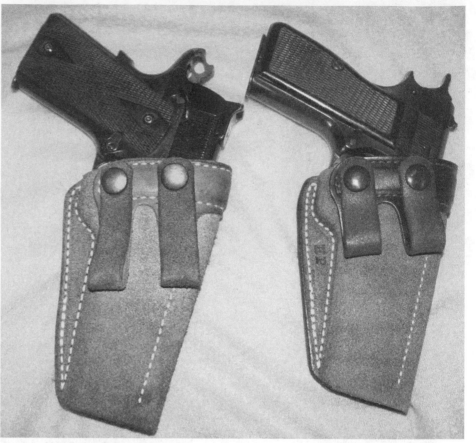

Designed by the late Bruce Nelson, these rough-out Summer Special IWB holsters were produced by Milt Sparks. Left, standard version for Morris Custom Colt 45 automatic. Right, narrow belt loop model to go with corresponding thick but narrow dress belt for suits, also by Sparks, here with Browning Hi-Power.

Author says at least one ambidextrous model is imperative to the holster wardrobe. This is Glock's own, in very economical polymer, with a Glock 30 45 auto.

The Pager Pal carries the gun, in this case a Kahr PM9, not only inside the waistband but below it. Fake pager *(shown)* or knife pouch or cell phone carrier disguises the concealment system.

Women's hips don't adapt well to male-oriented holsters. Note where Julie Goloski carries her S&W M&P 9mm as she pauses while winning 2006 National Woman IDPA Champion title..

Mitch Rosen's Workman holster, named after designer Dave Workman, was the first and defining "tuckable." Notice "V" of leather between gun and belt loop. Shirt, tucked into the V and inside the waistband, hides this Glock 26. Belt loop can be disguised by putting a key ring on it.

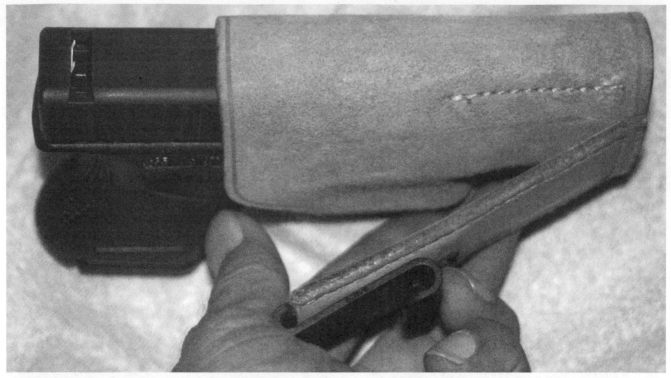

Galco's affordable Tuckable is suede-out (a.k.a. "rough-out") and secures to belt with low profile polymer J-clip. Pistol is Glock 26 9mm.

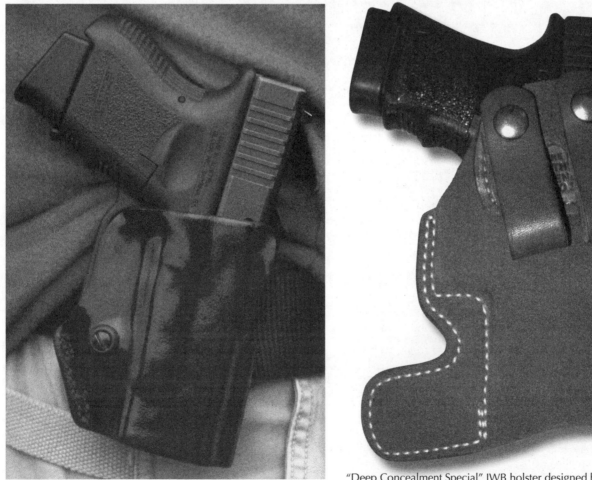

This Safariland synthetic OWB holds Glock 39 subcompact 45 GAP tight to the body of a state police instructor.

"Deep Concealment Special" IWB holster designed by Elmer McEvoy at Leather Arsenal has rearward flange to help keep holster from digging into body, or shifting. Pistol is Glock 30 in 45 ACP.

Exotic leathers have become a status symbol among CCW people. This ParaOrdnance SSP 45 automatic lives in this sharkskin OWB holster/belt combo by Aker.

"Plastic" CQC holster for Glock 17 here holds a longer Glock 34, which works fine in this instance despite exposed portion of barrel and front sight. It holds the gun tight to the body, and is very fast for IDPA-type competition.

One of the great classic IWB holsters is the #3 Pistol Pocket designed by Richard Nichols for Bianchi. Here holding a square butt S&W 357 Combat Magnum, it has wide, handy one-way-snap for easy on-off, leather reinforced mouth for easy re-holstering, and fast, secure thumb break. This one has been in service for decades and still works fine.

STREET TIP: If weight of gun is pulling pants down, don't pull it back up like this. It looks as if you're going for a gun. INSTEAD…

…pull whole belt up, with both hands, like this. Now, you're just another guy "doing a guy thing" and "hitching up his pants," and don't broadcast the fact that you're "carrying."

Author designed the popular Ayoob Rear Guard (ARG) holster for Mitch Rosen. It rides inside the waistband, weight of gun levered forward by rear-placed belt loop to prevent "printing." This example is in sharkskin and carries S&W 1911 45 auto.

Replaceable belt-clip modules of Kydex IWB holster by Mach 2, the Honorman, "flex" and help conceal this Glock 27 without shifting. Note also "body shield" to keep sweat away from gun, and sharp gun edges away from underlying skin and clothing.

Author demonstrates his "fingertip draw," which he calls "Reach Out and Touch Yourself." As draw from under open-front garment begins, all four fingertips touch abdomen's centerline...

... and, *fingertips maintaining torso contact,* hand sweeps back to gun. Note that knife edge of hand has begun to sweep the Woolrich Elite vest to the rear...

...and will instantly and positively sweep it *all the way* to the rear, and *hold it out of the way* until hand has taken its drawing grasp, shown. Carry combo is Beretta 92G 9mm in Milt Sparks Executive Companion IWB holster.

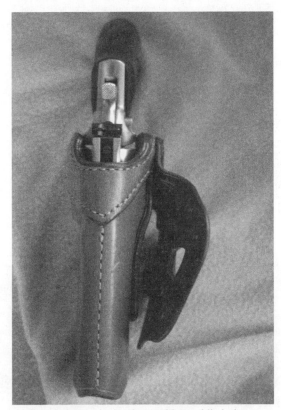

Author explains why he doesn't like paddle holsters, but why they can work for some people in some situations. This is one of the best of the breed, by Aker, carrying Ruger GP100 357 Magnum.

STREET TIP: When you feel the gun butt moving to the rear and "printing," DON'T adjust it like this. It will be obvious to anyone in line of sight that you're "carrying." INSTEAD…

…use your forearm behind your back to push the gun forward, stretch back a little, and you look to the world like someone with a sore back, not someone carrying a gun.

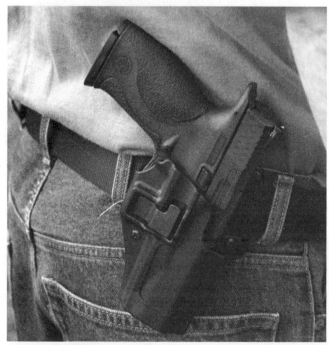

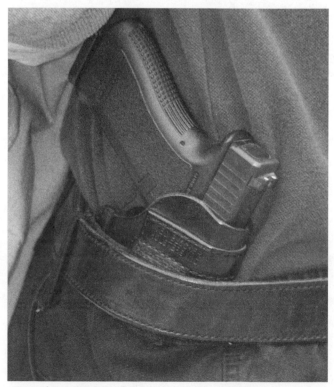

Blackhawk SERPA is a snatch-resistant, concealable rig that effectively hides this S&W M&P 9mm under a coat. It has been adjusted to desirable forward tilt angle. Finger paddle is easily released by owner's safely extended trigger finger when draw begins.

Concealment Rig by Ted Blocker makes this full-size Glock 17 concealable for its average-size male owner.

fast. For males, simply bringing the elbow straight back brings the hand almost automatically to the gun.

Disadvantages

The hip draw does not lend itself to a surreptitious draw – that is, starting with the hand already on the gun, unnoticed – unless the practitioner can get the gun-side third of his body behind some concealing object or structure. Because of the higher, more flaring pelvis and shorter torso, women don't find this carry nearly as comfortable or as fast as men. As noted elsewhere in this book, cross draw and shoulder carry seem more effective for many women.

Ayoob designed the LFI Concealment Rig with Ted Blocker, whose namesake company now in other hands still finds it a good seller. Velcro tab on holster *(and spare mag carrier, shown)* mates with Velcro lining inside the dress gunbelt to secure solidly, and allow wide options to wearer as to height, angle, and location. Pistol is SIG P220 ST 45, with Hogue stocks.

Author demonstrates proper hip draw continuum while winning Wisconsin State Service Revolver Championship, IDPA 2007. GP100 is blurring as it comes up to pectoralis position, in line to already hit a fast-coming, close range threat…

…and then extends for precise aim with mandatory one-hand head-shots from behind simulated cover.

STREET TIP: When driving, you don't want your hip holstered gun trapped by seat belt and concealing garment. Here, safety belt is fastened...

...but then driver should reach under seat belt and grab the concealing garment...

Christine Cunningham, an instructor and competitor in the Pacific Northwest, is also a holster-maker. She specializes in "by women, for women" concealed carry gear. Her stuff is tops in quality and function, and very well thought out. You'll find much good advice, as well as many useful products, at her website, www.womenshooters.com.

The gun behind the hip is positioned so as to be sensitive to exposure and bulge when the wearer bends down or leans forward. This simply means the practitioner has to learn different ways to perform these motions in public. See photos.

Belt Holster Options

Continuing with the "clock" concept, let's look at different spots on the belt for holster placement. 12 o'clock, centerline of the abdomen, will be comfortable only with a small, short-barrel gun. It's a quick and natural position, particularly for women thanks to their relatively higher belt-lines. My older daughter, tall and slender, prefers to carry her S&W Model 3913 9mm here, in an Alessi Talon inside the waistband holster, or a belly-band. It disappears under an untucked blouse, shirt, or sweater, but provides very fast access.

1 o'clock to 2 o'clock becomes the so-called "appendix position." An open front garment must be kept fastened to keep it hidden, but a short-barrel gun works great here for access during fighting and grappling. A top trainer who is still active in

...and *pull it free of the seat belt!* It's not the seat belt that usually traps a hip holstered gun, it's the coat that is trapped by the seat belt. Now...

...you're "ready to ride," and your hand can quickly get to your sidearm.

The Yaqui Slide is extremely popular for concealed carry. Here, the Galco version carries a custom .40 cal. Glock 23 with Caspian slide, BoMar sights, and Hybrid-Port recoil reduction system.

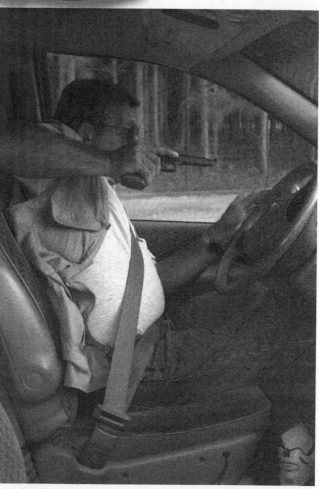

STREET TIP: Here's how to draw from hip holster while seat belted behind a steering wheel. Gun hand does "fingertip draw," which clears cover garment even in static position...

...and author rocks upper body sharply to left to create more range of movement for right arm, which draws Blackhawk dummy of Beretta 92 used for demo, *lifting it up and over steering wheel to prevent snagging there...*

...and driver is quickly in a ready-to-shoot posture.

undercover police work and teaches under the nickname "Southnarc" favors this location, with his retired cop father's hammer-shrouded Colt Cobra 38 snub-nose inside the waistband at the appendix. It is very fast. Some top IPSC speed demons, such as Jerry

Holster-makers are keeping up with tactical trends. This southpaw cop carries his department-issue Glock 22 with white light unit already mounted, in concealable Blade-Tech holster off duty.

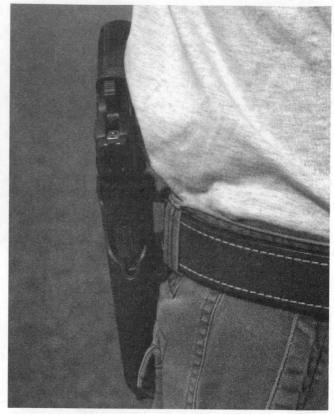

Comparisons in concealability. Dave Lauck Custom full-size 1911 45 leans out a little from the body in Lauck outside-the-waistband (OWB) Kydex holster...

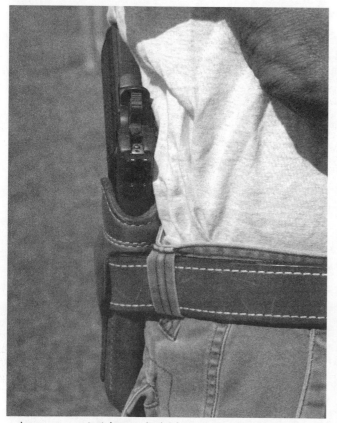

...but same gun is tighter to the body in Elmer McEvoy Quad Concealment holster worn "in the belt" (ITB), between belt and trousers. However...

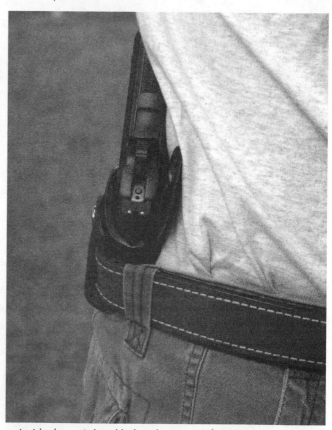

...inside-the-waistband holster by Secret Squirrel carries same gun even closer, and concealing garment can come all the way up to belt without revealing holstered gun.

With tunnel loop at back and rear-mounted belt loop, this Derry Gallagher scabbard carries an N-frame (.44 size) S&W Model 27-2 357 Magnum with 4-inch barrel with surprisingly good concealment.

"the Burner" Barnhart carry their competition guns in speed rigs at the same location. A small gun conceals well here under untucked closed-front garments. However, the appendix carry causes all but the shortest guns to dig into the juncture of thigh and groin when seated, and the muzzle is pointing at genitals and femoral artery. There are those of us who find this incongruous with our purposes for concealed carry, one of which is to *prevent* weapons being pointed at such vulnerable parts of our bodies.

Moving more to the side, the true 3 o'clock position is not ideal for all day concealed wear. Riding on the protuberance of the hip, the gun protrudes accordingly, calling attention to itself even under big, heavy coats. The holstered gun at 3 o'clock will grate mercilessly on the hip-bone. Cops get away with it in uniform because their holsters have orthopedically curved shanks, and the weight is distributed on their wide Sam Browne belts. Neither mitigating factor will be at work in a concealment holster.

3:30, just behind the hip, seems to be optimum for comfort, concealment, and speed. It's where most professionals end up parking their holsters.

By the time you hit 4 o'clock, there is more likelihood of the butt protruding. When you hit 6 o'clock, the true MOB (middle of back) or SOB (small of back) position, you're getting into dangerous territory. The SOB is an SOB in more ways than one. While accessible to either hand, it can be mercilessly

uncomfortable when you are seated. The rear center hem is the first part of an outer garment that lifts when you bend forward or sit down. The gun butt can catch the hem and completely expose the holstered gun. You can't see it and usually can't feel it, meaning you're the only one in the shopping mall who *won't* know that your weapon is exposed.

Another extreme danger of this carry is that any fall that lands you flat on your back will be the equivalent of landing on a rock with your lumbar spine. Very serious injury can result.

Yet another problem with SOB carry is that you can't exert

Milt Sparks Summer Special holster, worn from decades of service, still works fine. This classic IWB carries an equally well-worn Smith & Wesson Model 58 41 Magnum service revolver.

Author demonstrates "Hackathorn Rip," his preferred technique for drawing from hip holster under closed-front garment. Support hand grabs hem of shirt at appendix position...

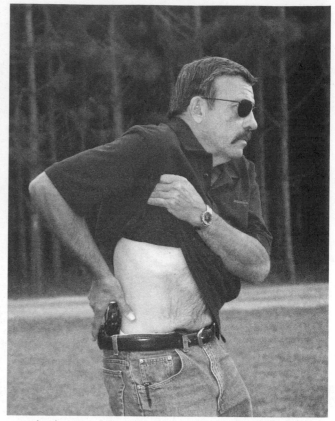

...and jerks it upward toward shoulder, as gun hand goes for sidearm, in this case full-size custom Beretta 92 in Milt Sparks IWB holster...

...as pistol "rocks and locks" upward into draw, support hand releases garment, and...

...shooter is on target in strong firing stance with maximum speed.

STREET TIP: Rocking hip to side away from holster (i.e., to left with right-handed draw) speeds draw from under closed front garment because it helps pull holster out from under pistol.

any significant downward pressure to hold the gun in place when trying to counter a gun snatch attempt. Moreover, biomechanically, you are pretty much putting yourself in an armlock when drawing. As a rule of thumb, any technique that requires you to put yourself in an armlock when defending yourself is a technique you should probably re-evaluate.

Inside or Outside the Belt

An inside-the-waistband (IWB) holster will conceal the gun better. Simple as that. The drape of the pants from the waist down blends the shape of the holstered gun with that of the body. The hem of the concealing garment has to rise above the belt to reveal the hidden weapon. This carry allows average size guys like me to carry full-size service handguns concealed under nothing more than an opaque, untucked tee or polo shirt, one size large. Held tight to the body by belt pressure, this design minimizes bulge.

Some have tried IWB and found it uncomfortable. This is because their pants were sized for *them,* and now contain them – plus a holstered gun. For preliminary comfort testing, unbutton the pants at the waist and let out the belt a notch, and try it again. If it's comfortable now, nature is telling you to let out the pants if possible, or start buying trousers two inches larger in the waist. As noted elsewhere here, this practice "keeps you honest" (i.e., keeps you carrying) because now the pants won't fit right *without* the gun in its IWB holster.

One-hand-only draw from under closed front garment is critical to know, says author, demonstrating his own technique. Support hand rises in close-range block position as thumb of gun hand catches shirt hem…

…and pulls it straight upward. Hand now drops into drawing grasp…

…and gun comes up on target in "rock and lock" motion for one-handed firing if necessary, from close-range "protected gun position."

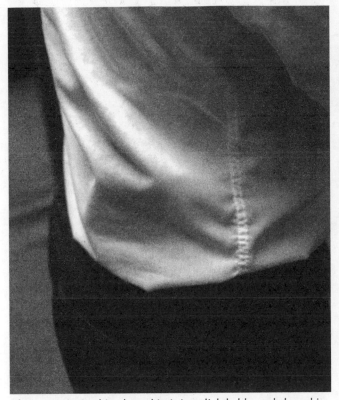

This executive's white dress shirt is just slightly bloused above his pinstripe suit pants…

…but pressing hand reveals the presence of a full-size Glock service pistol, completely hidden beneath in a belly band holster in strong-side hip draw position.

Belt clips don't secure as well as leather loops, for the most part. There are exceptions, such as the appropriately named Alessi Talon, the clips used by Blocker on their DA-2, and the modular Kydex clips on the Mach-2 Honorman holster. Cheaper IWB holsters are notorious for their poor clips.

The IWB holster stays in place largely through belt pressure, so you want a rigid holster mouth to keep the opening from collapsing and interfering with re-holstering. The classic Bianchi #3 Pistol Pocket, a Richard Nichols design, used stiff leather reinforcement for this. Most others followed the lead of the late Bruce Nelson in his famous Summer Special design, and used leather-covered steel inserts to keep the holster mouth open. On rigid Kydex, of course, the material does this by itself.

Inside the waistband, slimness becomes more important, one reason the flat Browning Hi-Power and 1911 pistols are so popular with those who prefer this carry format. The fatter the gun, the more the belt is pushed out from the body. This allows the pants to start sliding down in the holster area, causing frequent need for readjustment.

Because the gun is tight to the body, sometimes against bare skin or sweat-soaked shirts, many makers have built "shielding" into the design to protect the gun from sweat, and bare skin from sharp edges. This works pretty well, but can slow the thumb's access to a perfect pre-draw grasp, depending on gun design and hand size.

I've only designed two holsters in my life. Both were IWB. The first, designed with Ted Blocker, is the LFI Concealment Rig. It's comprised of a dress gun belt lined with Velcro, and your choice of open top or thumb-break safety strap holster with coordinated Velcro tab. This lets the concealing garment ride all the way to the *top* edge of your belt without revealing anything, and perhaps more important, lets you adjust the holster almost infinitely for your particular needs: high, low, *exact* degree of rake (orientation of muzzle) and tilt (orientation of butt) that you want. High versus low is important if, like me, you have to switch between suit pants and uniform pants that tend to ride at the waist, and jeans/cords/BDUs that tend to ride slightly lower at the hips. Now the gun is in exactly the same where-you-want-it spot no matter what you're wearing. The combination of Velcro shear factor and belt tension holds it in place. It's very secure, and I've taught weapon retention classes with one without it coming loose. Matching magazine pouches are available, and the LFI Concealment Rig also works as a cross draw.

The other was designed for Mitch Rosen, at his request. He wanted an open-top rig that would carry a heavy, full-size fighting handgun without the weight of the loaded magazine in its butt tilting it backward to "print," or expose itself through clothing. I designed an FBI-tilt IWB scabbard with a single strong belt loop at the *rear*, behind the gun, where the loop's bulk wouldn't add to the holster's. In this position, the holster "levered" the gun forward and prevented it from tilting backwards. I called it the Rear Guard, because the loop at the rear guarded against rearward

This Don Hume IWB holster, here in lefty version holding Glock 19, is an excellent value.

holster shifting. Mitch was kind enough to call it the Ayoob Rear Guard. It was shortened to ARG, which I've always pronounced as Ay-Arr-Gee. Unfortunately, folks started pronouncing the acronym in one syllable, which sounded like "Arrgghh." I suppose I should just be glad I didn't name it Super Holster Inside Trousers. After 9/11/01, Mitch changed the name to American Rear Guard. Still the same excellent holster, though.

The belly-band is a variation of inside-the-waistband carry, approximately four inches of elastic strapping with a gun pouch. It is worn best at belt level, "over the underwear and under the over-wear." The first of these I ever saw was a John Bianchi prototype in *Gun World* magazine, circa 1960. Bianchi didn't bring it out back then, but in a few years, a firm in Brooklyn named MMGR did. I wore an MMGR belly-band to my grad school tests one hot summer day when I was 21, and noticed the day I got home that the beautiful blue finish of my S&W Model 36 Chief Special had turned brown on the side next to my body. Some later belly-band designs, such as the Gould & Goodrich, used a separate plastic shield on the gun pouch to protect the weapon from this, but expect some degree of sweat exposure with this type of carry. The Tenifer finish of the Glock pistols seems to stand up to this best, followed by the similar Mellonite finish used on S&W M&P autos, followed by industrial hard chrome finishes and stainless. The Glocks will discolor after

long carry in this fashion, but won't actually rust.

While I prefer the belly-band in the front cross draw position for a 2-inch 38, larger guns work best behind the hip. They're a great alternative under a tucked-in shirt for those who work in business suit environments and must take the suit coat off in the office, but can't afford for the gun to become visible. A "Hackathorn rip" movement is the best drawing option here. I also know medical professionals in gun-free zones in high crime areas, who wear small handguns this way under their scrubs.

There are many good belly-bands. My personal favorite has always been the unfortunately discontinued Bianchi Ranger, with built-in money belt. It has been my companion all over the world. I've carried S&W 4-inch 44 Magnums in it, perfectly concealed on the streets in cities from South Africa to Europe.

Since they offer little protection against sharp edges, belly-bands work best with edge-free guns. That said, properly adjusted they can be incredibly comfortable. One downside to them, though, is that you practically need a shoe-horn to get the gun back in. The near-impossibility of quickly reholstering means that regular range practice is out of the question, and you have to have an action plan that includes putting the gun away in pocket or waistband after making a belly-band draw on the street.

The "tuckable" is a different breed, the latest

Author only trusts a few metal belt clip-type IWB holsters to stay in place. One is this Don Hume, here holding a 4-inch custom Kimber.

development in this area and one of the most widely copied. It goes back to Dave Workman, a holster-maker who is also a leading Second Amendment advocate and gun author. For those with office dress codes, Dave came up with an inside the waistband holster that had a separate paddle that secured on the belt, creating a deep "V" between the holster and that securing portion, into which a dress shirt could be tucked. Worn at 3:30, or in the appendix position, or at 11 o'clock in a front cross draw, it hid the gun perfectly. The snap-on belt loop could be disguised as a key holder simply by putting a small key ring in the loop. When he looked for a larger manufacturer to handle the design, I steered Dave to Mitch Rosen, who introduced it to the world as The Workman. It instantly became the most copied new rig in the holster field. This style also functions perfectly well as an ordinary inside the waistband holster.

Another IWB variation that goes *deep* inside the waistband is the Pager Pal. A flat semi-disk of leather contains a small revolver or auto that rides inside the pants and *below* the belt, hooked onto the belt by a camouflaged pager, cell phone carrier, knife pouch, etc. When carried cross draw, the support hand grabs the pager or whatever and pulls upward, exposing the holster for the gun hand's draw. I found that if you don't have a large butt, you can carry it on your strong side behind the hip and knife the hand down inside

the pants to get at the gun. Not my first choice, but an interesting option that some have found useful.

Outside the Belt

Outside-the-waistband (OWB) is more comfortable, but requires more effort for concealment. The most concealable designs copy to some degree the Pancake holsters of Roy Baker. Rounded, thus their eponymous shape, Baker's holsters and some of today's copies have three belt slots, one in the rear and two in the front. This allows the shooter to set up for forward "FBI" tilt, straight up hip-draw, or straight up cross draw. With the belt tensioning the holster fore and aft of the actual scabbard body, the gun is pulled in tighter to the hip for better concealment.

The Yaqui Slide holster, a "skeleton" design popularized by Milt Sparks, is handy in that it fits a number of different barrel length guns with the same frame. Points to note with it, though: 1) If sitting in an armchair and the arm of the chair bumps the gun muzzle, the whole gun can be pushed up and out of the holster. 2) Carbon and dirt on the gun after firing can, while it's holstered, transfer to the underlying trousers. 3) Sharp-edged sights, or deep Picatinny-style rails on the dust cover (lower front of frame) of some modern military style auto pistols, can snag on the bottom edge of the Yaqui Slide, dangerously stalling the draw. 4) Back in the '70s, a selling point

Skeletonized holsters and aggressive M1913 rails don't mix. This first-generation Glock 21SF so equipped appears to fit perfectly in a regular Galco Yaqui Slide for standard G21 but, in drawing, the deeply-cut accessory notches can catch the edge of the holster and dangerously snag the draw.

revolver, or a similar size auto, may actually conceal better because the longer barrel bears lightly against hip or leg, pushing the butt in toward the torso to better maintain concealment.

The In-Between Option

For some, at least in some circumstances, the most viable option is a gun carried ITB, or in the belt, that is, between the belt and the trousers. This allows the user to wear trousers that fit him normally, but the belt pressure pulls the gun in tight as on IWB. However, the IWB advantages of allowing the bottom of the garment to rise higher without revealing the gun, and of breaking up the outline of the holstered gun, are lost. Mitch Rosen's appropriately titled "Middleman" is one holster designed expressly for this purpose. Another that is perfectly adaptable to this is the Quad Concealment from Elmer MacEvoy's company Leather Arsenal. Its name comes from the fact that this ingenious and extremely useful rig can be worn outside the belt or between belt and trousers, and can be worn either way ambidextrously.

Paddle Holsters

Some belt holsters are made with a paddle that goes inside the waistband, securing on the belt and holding the holstered gun outside the pants. The one strong point of this design is convenience: easy on, relatively easy off. I don't care for them for the following reasons. 1) I've seen too many fail to secure, resulting in the holster coming out with the gun. It's funny at a match or a class, but on the street, it would get you killed. The only thing that would save you would be if your opponent was laughing at you too hard to shoot straight. 2) Since the belt is securing on the paddle rather than the holster itself, guns carried in this fashion tend to lean out away from the body, compromising concealment. 3) The juncture of paddle and holster body is, by nature, weak. I've seen even the best brands break here, yielding the holstered gun to the "attacker," in weapon retention drills. 4) The convenient on/off nature of this holster fosters an "I'll wear it when I need it" mentality, causing the gun to be left behind and to not be present when, unpredictably, it *is* needed.

of this design was that it could stay on the belt with the gun removed, and would often go unrecognized as a holster. This is probably not the case today. The Don Hume version is certainly a best buy for quality vis-à-vis price today, and a key objectionable point to this particular style is removed with models that have thumb-break safety snaps, as offered by Bianchi, Ted Blocker, and others.

With any strong-side hip holster, a 4-inch barrel revolver or 5-inch barrel auto pistol are about the max in overall length that will carry comfortably before the muzzle hits the chair or seat when you sit down, causing some awkwardness and discomfort factor. Larger men, with larger butts and higher beltlines, can perhaps get away with longer handguns.

An outside-the-belt holster is particularly vulnerable to the gun leaning outward because of the butt portion's weight. Each generation of pistol packers seems to discover that a 3-inch or particularly 4-inch

There are many companies that make high quality paddle holsters, but none can get past these inherent weaknesses in the paddle concept. Go to the same maker, turn the page of their catalog, and order one of their holsters that *properly* secures to a good dress gun belt.

Construction

Leather or synthetic? Leather is the classic, and so long as it gets an occasional application of neatsfoot oil or other leather treatment, won't "squeak." Cowhide is by far the most common. Horsehide has its fans: it is thinner and proportionally more rigid, but seems to scratch more easily. Sharkskin is expensive, but extremely handsome and very long-lasting and scuff-resistant. It may last you longer than it did the shark. (I often wear sharkskin belts in court. Doesn't ward the lawyers off or anything, but seems appropriate, especially during some cross-examinations.) Elephant hide? Hellaciously expensive, but certainly tough, and predictably thicker than you probably need. Alligator and snakeskin holsters seem better suited to "show" than "go." For the most part, cowhide and horsehide are where it's at.

Rough-out or grain-out? The latter rules with outside-the-waistband carry. The only guy who ever seemed to like rough-side-out belt scabbards was John Wayne, who wore a personally-owned rig of that kind in many of his cowboy movies. It tends to hold sand and dust. The guy who popularized rough-out holster design in concealed carry was the late, great Bruce Nelson, whose Summer Special design was hugely popularized by another departed giant of the industry, Milt Sparks. They found that inside-the-waistband, the rough outer surface had enough friction with clothing to help keep the holster from shifting position; early versions had only one belt attachment loop, and were less stable than the later, improved two-loop Summer Special variations. As a bonus, the smooth grain of the leather was now toward the gun, less likely to trap sand and dust and cause wear on the finish. Some theorized that this also made the draw smoother. However, sweat tended to rapidly migrate through these holsters to the gun, much more so than grain-out IWB holsters that seem to repel perspiration better.

Plastics, particularly Kydex, do not loosen with age like leather, nor do they tend to start out too tight and need a break-in, again a common thing with good leather. Kydex certainly provides more sweat protection to the gun. However, I'm not persuaded that they're longer lasting. The reason is that their belt attachments are more likely to break. In retention training, with constant struggles for the neutralized guns between two men moving full power, I've seen a lot more Kydex and generic plastic holsters break than leather ones. The most secure of the Kydex holsters are the inside-the-belt variations. A genuine tactical problem with Kydex is that it makes a distinctive noise when the gun is drawn or holstered. Sometimes, the concealed handgun carrier wants a *surreptitious draw,* in which the weapon is slipped out of the holster unnoticed. This is much more difficult with Kydex and requires aching slowness. Score a point for traditional leather in that situation.

However, one advantage of Kydex holsters is that the better ones come with spacers in their belt loops to allow the wearer to adjust the holster to properly fit belts of different widths. For the person switching between casual pants and dress pants, the latter generally mandating narrow belts due to fashion pressure or belt loop size, this can be an advantage. The better Kydex holsters today, such as the Blade-Tech, can ride sufficiently tight to the body for good concealment. They also lend themselves better than leather to carrying a pistol already mounted with flashlight, with reasonable concealment.

There are very few fabric holsters, i.e., ballistic nylon, which will stand up. Most make it difficult to re-holster. For the most part, the "cloth" holsters are at their best as cheap "belt-mounted gun bags" that hold the gun for plinking sessions at the range, and not for daily carry in what might become a dangerous tactical environment.

Security Devices

"Snatch-resistant" concealment holsters are discussed in the Open Carry chapter. However, they should not be neglected in concealed carry. People who haven't learned to properly activate retention devices call them "suicide straps," and prefer open top. They will tell you, "It's concealed, so you don't have to worry about someone grabbing it." *Rubbish!* Your attacker may know from previous contact with you that you carry a pistol, and even where you carry it. He may have spotted it when scoping you out. Or you might get into a fight and the other guy wraps his arms around your waist for a bear hug or throw and feels the gun, at which time the fight for the pistol is on.

It is good to have at least one "level of security," that is, one additional thing the suspect has to do to shoot you with your gun in addition to the obvious movement of pulling it out of the holster. An on-safe pistol should count as one level of security. So should a thumb-break safety device. A hidden or "secret" release device may count as two levels. A holster requiring a push in an unusual direction to draw is another level. It's not a bad idea for the holster to have at least one "level of security."

A safety strap can also keep the gun in the holster when something other than a hand pulls at it. The gun butt can catch in brush when sliding down a hillside, or on a counter you're pushed against in a physical fight, or simply come out if you take a tumble butt-over-teakettle. There have been cases of guns falling out of holsters on amusement park rides that put the rushing riders upside-down.

Some, like me, justify the occasional wear of open-top holsters with their extensive experience in handgun retention training. However, even we are likely to have at least a safety strap when out in the brush or performing other strenuous physical activity, or when "open carrying" as police investigators at

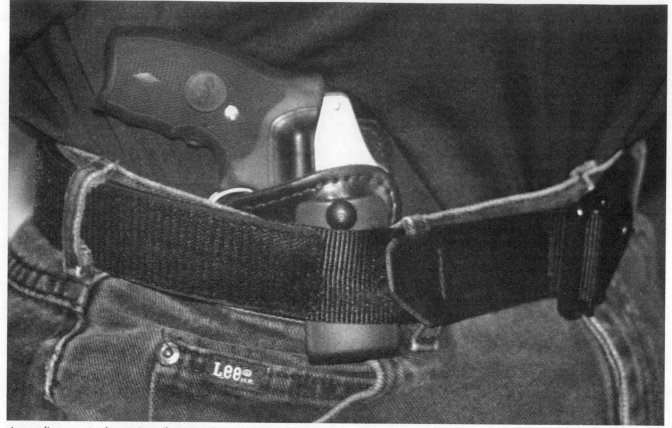

Appendix carry. As shown, it works particularly well for females. Combo is S&W 342 with LaserGrips in Safariland J-hook IWB designed by Bill Rogers.

the station or other environments that increase the likelihood of a gun-snatch attempt.

With practice and proper technique, the difference between open-top and thumb-break in drawing speed is a very thin fraction of a second, a fair price to pay for the added security.

Belt Factors

Holsters and belts are as symbiotic as automobiles and tires. We firearms trainers can tell you *ad nauseum* of students who come in with expensive guns in holsters that should have a Fruit of the Loom label, or may be proof incarnate that you can skin a chicken and tan its hide and make a holster out of it. However, we can also tell you about the students who come in with fine guns in top quality holsters that are hanging off crappy, floppy, narrow little belts whose institutional memory is probably the words, "Attention K-Mart shoppers!"

Even the best holster will, on a poor belt, hang outward from the body. It will shift its position constantly, violating the twin needs of discretion and comfort. There may be so much slop between the belt and the holster's belt loops, and so much undesirable flexibility in the belt itself, that you can exert the drawing movement for an inch or more and the gun has not begun to leave the holster.

The belt should be fairly stiff, and should be fitted tightly to the holster loops. Often, the easiest way to achieve this is to use a "mated" gun and dress gun belt

from the same maker. This also gives a certain pride of ownership. Looks great at an open carry barbecue. Of course, we carry them *concealed* for the most part, so it's not really a fashion statement, just a matter of personal satisfaction. I personally don't care who made the belt and the holster, I care that they go together.

You wouldn't save up to buy a Volvo or a Mercedes to keep your family safe, and then put on two-ply retread tires. Counterproductive. Ditto a good gun in a crappy holster, or a good gun in a good holster on a crappy belt. I would rather have a $300 police trade-in handgun in a good holster on a good belt, than a $3000 custom pistol in an inappropriate holster on an inappropriate belt. The man with the latter combination will inevitably lose a quick-draw contest to the equally skilled man armed with the former.

For those who don't care for leather, top-quality nylon dress gun belts such as the defining Wilderness Instructor's Belt will work fine with casual clothing, and companies like Blackhawk make narrow *faux* leather belts with matching-loop holsters that will work well in concealment. "Armed and green," as it were.

A larger gun in a well-selected holster will carry more comfortably and in more discreet concealment than a smaller gun in a poorly-selected holster on an inappropriate belt. Gun, holster, and belt are all part of a system, and if any of those links fail, the whole chain will fail. We're talking about life-saving emergency rescue equipment here. Failure is unacceptable.

Chapter 8

CROSS DRAW

Polymer-framed 9mm Kahr PM9 rides inside and *below* the waistband, and was designed for cross draw wear.

The cross draw holster – carrying the handgun butt forward, on the hip opposite the dominant hand – seems to be one of those "love it or hate it" issues among experienced *pistoleros*. There are several handgun sports that actually ban them as safety hazards. But there are also some folks out there who find them perfect for their needs.

Let's look at the upsides and downsides, and at how to streamline the cross draw concept in ways that may help get past the concerns of the detractors. First, let's define some terms.

Assorted Cross Draw Concepts

There are cross draws, and there are cross draws.

Conventional cross draw generally puts the gun all the way over on the opposite hip.

Front cross draw brings the gun to a point between

Transparent raincoat is used to demonstrate cross draw. If garment is closed, front position shown can work well, but zippered garment like this should be fastened no higher than abdomen, and buttoned garment should have unbuttoned open space near the gun…

…assuming target/threat is in camera's position, first movement is to step back with dominant side hip. Support hand begins to rise, partly to block attack and partly to clear it from path of practitioner's own muzzle. Gun hands fingers begin to form "spear hand" configuration…

hip and belt buckle, what would be the appendix position for a southpaw. This was the position once favored by IPSC shooters, and by the Illinois State Police back in the Seventies and earlier. It's also a favorite location for belly-band carry.

This is also a top choice for placing the second single-action revolver required in Cowboy Action shooting.

Fanny packs are often worn in a position that, effectively, puts them in a cross draw location.

Shoulder holsters require a variation of cross draw to bring the handgun into action.

Backup gun rigs attached to body armor are normally worn like vertical shoulder holsters, and therefore call for cross draw techniques and tactics.

The Kramer Confidante, a tee-shirt with built-in gun pockets under the armpits, is designed for wear under a dress shirt or casual shirt. The draw is the same as that from a conventional shoulder holster: a variation of cross draw.

Cross Draw Advantages

Many of those who choose the cross draw do it because of **range of movement issues.** Proportionally more female than male cops and CCW civilians carry cross draw than their male counterparts. This is because with a female and a male of the same height, you can expect the woman to have a shorter torso, a higher pelvis, and relatively longer and more limber arms (vis-à-vis the torso) than men. A woman can reach farther under her off-side arm for a shoulder holster, and farther toward her opposite side hip, for these reasons. A cross draw belt holster or shoulder rig that might be literally out of reach of a brawny, broad-shouldered man might be perfectly accessible when worn by his sister.

For women, the cross draw is also an alternative to the problems that come with strong-side hip holsters that have been designed "by men, for men." The higher hips and more pronounced buttocks of the average woman push the muzzle area of a strong-side holster outward, which concomitantly pushes the butt

...as support hand continues to rise, spear hand "knifes" through coat opening for smooth access to gun ...

...access is achieved on Com-Tac dummy Glock 19 (used here for safety purposes), trigger finger straight and clear. Now...

in toward the body. Because of the higher belt line, a gun "handle" that sits comfortably in the hollow beneath a man's ribcage can press with excruciating discomfort into a woman's ribs. When the most popular solution doesn't work, you need to explore less popular alternatives, and cross draw/shoulder carry is one.

It's not just a woman's issue. One of my fellow gun writers has some serious arthritic issues that limit the range of movement of his shoulder. He finds the conventional hip holsters of his youth to be awkward and uncomfortable, and excruciatingly slow. So, he wears his sidearm, usually a 1911 45 auto, cross draw on the opposite hip. *Voila:* problem solved.

Many bodyguard chauffeurs and others who must constantly be seated, especially at the wheel of an automobile, have come to appreciate across-the-body carry. Many types of car seats inhibit the elbow's flexion and therefore the reach of the gun hand when going for a strong-side hip scabbard while sitting in a vehicle. A quick reach down across the front of the body is generally faster. In the 1990s, a new breed of holster called the "counter-car-jack" rig made a brief appearance, though it did not seem to catch on. It held the pistol butt down, with the barrel almost horizontal, just to the off-side of midline of the abdomen. Men behind the wheel found it deadly fast. It did, however, have some downsides when one got out of the vehicle.

Hunting advantages. In the game fields, I learned to appreciate a sidearm in a cross draw holster. If it was backup to a long gun, the main gun's stock was no longer banging into the handgun's butt all the time. If travel involved ATVs and such, the cross draw seemed more accessible. Shoulder holsters have always been hunting favorites because the outer coat totally protects even big handguns from inclement weather.

I'm not a horseman – the closest I've come to hunting with a horse has been driving to the deer woods in a Ford Bronco – but friends who have hunted a lot on horseback tell me the cross draw

...pistol is drawn across chest, rocking up toward threat ...

...and body is ideally positioned for classic Weaver stance.

is much more accessible to a person in the saddle. This is one reason cross draw was so popular among genuine cowboys in the Old West. At the OK Corral shootout, witnesses said Billy Clanton drew his 44-40 Colt Frontier Six-Shooter from a cross draw rig. And he was pretty quick with it. Wyatt Earp had gone into the fight with his own Colt 45 in the capacious, custom-made pocket of his overcoat, with his hand on the gun to start. Yet, when Clanton went to draw, he was so fast from his cross draw scabbard that both Wyatt and Virgil Earp testified later that Billy and Wyatt had fired simultaneously at the opening moment of the gunfight.

Weak hand accessibility. If you need to get to your sidearm with your non-dominant hand, nothing is faster than a gun already holstered on that hand's side. With a regular cross draw rig on the belt, you simply use the "cavalry draw." Turn your weak hand so the thumb is pointing to the rear and the metacarpal bones are toward your torso. Grab the pistol and lift. As it starts to clear the holster, point the muzzle down in front of you. The gun will now be upside-down. Rotate your hand to conventional gun orientation as you bring it up on target, and you'll avoid the common

"cavalry draw" mistake of crossing your own body with the gun muzzle.

Is this fast? Well, on the Old West frontier, there were those who carried their guns butt forward and *always* did a cavalry draw from them! These included the men of the U.S. Cavalry itself, who carried their sabers on their left hips positioned for draw with the presumed-to-be-dominant right hand, and their service revolvers on their right hips in butt-forward flap holsters. The rationale was that if the cavalry trooper needed a weapon in either hand, a revolver was easier to manipulate with the "weak hand" than a saber, and a conventional cross draw would be executed with the weak hand. If the dominant hand reached for the gun, it would do so with the "cavalry draw" described above.

James Butler "Wild Bill" Hickok carried a matched pair of Colt Navy 36-caliber revolvers at his waist, butts forward at the points of his hips. He used the cavalry draw exclusively...and he shot his way into history as, some said, the deadliest gunfighter of his time.

Compatibility with heavy winter coats. A knee-length overcoat is not the easiest thing to sweep out of

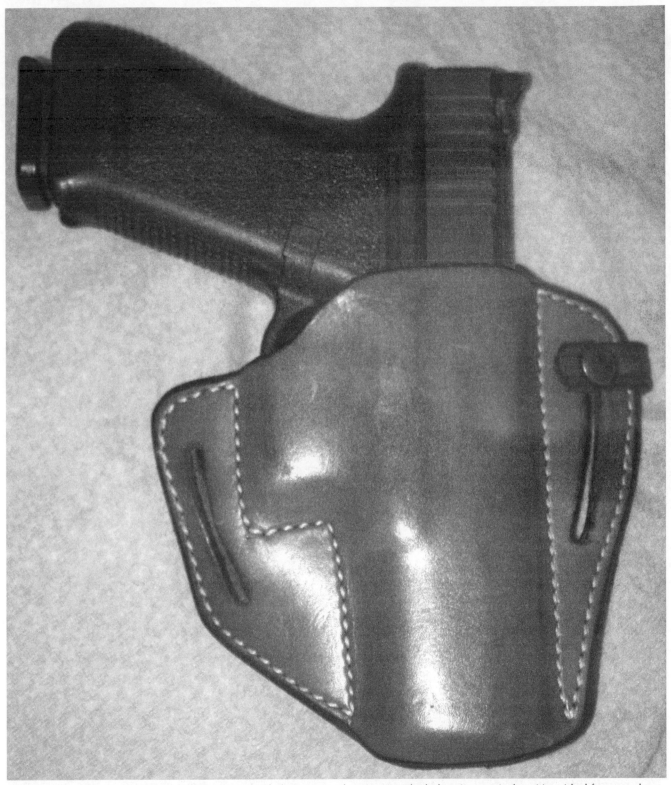

Slider loop in right *(forward)* slot of Blocker DA-2 hip holster is moved up to orient the holster in a vertical position, ideal for cross-draw carry. Pistol is Glock 17 full-size 9mm with Heinie night sights.

the way when you need to suddenly, reactively draw a handgun from a strong-side hip holster. On the other hand, a shoulder or cross draw belt rig is very fast for a right-handed man or a left-handed woman to reach, through the *front* of the winter coat. All that is required is a coat design that allows one button to be left undone to allow access. (I say right-handed men and left-handed women, because men's coats button to the left and women's, to the right.)

One bitterly cold, dark night in the winter of 1970 I was wearing a heavy winter overcoat over a suit as I stepped out of a hotel and made my way through the

The cavalry draw. Assume this old fat guy's right arm has been hit by first opposing fire, and his only gun is in a cross draw Aker holster, butt forward on his left hip…

…left thumb sweeps back coat as palm turns outward and slides between gun and torso…

biting wind to the far, dim corner of the parking lot where I'd had to leave my car. To make a long story short, I "saw the muggers coming," and unbuttoned both coats so I could get at the Smith & Wesson 38 I was carrying in a Bucheimer scabbard behind my right hip. When they made their move, I made mine, and once my gun came out it was all over. On the way home, I kept thinking about how it might have ended if they'd been more stealthy, and my gun had been buttoned under two coats when I needed to get it quickly. From then on, for a long time after, I carried my gun in a cross draw or shoulder holster in deep winter.

Compatibility with likely "hand start" position. Back in the Seventies, when IPSC (the International Practical Shooting Confederation) first got up and running, the front cross draw was hugely popular. Concealment has never been an issue in IPSC, so a big 45 auto just to port of the belt buckle posed no problems in that regard. Ray Chapman, and many other champions of the day, shot from cross draw. Ray designed the popular Chapman Hi-Ride holster for Bianchi, and the (Ken) Hackathorn Special was

a bestseller for Milt Sparks Leather, often worn butt forward.

Why the popularity? Only a few of us seem to remember that back then, one of the most popular start positions at the beginning of a course of fire was with the hands clasped at midline of the body. This put the gun hand just an inch or two above the grip-frame, and gave the user of a front cross draw holster a "running start." Many of the hip holsters "back in the day" were low slung, even using thigh tie-downs and riding on buscadero-like belts. The also popular "hands up" start position put a high-riding cross draw closer within the shooter's reach than many of the strong-side rigs. As time went on, it was discovered that moving your Chapman Hi-Ride or your Hack Special to the gun-hand side of the belt buckle made things just as quick, and soon the cross draw was a relic of the past among IPSC's top contenders.

The Bianchi Cup has always used a hands-up start position. I was there when Ron Lerch won the first, drawing his Colt 45 from a front cross draw, and for the years following when Mickey Fowler *ruled* the Cup, drawing his custom Government Model from the ISI front

...with "hand backward," conventional grasp is taken. Thumb would pop safety strap if there was one, and then take grasping position as shown...

...gun is pulled straight up along given holster's natural drawing path, and when barrel or slide area have cleared, gun is rotated butt outward...

cross draw rig he had co-designed with manufacturer Ted Blocker, and named after International Shootists, Inc., the school he founded with training partner Mike Dalton, another ace gunner.

What does any of this have to do with serious pistol packing? Only this: there were times and places where men who knew where their hands would be when they began their draw, and had a lot riding on the outcome, chose the front cross draw position because it was faster to reach.

If you carry a gun for defense, when the day comes, you'll have a lot bigger stakes on the table than even so prestigious a trophy as the Bianchi Cup. If you can figure out a way to have your hands closer to the gun before trouble starts, in situations where you can't just haul it out when you smell danger, the cross draw tends to lend itself to early readiness.

Fold your arms at your chest, and let your gun hand slip inside your jacket. Ta-da! Your gun hand is already on your shoulder-holstered pistol, and ready to draw. The two key portions of a draw are *access*

and *presentation*. Access – getting to the gun and taking a drawing grasp – is the toughest part. Our tests show that starting with the hand on the gun cuts your draw-and-fire time roughly in half. With the cross draw shoulder rig, arms folded across the chest puts you discreetly in position.

Cross draw holster on the belt? The same technique works, simply lowering the folded arms midriff high. Belly-band holster in a front cross draw position? Slide the gun hand in through the opening above the belt that you'll have if you leave the second button above that belt undone. Take your drawing grasp. Let your free hand fold over that gun hand. Slouch forward a little. You look like a scared guy wringing his hands in a body language "surrender" position...but the belly gun is already in your hand, and you're ready to draw with the fast, efficient technique that made Chapman, Fowler, and Dalton the famous champions they are.

This, I submit, is a good thing to have on your side of a fight.

...and that way, muzzle never crosses own body as Odin Press dummy of S&W 38 is thrust forward and simultaneously rotated upright ...

... and shooter is in a strong firing stance, here using "McMillan/ Chapman tilt."

Disadvantages of Cross Draw

Cross draw is nowhere near as popular as it used to be. Remember the old TV series *Dragnet,* where Jack Webb as Joe Friday always had his snub-nose 38 butt forward on the opposite hip? Remember how many other cop shows of the Fifties and even the Sixties had detectives carrying their guns the same way?

That's almost gone now. I very rarely see cross draw holsters on plainclothes cops anymore, and when I do, they're usually on the hips of female officers for reasons discussed earlier. Shoulder holsters are somewhat more common, but less so than they once were, even though today's shoulder rigs are the best and most comfortable that have ever existed.

As far as uniform wear, the cross draw duty holster has been relegated to the police museum. When I was young, cross draw was standard uniform equipment for Metro-Dade officers in Miami, and for the state troopers of Florida, Illinois, Iowa, Michigan and Washington. The last stubborn holdout, the Iowa State Patrol, switched to Safariland security holsters on the strong-side hip just a few years ago for their S&W

4046 Smith & Wesson 40s. They recently replaced those guns with S&W's new Military & Police autos in the same caliber, but stayed with the strong-side Safarilands. Today, there is not a single major police department in the United States that issues or, to my knowledge, even authorizes cross draw holsters for personnel in uniform.

One of the biggest complaints about the cross draw was that the forward butt made the gun altogether too accessible to an opponent you were facing. Indeed, with the gun all the way over on the opposite hip, it was literally more accessible to a facing man than to the wearer, if they were positioned to each other squarely. Bill Jordan warned against cross draws for just this reason.

The late, great gun expert Dean Grennell was a good friend of mine, and one day he told me that early in his short police career, he equipped himself with a 3 1/2-inch barrel S&W heavy frame 357 Magnum in a cross draw holster that looked just spiffy, and seemed handy to reach when he was at the wheel of the cruiser in the Great Lakes area community he

Snub revolver like this S&W 340 M&P is ideal for front cross-draw (navel or weak-hand side of abdomen) at belt line with belly-band like this. It's the author's favorite, an old Bianchi Ranger that also serves as a hidden money belt.

Polymer-framed 9mm Kahr PM9 rides inside and *below* the waistband, and was designed for cross draw wear. This is the side that faces the wearer.

served. Then, one day after lunch, he was washing his hands at the rest room sink and, looking in the mirror, realized just how inviting that forward-projecting gun butt would look to a man standing in front of the uniformed officer. On his next shift of duty, he told me, his Smith & Wesson Magnum was in a strong-side hip holster.

Another big problem, particularly when the gun was worn as a true cross draw all the way over on the opposite hip, was that the draw could sweep the range officer behind the shooter on the range, and would definitely sweep the shooter on the holster side. This is why cross draw has been banned from police combat/PPC competition since its inception in the late 1950s. This is why it has been banned in IDPA (International Defensive Pistol Association) competition since that organization was founded in 1996. I recall visiting the Iowa State Law Enforcement Academy about thirty years ago, back when Iowa state troopers carried S&W Model 13 357 Magnum revolvers in cross draw flap holsters. I learned that when Iowa State Patrol recruits came through the Academy, they were forbidden to use their issue duty

Cross draw lends itself well to surreptitious draw. Regular jacket would hide what this transparent one reveals: standing with arms crossed, author already has drawing grasp of dummy Glock in cross-draw LFI Concealment Rig.

Another option for cross draw. If concealing garment is open as shown…

…support hand can grab garment as shown and peel it back, giving drawing hand faster and clearer access to the LFI Concealment Rig worn here cross draw …

…but this technique takes somewhat more effort to keep support hand out of gun muzzle's drawing path, and that hand may be busy warding off an attacker.

holsters, and instead were furnished by the Academy with FBI-style straight-draw scabbards for the strong side hip.

A third concern with the cross draw holster is that it has to ride farther forward on the hip than a strong-side rig. This causes concealment problems. The strong-side concealed carry holster generally is located *behind the hip.* In cross draw, if the man carrying it is to be able to reach the gun quickly enough to save his life, the butt-forward scabbard has to ride either *on* the opposite hip, or *ahead* of it. This makes it much more difficult to conceal when that winter coat is taken off at restaurant, office, or a friend's home, unless the underlying suit coat or other concealing garment remains closed in the front.

Shoring Up the Weaknesses

Whatever the concept, my rule is "go toward your strengths and shore up your weaknesses." The strengths and weaknesses of cross draw carry have already been identified. Let's look at how to shore up the identified weaknesses if you've decided to, at least sometimes, carry the gun opposite your gun hand.

Handgun retention. Take a tip from the Illinois State Police. For the last several years of cross draw carry with their Smith & Wesson Model 39 9mm autos before switching to strong-side holsters in the late 1970s, they wore their flap duty rigs in a *front* cross draw position, with the gun tilted about 30 degrees toward the dominant hand. Like the Iowa State Patrol and the Michigan State Police, they taught troopers to lift the flap with their nearby weak hand, and draw with the strong hand.

The draw would start from the interview position, with the weak side (which, with cross draw, is the holster side) of their body toward the threat. When this stance is combined with the 30-degree angle of holster rake, the butt is no longer "offered" to the man in front of you. Indeed, it's your muzzle that's pointing toward him. This is a *much* more defensible posture from which to start a struggle for the holstered weapon!

With a cross draw holster on the belt, the Lindell System (Kansas City system) proven for three decades now and created by Jim Lindell, will work. You simply treat the right-handed cross draw holster on your left side as if you were a left-handed person carrying your weapon on your dominant side. The entire repertoire of techniques will work fine.

The Lindell System has never really addressed shoulder holsters. I teach my students a set of shoulder rig retention techniques that were developed by Terry Campbell, late of the Marion County (Ohio) Sheriff's Department, one of the toughest and best defensive tactics instructors I've ever had the privilege of training with. No handgun retention technique (at least, none of the ones that actually work on the street) can be taught in a magazine article or a chapter of a book. But, make no mistake, retention techniques that will protect cross draw and shoulder holsters do in fact exist.

Reaching through a conveniently unbuttoned opening to belly-band positioned for front cross-draw is one of the fastest ways to bring a little J-frame snub into action.

Cross draw as shown is best access to AirLite S&W, worn in hidden pocket behind breast pocket of this Woolrich Elite shirt designed by Ferdinand Coelho. Thumb is on top of hammer area to reduce the combined width profile of the drawing hand and the gun, smoothing and accelerating the draw.

"Sweeping" and Safety Problems.
Yes, the cross draw is banned in IDPA, PPC, and most police academies. That said, it's still allowed to my knowledge in NRA Action Pistol Shooting (including the Bianchi Cup), IPSC, and of course, cowboy action matches. The requirement that makes it safe in those venues is the one you want to use religiously for your own practice "for the street."

Always remember: "If it's not safe to practice on the range, you'll never build enough repetitions to make it work reflexively and safely in the real world."

To make the across-the-body draw safe and efficient, drill in the following steps. They'll work with conventional cross draw, front cross draw, belly-band, fanny pack, shoulder holster, *et. al.*

Step one: Take a step back with the leg on your gun hand side, turning the holster side toward the threat.

Step two: Drop the gun hand straight down to the grip-frame. As you do so, raise your non-dominant hand as shown in photos, into a blocking position. This will keep your gun arm clear of your muzzle's path.

Step three: As you draw, bring the pistol back across your body toward your strong hand side until the muzzle comes up and into the target. There should be no "sweep" laterally: the muzzle should come right up out of the holster and toward the threat.

Step four: Punch the gun toward the target.

Step five (Optional): If there is time for a two-hand hold, bring the support hand down and forward, coming in on the gun from above and behind so your support hand is never swept by the muzzle. Because of the torso angle, this type of draw lends itself very well to the classic Weaver stance, or the modified Weaver stance popularized by Ray Chapman. To go to Isosceles if that's your preference will require an additional movement, a turn of the hips that squares the target to the threat while leaving the non-dominant side's leg forward and the dominant side's leg to the rear, leaving your feet still in a boxer's stance.

Only the smallest and shortest of combat autos, such as this 9mm Kahr MK9, work well in front cross draw inside belly-band. This rig is from Action Direct.

The Chapman Hi-Ride was Bianchi's competition holster commonly used as front cross draw. This one was custom made by the factory for long-slide competition pistol. Les Baer 45 is shown here.

In Summation

The cross draw holster is not at its height of popularity right now. That doesn't mean that there aren't some people for whom it's the best choice. Nor does it mean that each and every one of us might not find some special purpose that is best fulfilled by some sort of across-the-body carry.

It's like so many other things. It's safe if you do it correctly, and may even be more efficient. But when any of us go to a new technique – or resurrect an old one, like this – we have the responsibility of making sure we're doing it correctly, and making the right choice for the right reason.

Chapter 9

SHOULDER HOLSTERS

Bianchi X15 shoulder rig that must be a quarter century old, but still works perfectly.

The driving rain sweeps the night streets and sidewalks of the city, making them look like glistening pools of ink, streetlights and automobile headlamps sending swords of light across their oily surfaces. You pull up the collar of your trench coat, and tug the brim of your dripping fedora a little lower down over your eyes. You reach inside the coat to feel the reassuring solidity of the gun in your shoulder holster...

Ah, yes, the shoulder holster is a part of

Recommended draw from vertical shoulder holster. Transparent raincoat used here for illustration purposes reveals a vertical shoulder holster, with Odin Press dummy 1911 pistol used for safety reasons.

Movement begins with gun hand side quartering back from threat, support hand rising to block attack, and to get it out of shooter's own gun-path. Gun hand fingers form "spear hand" that knifes into opening of coat, which is fastened up to solar plexus…

whole *noir* scene, in movies and novels alike. Frank Sinatra carried a Colt pocket model in a Heiser-type shoulder holster in *Suddenly,* and one biographer says he wore the identical combination, loaded, under his custom tux and suit coats, in a time when most carry permits were discretionary and most movie stars could get them. Robert Stack as Eliot Ness carried a Colt Official Police 4-inch in a butt-up spring clip shoulder rig of the Heiser style, as did all his men on the TV show. Playing the same role in the movie *The Untouchables,* Kevin Costner wore a Colt 1911 auto in a shoulder rig. As a matter of fact, the real Eliot Ness *did* wear a shoulder holster, and a Colt. However, Ness' Colt seems to have been an early 38 Detective Special with a 2-inch barrel.

On the printed page, the mid-20th century saw Mickey Spillane's classic "hard-boiled private eye,"

Mike Hammer, carrying a 45 automatic in a shoulder rig. In one book – I want to say "Vengeance Is Mine," but I'm working from memory here – Hammer replaces a lost 45 with a military surplus Colt 1911 bought from a New York City gun dealer. In the last of the novels, *The Black Alley,* Hammer's shoulder holster carries an updated, commercial Colt 45 auto, the Combat Commander. A popular paperback private eye of the 1960s, Shell Scott, was armed by author Richard S. Prather with a snub-nose Colt Detective Special 38 in a "clamshell shoulder holster," which I always pictured as a Berns-Martin Lightning.

The glamorous image of the shoulder holster went beyond private investigators. One of today's best-selling novelists is Laurell K. Hamilton, who's most popular character is "Anita Blake, Vampire Hunter." Set in an alternate reality in which vampires and assorted

…and takes firm drawing grasp. Now…

…gun hand draws, NOT down and out, but STRAIGHT ACROSS CHEST, which will clear support arm now and also …

were-beasts are out of the closet, politically active, and legally protected, they can only be slain if a judge signs a warrant and dispatches a Licensed Vampire Hunter like the heroine. A petite female, Anita Blake was armed by her creator with a Browning Hi-Power and a Star StarFire, both loaded with all-silver 9mm hollowpoints, and one carried in a shoulder holster with the other backing it up in an inside-the-waistband holster.

What character in modern adventure fiction could be more famous than James Bond, Agent 007? The late Ian Fleming equipped him with a Beretta 25 in a chamois shoulder holster in the early novels. (This ignored the fact that chamois would probably hold moisture and rust the gun it contained, which is probably why you never see anyone in the holster industry actually making the things out of chamois.) In *Doctor No,* Fleming summoned the assistance of

leading British handgun authority Geoffrey Boothroyd, who more or less played a cameo as himself in the novel, but apparently Fleming didn't keep good notes of Boothroyd's advice. 007 wound up with a 32-caliber Walther PPK in a Berns-Martin Triple Draw holster, which could be worn as either a belt or shoulder rig. Problem was, this design secured on the cylinder and was available for revolvers only, not autoloaders such as the Walther.

When the Zodiac Killer stalked San Francisco, the crack SFPD investigator who hunted him was the famed Dave Toschi. Photos of the period show Toschi wearing a short-barrel revolver in a shoulder rig. Toschi is said to be the real-life model for the character Steve McQueen played in *Bullitt,* and in that move McQueen wore a 2 1/2-inch barrel Colt Diamondback 38 Special in an upside-down Safariland shoulder holster.

...more quickly get the muzzle on the threat ...

...and smoothly flow into a classic Weaver stance.

Real Life

Why so much "reel life" before getting to "real life" use of shoulder holsters? The reason is, no holster choice has been so much influenced by the entertainment media – print, film, and television – as the shoulder rig. In their classic *non*-fiction text on holsters, *Blue Steel and Gunleather,* John Bianchi and Richard Nichols said, "Perhaps no other category of holsters has more nostalgic appeal. Although such holsters were first used many decades earlier, the cops-and-robbers movies of the Thirties, followed by subsequent prohibition movies of the Forties and Fifties brought shoulder holsters to the attention of the public. The old gangster-versus-police films featuring James Cagney, Edward G. Robinson, and Humphrey Bogart (who were alternately cast as good and bad guys), were liberally sprinkled with a wide variety of shoulder holsters. Wardrobe and property departments made liberal use of the dramatic impact of these harness rigs."

The fact is, though, that art was imitating life, as it should have been. Nichols and Bianchi were correct to note that the shoulder holster had long preceded cinema. Dr. John "Doc" Holliday was known to frequently wear one, and as noted, so did the real Eliot Ness. Shoulder rigs were seen on the other side of the law in the Roaring Twenties and the Depression years, as well. Baby Face Nelson was partial to shoulder rigs. So was John Dillinger, who had been observed wearing a twin shoulder rig with a pair of Colt 45 automatics by the nervous folks who dropped

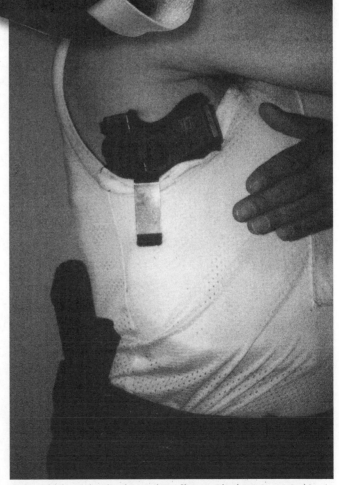

Old and new. New Ed Brown Executive Carry .45 auto rests in a Bianchi X15 shoulder rig that must be a quarter century old, but still works perfectly.

a dime on him at the Little Bohemia Lodge and set the stage for what was then the FBI's most humiliating debacle. (Dillinger didn't wear shoulder holsters or 45s when they weren't suitable for his lifestyle, though. On the hot summer night when he was killed outside the Biograph Theater in Chicago, he was coatless, and carrying a Colt 380 automatic in his pants pocket, and a spare magazine of UMC 380 ball ammo in another pocket.)

Real Life, Not Reel Life

Shoulder rigs were more popular in the time of Eliot Ness than now. Part of that came from most folks not yet having figured out that good gun belts were necessary for hip holsters, and part of it was that hip holsters hadn't yet come anywhere close to today's state of the art.

Nowadays, cops and armed citizens alike vastly prefer belt carry to shoulder carry, but that does not by any means make the shoulder holster obsolete for gun concealment. There are several situations where they come in handy.

Female Practitioners

Female users seem proportionally much happier with shoulder rigs, particularly detectives who wear guns constantly and daily. Many of the factors on the male body that make the strong-side hip holster a guy's favorite, are not present on his sister, even if she's the same height. The female torso is proportionally shorter than the male's, and her pelvis proportionally much higher and usually a lot more flared. The gun butt that rests just perfectly below the ribcage behind the brother's hip digs painfully into his sister's floating ribs, due to the higher pelvis and shorter torso. Moreover, the flare of her hip pushes the

Baby Glock 27 that backs up this officer's Glock 22 is carried in holster clipped to body armor, reached with support-side hand shoulder holster style.

Shoulder holsters lend themselves to weak-hand draw. Here, with vertical rig, left hand comes in palm out to take drawing grasp…

…and is rocked out muzzle forward, upside down, to keep gun from crossing its own user …

bottom of the holster outward at the barrel end, which concomitantly forces the butt end uncomfortably into her side. As if this is not enough, the weapon sits so high that she practically has to disarticulate her shoulder joint to perform a proper hip draw.

If the hip holster is a "by males, for males" design that is ideal for most men and difficult for many or even most women, the shoulder holster turns out to be the exact opposite. A great many men, particularly big guys, have tried shoulder rigs and found them mercilessly uncomfortable, while women do not have the same problems with them as their brothers.

Once again, it's a case of *vive la difference*. A woman's torso tends to be narrower through the chest and rib cage area than that of a man the same height, and her arms will be proportionally longer and usually, more limber. This makes certain angles of shoulder holster carry – notably the 45-degree muzzle up/butt down position, and especially the muzzle straight up position – difficult for the male to reach in terms of proper grasp and draw. This becomes increasingly worse as the male gets more broad-shouldered (forcing his arm to reach farther)

and more broad-chested (also impeding his reach in that direction.)

Try this simple test. Put together a man and a woman of roughly the same height, and ask each to raise their left arm and reach their right arm across the left armpit area where the shoulder holster would hang. See how far they can reach. Most males will run out of range of movement with the tip of their longest finger somewhere in the armpit area. Typically, though, the *female* will be able to reach around so far that she can pat herself on the shoulder blade, and I've seen a very few women so slender and flexible, their middle finger could touch their spine.

In other words, *she* can reach much farther in the direction a shoulder holster draw requires, than *he* can.

There are other reasons so many women prefer shoulder rigs. Only the most casual female wardrobe will allow the sort of quality dress gunbelt that men can wear even with business suits. The self-suspensory nature of the shoulder holster solves that problem nicely. Hanging a spare magazine or two under the off-side arm from a flat, soft, well-designed piece of

...and is rotated upright as it is thrust forward into the threat. Dummy .45 is from Odin Press, used here for photographer's safety.

This horizontal shoulder rig, the Stylemaster by Mitch Rosen, conceals even on an average size torso with the "baby Glock."

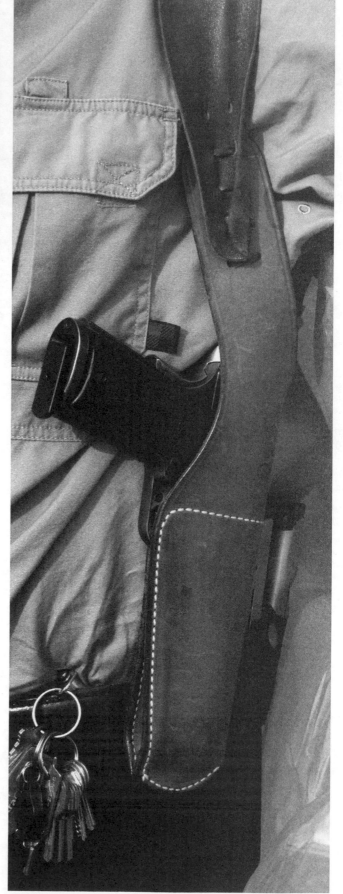

leather or synthetic seems to be more comfortable and less protuberant than hanging it on the belt. And, if she has a narrow waist, space there is at a premium, but there's a vacant place to hang gear right there under the armpit.

Constantly Seated Practitioners

Some occupational requirements force the person wearing the gun to be constantly seated. A teller's cage. An office or cubicle. Behind a steering wheel. A wheelchair. Many practitioners have found a comfortable shoulder rig to work well in these applications. However, the optimum word is "comfortable."

You can achieve the same goals with a cross draw belt holster, but the shoulder rig has some advantages. Depending which side of the seat you're on, the armed driver or bodyguard/chauffeur may find seat belts getting in the way of the cross draw holster. A "shoulder system" with spare ammo suspended beneath the armpit opposite the holster may also give faster access to spare magazines than would a belt pouch for a seated person.

These "reach" factors may significantly favor the person who is constantly planted in other types of seats. An armchair's arms, and those of a wheelchair, can catch a hip holster on either side of the body. The shoulder rig will literally be "above all that."

There can be a downside, however, and again it goes to comfort factor. "Concealed means *concealed,*" and in an automobile, that means a covering garment must constantly be worn. The long-haul driver with a handgun holstered on either side of his belt can generally take his coat off, and it will probably go

Bianchi's classic X15, shown here with Kimber 45 auto.

Horizontal shoulder holster needs subtly different draw from vertical style. Here dummy Glock is visible in Rosen holster under arm, thanks to transparent jacket…

…as draw begins, gun-hand-side leg steps back, pivoting body as shown, while support hand rises to blocking position and fingertips of drawing hand knife through opening in coat, which as shown should be fastened no higher than solar plexus…

unnoticed by anyone not in the vehicle with him, or not leaning into the vehicle and peering in. Not so the shoulder rig. Failure to realize this led to the fortunate arrest of American terrorist Timothy McVeigh, who was stopped by a lawman who spotted McVeigh driving while wearing a Glock 45 auto in an uncovered shoulder holster. The policeman drew his own Glock and arrested McVeigh at gunpoint. Apparently more comfortable blowing up children with explosives from a safe distance than he was facing armed good guys, McVeigh meekly surrendered.

The shoulder holster works well for "drivers" of conveyances other than automobiles. Most of the police pilots I've flown with – and virtually all of the police *helicopter* pilots – wore shoulder holsters.

That goes for farm vehicles such as tractors, as well. Don't forget, part of a day's labor on a working farm is getting under the tractor or the machinery to fix it. If a snake slithers along at that point, it might be difficult to get at your hip. No one has a better perspective on this than my old friend Frank James. A well-recognized authority on firearms and the gun industry, Frank also owns a successful working farm. In fact, his good-natured nickname among friends is "Farmer Frank." One of those friends is noted weapons expert Rich Grassi. In the 2008 edition of Harris Publications' *Concealed Carry* annual, Rich asked half a dozen of us what we carried on our own time and why, and called the article "Carry Guns of the Professionals." Frank James had the following to say:

"Unlike many in the gun-writing field, I am an advocate of the shoulder holster because in my experience, waist or hip-mounted holsters are poor choices during operation and/or the repair of farm machinery.

"Throughout the harvest, I usually rely on an S&W M657 41 Magnum with a custom 4-inch barrel and a Walt Rauch-designed gold bead front sight. This revolver is routinely carried in an A.E. Nelson Model 58 shoulder holster with the old-style Al Goerg shoulder harness. On certain occasions I will substitute a custom-built Heinie Springfield Armory 10mm 1911 pistol for the S&W M657. This is my second Heinie 10mm 1911 pistol, since I wore the first one (built on

…gun hand takes firm grasping hold with all but trigger finger, as thumb releases safety strap. Meanwhile, support arm has risen higher than usual to Najiola-style block …

…and now pistol is drawn straight rearward across chest, quickly coming to bear on opponent and without crossing shooter's own left arm …

a Colt Delta Elite) out, but I've also worn out three different S&W 41 Magnum revolvers. The holster used with the 1911 is the Galco Miami Classic, but I adjust the holster to a highly angled rake with the muzzle up and the butt down because that makes the whole thing less prone to snagging on hoses, levers, and other stuff," Frank concludes.

Shoulder System Users

The man who invented both the concept and the term "shoulder system" is generally conceded to be Richard Gallagher, with his early Jackass Shoulder System line that became the cornerstone of his later Galco gunleather empire. Here we had a comfortable figure-eight harness that did not put direct pressure on the neck. Under the armpit opposite the dominant hand swung the holster, which could be adjusted from horizontal draw if the gun was short enough to conceal that way, to 45 degrees or more angle of muzzle up/butt down. And, on the opposite side, there were pouches for ammunition – loose revolver cartridges, auto pistol magazines, even speedloaders later – and handcuffs.

This absolutely captivated the type of plainclothes officer who is uncomfortable carrying a gun all day.

By pulling open the desk drawer when an emergency call came in, this practitioner could don the shoulder rig as easily as throwing on a coat, and *voila!* Gun, ammo, and cuffs were suddenly onboard and ready to go in one smooth swoop.

There are those of us who don't care for this approach, since we know that one might be away from that desk drawer, or wherever the shoulder rig is stored, when the call to arms comes. We prefer to put our gear on in the morning and take it off when we are certain we will no longer need it. However, we have to realize that not everyone who carries a gun on the side of the Good Guys n' Gals shares this attitude. A quickly donned set of gun-and-gear beats hell out of *no* gun and gear, and that's why, even if this had been Richard Gallagher's only design, it would have earned him a place in the history of great holster designers.

Another useful purpose for the shoulder system is the bedside "roll-out kit." Only the most paranoid (or those at genuinely red alert level of risk) sleep with their guns on. When the burglar alarm goes off or the glass breaks, a shoulder rig right by the bed allows the awakened home defender to do exactly what that lax-about-carrying cop does with *his* shoulder

...and the draw smoothly flows into a classic Weaver stance.

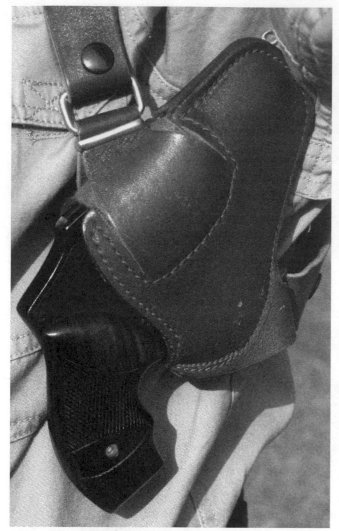

Upside-down shoulder holsters (muzzle up, butt down) work best with smaller, lighter guns, author has found. This is the old Bianchi 209, carrying an Airweight S&W J-frame 38 Special with Eagle "secret service" grips.

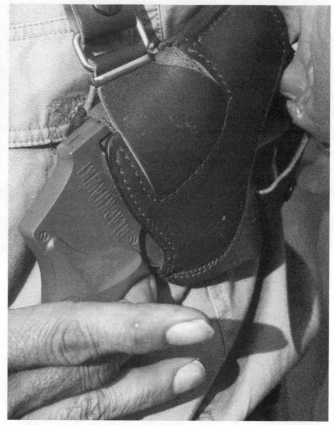

Many men have difficulty reaching far enough across their chest to get good drawing grasp on upside-down shoulder holsters. Here's Ayoob's suggestion: snag it with your middle finger…

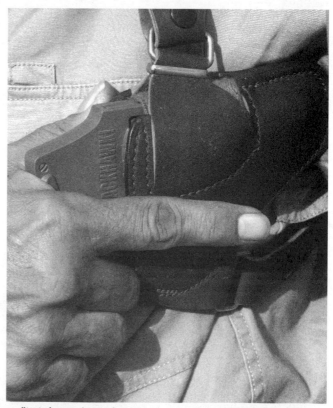

…flip it forward into drawing grasp, and *then* complete the draw. This is Blackhawk dummy version of S&W Centennial revolver, in Bianchi 209 shoulder rig.

system. In a trice, with little more than a shrug of the shoulders, the necessary gear is strapped to him even if he doesn't have time to fully get dressed. A small, powerful flashlight clipped to the shoulder strap, perhaps even a pouch attached for a cell phone, and the defender is equipped to "roll out" and handle necessary defensive task.

The "Orthopedic" Shoulder Rig

One reason I keep shoulder holsters in my personal wardrobe is that over the years, I've occasionally "thrown my back out." It always seemed to be something in the lumbar region. There are also hip injuries that can make anything heavy worn on a belt (or even a belt itself) intolerable. In situations like that, a shoulder holster can be a Godsend.

Indulge me in a little personal remembrance. In the early 1990s, I managed to throw my lower back out big time. The doc told me in no uncertain terms that I was not to have *any* weight on my belt. If I was going to do police work, he said, it would have to be

Shoulder holsters lend themselves well to surreptitious draw. Even with transparent raincoat, folded arms hide the fact that Ayoob's shoulder holstered 38 is already *in* his gun hand and ready to draw.

administrative or investigative, so I wouldn't need to be in uniform, because he had treated a lot of police back patients and knew how heavy the Sam Browne duty belt was.

"No problem," I told him. "I'm sure my chief will let me do plainclothes for a while. I'll just wear a shoulder holster."

He looked at me, dead-level serious, and answered, "Make sure you wear one on each side."

There was a long moment of silence. I ventured uncertainly, "Uh, you're kidding me, right?"

"Not at all," snapped the doc. "Think about it. Your lower back is trying to heal. Your lower back supports your upper body. If weight is off-center on one side of your upper body, your lower back isn't going to heal, is it?"

I went home to the holster room and cobbled together a double rig for a pair of Smith & Wesson revolvers. The harness and the left-hand holster were from an early Bill Rogers design, and the right-hand holster was from an old Jackass Shoulder System. It

Note orientation of muzzle of upside-down shoulder holster: subclavian artery and other vital parts are in line of the muzzle. With these, author recommends draw begin with this Kerry Najiola block, elbow high, clearing brachial artery out of the way and giving head good protection against physical blows and contact weapons. Draw is otherwise the same as with horizontal shoulder holster.

Master concealment holster designer Chic Gaylord observed that an advantage of horizontal shoulder holster is that it carries the gun already pointed at mugger or rapist who jumps you from behind. Unfortunately, it will also be pointed at *anyone else* standing behind you, and is probably the most antagonistic holster with which to practice open carry.

Cold Weather Carry

The shoulder holster has much to recommend it in very cold weather. By leaving one button undone, the hand can knife through the opening in the coat to grasp the pistol, even when bundled up against sub-zero weather. Living more than half a century in New Hampshire, which can become a frozen wasteland in winter, I found that when I took my overcoat off in an office or restaurant, the sport coat or suit coat beneath it generally stayed on, and the thermostat in the given place was generally adjusted to allow for that.

Others had noticed it long before I came along. Hunters in particular learned to appreciate shoulder holsters. Part of that was that big-game hunting season generally falls in the cooler months, and part of it was that the outer garment made a perfect protector of the shoulder-holstered handgun from inclement weather in the great outdoors. When the handgun is backup to the rifle or shotgun, it also keeps the stock of the long gun from getting scratched against the handgun on the same-side hip, or the adjustable sights on the holstered 44 Magnum from being inadvertently knocked out of alignment by the butt of a long gun. Pioneering handgun hunter Al Georg, in the 1950s, did a great deal to popularize the shoulder rig among handgun hunters.

The hunter's concealed handgun can protect him from more than dangerous wild game. The following account appears in the book *Street Stoppers* by Evan Marshall and Ed Sanow, published by Paladin Press.

"While hunting bear in the northwestern United States, he carried a S&W Model 57 41 Magnum with an 8 3/8-inch barrel in a shoulder holster as backup, loaded with Winchester 170-grain JHPs. He and his hunting partner had spent a frustrating day without even seeing a bear. They had returned their rifles and related equipment to their motel room before going out to dinner.

"They were returning to their car when they were approached by a shabbily dressed individual who asked for money. The hunter gave him $5, but the man made a sarcastic remark about the bigger bills in his wallet. Ignoring him, the hunter turned toward his car when he was struck in the back. Thinking that the panhandler had hit him with his fist, he turned around to see the man holding a large knife in his hand. Realizing that he had been stabbed, he pulled the revolver from the shoulder holster and shot him twice."

The shoulder system also works very well in cold weather for uniformed police officers. When you're working a dangerous job, a second full-size fighting handgun can be a comforting thing. In a tailored uniform, with some piece of equipment already occupying every inch of space on your duty belt, it's all you can do to tuck a snub-nosed revolver into a

was exactly balanced. The short-barrel K-frames were adjusted to horizontal carry, held securely in place by thumb-snaps, and were very quick to get at. And, sure enough, my lower back sighed in relief.

And I felt like Sonny Crockett's older, stranger brother.

Sonny Crockett was the character played by actor Don Johnson on the then-popular TV series, *Miami Vice*. Show creator Michael Mann was big into both cutting edge guns and authenticity. He had the Crockett character carry a little Detonics 45 in a black nylon ankle holster for backup, and as primary, a Smith & Wesson Model 645 45 auto or, for much of the series, an oh-so-trendy Bren Ten 10mm auto. Both were big, heavy pistols, so the Crockett character wore whichever he carried in a given season in a shoulder system. The shoulder rig *du jour* was either a Ted Blocker or a Galco, again depending on the season of production.

I spent a little time with a postal scale, and determined that a Colt Lightweight Commander pistol loaded with 185-grain jacketed hollowpoints *exactly* balanced out with two spare loaded magazines, a pair of handcuffs (I forget which set, but they may have been the old S&W Airweights made of aluminum like the Commander's frame), and finally a Spyderco Police Model knife clipped onto the harness on the opposite side. That was the rig that carried me through to recovery, at which time I went back to my old, familiar hip holsters and belt-mounted magazine pouch.

hideout holster somewhere. But, with a jacket on, a shoulder system lets you not only utilize that unused space beneath your armpit, it lets you carry something more substantial there.

On NYPD's legendary Stakeout Unit, each officer was *required* to carry two handguns and have a long gun within reach while on that particular Job. Some used a service revolver and an off-duty snubby, but many carried two full service-size guns, and a shoulder holster was often the choice for one of them. Since they were quasi-uniformed in heavy vests stenciled POLICE in big letters on the front, convenience was a greater concern than concealment. Not all used the shoulder rig. The late Jim Cirillo, the SOU's most famous alumnus, carried one 4-inch barrel S&W Model 10 in a strong-side hip holster, and a second in a cross draw belt scabbard where he could reach it with either hand. However, Jim's frequent partner Bill Allard – probably the one guy on the squad who killed more criminals in the line of duty than Jim – was fond of the shoulder rig. He carried butt up/muzzle down, and the gun under his arm was generally either a heavy barrel 4-inch Model 10, or the Colt National Match 45 auto that he had special permission to carry on duty, and with which he killed at least three gunmen that I know of. A 38 Special revolver was generally in the holster on his right hip.

I had the chance to ride with Dave Venezian and Frank Bianculli, known on NYPD as "the Batman and Robin of Queens." Each carried one gun on the strong-side hip, and the other in a shoulder rig. They worked plainclothes, and they were able to conceal their shoulder rigs in spite of sultry heat in New York summers.

Remember the Y2K thing? We laugh about it now, but when the clocks and the computers ticked over on New Year's Eve that year, many people believed it was going to be TEOLAWAKI, the end of life as we all know it. And it wasn't just paranoid computer geeks. A few months before, I had been at a conference of the New England Chiefs of Police Association, where planning for Y2K was a major theme of the event. We were told by some *very* heavy-hitters that there was an excellent chance that the entire New England power grid would go down for an indeterminate period of time. Moreover, solid gang intelligence indicated that criminal groups in the Boston and New York metroplexes were under the assumption that a power failure would somehow magically unlock vault doors inside banks, and all the bangers would have to do would be to run stolen dump trucks through the front doors and gather up the loot. Informers also indicated that small banks in suburban and rural areas, where "the thin blue line" was thinnest, were deemed by the gangs to be prime targets.

This was by no means just a New England perception. In New York City, generators and thirty days' supply of food were stockpiled at every precinct house. Across the nation, law enforcement and other emergency services personnel found leave cancelled. Manpower often doubled for the shift that would see "the turning of the clock."

In the small town I served then and now, two banks were located a few hundred yards from each other, and in line of sight from a major interstate highway. Given the intelligence we had been provided by unimpeachable sources, these two locations might as well have had bulls-eyes on them.

My department, like most, had its people out in force  that night. We had issued M14 7.62mm NATO rifles to supplement the Ruger Mini-14s and the 12-gauge autoloading shotguns that were already permanent fixtures in each patrol vehicle. It was a typical, cold New England night, so as I and another officer stood watch over the two banks from a suitable vantage point, I had a spare pistol on under my uniform coat in a Bianchi Tuxedo shoulder rig. Since our department issue sidearm at that time was the excellent Ruger P90 45 auto, I simply kept one of those in my Safariland SSIII uniform holster and a second P90 in the Bianchi shoulder rig under my coat. My primary weapon, however, was a match-grade M1A Springfield Armory 308 with Trijicon scope.

And, of course, the clock ticked past midnight and power *didn't* go out, and life was good. The point was, on that bitterly cold night when hard intelligence indicated we could expect very serious problems from very dangerous people who run in packs, I for one had found it comforting to be able to wear a second full-size service pistol under my uniform coat to back up the one in my security hip holster…and a shoulder holster proved to be the most convenient way to do that.

Design Features

The first selection criterion for shoulder holsters is comfort, because for well over a century, that has been the end user's biggest complaint. Narrow straps can cut cruelly into the shoulders, and will do so more in proportion to how heavy the gun and accessories suspended from those straps might be. Wide, soft harnesses that distribute the weight are critical here.

All leather (or all plastic) straps that can't stretch as you move your arms or bend your torso will not only be uncomfortable, but will tend to limit your range of movement. This is why judicious use of elastic in the harness can make or break the comfort and practicality factors. The all-elastic off-side shoulder strap of the classic Bianchi X15, and elastic around the centerpoint of the harness on Mitch Rosen's Stylemaster holster, are reasons both designs were successful. Galco's use of strategically placed swivels in one of its harness designs was another approach to achieving the same objective.

When you're working a dangerous job, a second full-size fighting handgun can be a comforting thing.

If you're going to be wearing the shoulder rig for more than a few hours, you don't want one whose harness crosses the back of the neck. The pressure it applies will quickly cause fatigue, and could probably exacerbate existing neck injuries. A harness that describes a figure 8 turned on its side will generally be more comfortable for that reason, all other design factors being equal. This design is sometimes called "H-type," because if the holster and other gear are removed from the harness and the harness is laid out sideways, it may resemble a capital letter "H." Some others will resemble an "X".

As to gun carry position, shoulder holsters intended for concealment use will actually break down into about four types. Terminology differs from manufacturer to manufacturer.

What I'll call here **butt up vertical carry** is the oldest configuration. The gun muzzle is pointed straight down to the ground, and the gun butt projects forward from under the armpit of the non-dominant arm. These go back to the 19th Century. The early ones were simple pouches, from which the revolver had to be lifted up and out. Later came spring-loaded designs such as the classic Heiser, which allowed the gun to be pulled down and out through the front of the rig. These were the sort worn by Eliot Ness, and accurately depicted on actor Robert Stack, who played him in the classic television series *The Untouchables*. A more effective version, the Hardy/Cooper, was named after famed gun expert Jeff Cooper, who designed it and preferred it in the 50s and part of the 60s.

Shoulder rigs of this style are still manufactured, by companies including A.E. Nelson, Bianchi, Galco, and others. They usually work best when anchored to the belt, with a leather or fabric strap that is provided for that purpose. Otherwise, the holster wants to come along with the gun when you tug it forward. With a short handgun, such as a snub-nose revolver, the belt-strap anchor doesn't seem to be needed.

These are your best bets for concealing large frame, longer barreled guns. Some books on holsters, and even some manufacturers' instructions, suggest drawing from these by ripping the handgun down through the entire open front of the spring-mouthed holster. You can do this, but the gun ends up down at belly or midriff level, instead of up in line of sight where you can see where it's pointing. This sort of draw also requires the concealing garment to be open in front.

A faster, more efficient, and more useful draw is to grasp the butt firmly, rock the butt forward until the area of the rear sight is clear of the leather, and then simply pull *up* and out, bringing the gun across the chest. This also allows you to draw from this type of shoulder rig while wearing heavy cold weather coats. Simply leave the area at the sternum unbuttoned or unzipped. So you don't suffer pneumonia in exchange

If you're going to be wearing the shoulder rig for more than a few hours, you don't want one whose harness crosses the back of the neck.

for faster draw, make sure your overcoat is cut so that the upper front will remain in position, blocking wind, even if it is unbuttoned.

Butt down vertical carry, sometimes called "upside down carry," came along circa 1930 with the Berns-Martin Lightning holster. Riding high in the armpit, it was designed for snub-nose revolvers, though I've seen them used over the years with up to four-inch barrel guns. Hugging the gun high and tight to the armpit, it proved very concealable. A rip to the front pulled the gun through the strong springs that held its split front closed, and this brought the gun naturally upward toward line of sight. It tended to work best with an open-front garment, such as an unbuttoned sport jacket.

Because the butt is toward the rear in this type of carry, the hand has farther to reach to take a drawing grasp than with any other angle of shoulder holster. A guy with a big chest and thick arms may have to catch the gun's "handle" with the middle finger, the longest digit on his hand, and pull it forward before he can complete the drawing grasp with the rest of his fingers. Another liability with this design is that the muzzle is pointed straight up toward the armpit. There are stories of guys dying when they accidentally triggered their gun while reholstering, and put a bullet through their own subclavian artery. (There is no outside pressure point for first aid hemorrhage control of a severed subclavian.)

Horizontal carry was first proven to work in the 1950s by the great concealment holster designer of that generation, Chic Gaylord in New York City, whose spirit is carried on in holsters manufactured today by Bell Charter Oak. Gaylord wrote circa 1960 that horizontal was simply the fastest of the shoulder holsters. All these years later, I have to agree with him.

As the name implies, a horizontal shoulder holster carries the gun with the butt forward and down and the barrel parallel to the ground. Good news: it's no longer pointing at your hip as in butt-up vertical carry or at your own armpit as in butt-down vertical carry. Bad news: it *is* now pointed at anyone standing directly behind you. (Gaylord felt this was a good thing, since if the mugger was directly behind you with a forearm across your throat, your gun was already pointed at his chest and all you had to do was pull the trigger and fire through the back of your coat. This theory will be lost on those standing behind you in a police squadroom with your gun muzzle pointed at *their* chests.)

This rig is fast because of all shoulder holster designs, it puts the grip-frame the closest to your reaching hand. Even if you have giant pecs and biceps, if you can scratch your armpit you can make a quick draw from a horizontal shoulder holster. As the gun is presented, its muzzle swings neither up nor down: it's already at chest height, and all you have to do is get

WE DON'T DO IT THIS WAY ANYMORE!! This is the old-fashioned draw that got shoulder holsters banned from police academies and action shooting matches. Shooter starts facing target squarely…

…and, pausing only to slow himself down with extra movement, shooter rips gun down and out. He is now muzzle-crossing range officer behind him. This requires open front garment, and …

…swinging horizontally to his target – and having just muzzle-swept anyone to his left on the range – the shooter must now slow down at the worst possible time, or risk over-swinging past his target…

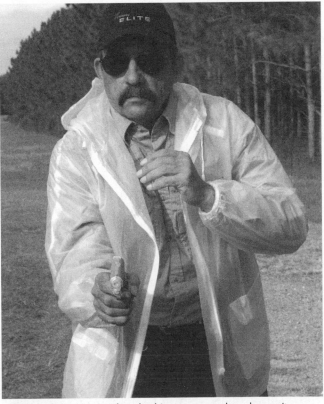

…and ends up in a cowboy-looking posture where he can't see where his gun is pointed. Did we mention that WE DON'T DO IT THIS WAY ANYMORE!?!?

it 180 degrees from where it rests to where you need it pointed. It comes out and on target with the least possible movement.

One downside is that it wants a fairly small gun. I suppose there are body builders out there who can carry Colt Government Models in this fashion and conceal them. There may also be sumos who can carry even longer guns. I'm not a big guy, though, and for me a baby Glock autoloader or a 2- to 2 1/2-inch barrel revolver are about the max I can conceal before the gun muzzle starts tenting out the back of my jacket under the armpit. How big a gun you can carry in a horizontal shoulder holster will be determined directly by how deep your chest is.

45 degree butt down carry was popularized by Richard Gallagher with the previously mentioned Jackass Shoulder System, which started the Galco holster empire. Some makers offer tie-down straps that secure on a belt. This feature keeps the gun and gear from slapping against your ribs if you have to run (and believe me, that can whale on your rib cage when it happens), but it also seems to restrict range of movement a little, as it does when a butt-up vertical carry shoulder rig is secured the same way. It's up to the end-user. Most people who like this type of holster, I've noticed, don't use tie downs.

Good news: this is another shoulder holster style that generally won't have the gun muzzle pointed at some part of the wearer's body. Bad news: when the coat is off, it will now be pointing at the faces of colleagues behind you, instead of at their chests. Back in the '70s, when Dominic Napolitano was doing police sales for Heckler and Koch, he and I went on a deer hunting trip with some guys from the SLED (South Carolina Law Enforcement Division) near Edgefield. SLED SWAT used all HK guns at that time, and that was the plan for the hunt as well. Dominic and I wanted to take our Bambis with handguns, so we each had an HK P9S, Dom's in 9mm and mine in 45 ACP. Each of us was carrying our pistol in one of Gallagher's shoulder systems. It was a warm day, punctuated by a noon barbecue, and our concealing garments were off. More than one of the locals took umbrage at looking down the muzzles of our pistols when they stood in the food line behind us. I wound up parking the shoulder rig with my gear and stuffing the 45 into my waistband "Mexican style" for the rest of the lunch.

Final Thoughts on Shoulder Holsters

For a handful of people, the shoulder holster is The Answer for constant, daily wear of a concealed handgun. For some, it's just not in the cards. X-number of folks just think it's too "Hollywood." For most who get into concealed carry, though, there's at least one shoulder rig in the holster wardrobe, and I for one think that's a good thing.

For a majority of concealed carriers, there will be certain times when this thing just comes into its own. The back problem I mentioned, or the leg injury that has me at the moment writing this with a laptop literally in my lap, and my right leg elevated in a recliner chair. The chair's design makes it awkward for me to get at my usual hip holster. A Rosen Stylemaster double rig, perfectly balanced with a baby Glock under each armpit, keeps everything out of the way and has come in as handy as the cane.

F or a handful of people, the shoulder holster is The Answer for constant, daily wear of a concealed handgun.

Shoulder holsters do present safety problems that the wearer must deal with conscientiously. Because of the potential for the gun to cross the shooter's own weak side arm, and the whole body of the shooter next to him on the firing line when he draws, absolutely *scrupulous* care must be taken not to let the finger or anything else touch the trigger until you are in the very act of intentionally firing the weapon. On the range, turn your back to the target before you reholster, so the muzzle never goes uprange or points at anyone on either side of you.

One little-recognized downside of the shoulder rig is that it may be inaccessible to you if your opponent has you in a chest-crushing bearhug. If the attack comes straight on, you'll be front-to-front with the assailant, and your gun hand's reach to the weapon beneath the opposite armpit may be blocked. Access by the support hand will probably also be blocked, at least to some degree. Ed Lovette tells the following story in the pages of his excellent book from Paladin Press, *The Snubby Revolver* (second edition).

"Jim, a detective buddy of mine, and his partner go into a trailer home to serve a warrant. At the knock, the suspect opens his door and permits them to enter. But as soon as they step into the trailer a fight breaks out, and my friend reaches for his handgun – a Colt 45 Gold Cup that he carries in a shoulder holster. As his hand wraps around the butt of the weapon, the bad guy grabs him in a bear hug, effectively trapping the 45 and Jim's hand between their bodies. (Jim tells me later that his left hand is free. Had he had a snubby in his pants pocket he could have easily gotten it into action.) Fortunately, Jim's partner pulls her trusty Colt Diamondback – the 38 Special version with the 2.5-inch barrel, certainly one of the handsomest and most accurate snubbies ever – and restores order to the fracas," Brother Lovette concludes.

The photo sequences in this book show safe draws from all four angles of shoulder holster carry. Burn them into your program. Safety is one reason that some police departments – and most shooting academies – *forbid* shoulder holsters.

All that said, shoulder holsters do have a place.

And that place goes far beyond Hollywood.

Chapter 10

POCKET CARRY

In all kinds of weather, pocket carry makes sense. For many, it's the ideal answer.

Left-hand trouser pocket holster by Bill Rodgers for Safariland conceals J-frame S&W Airweight 38 with Eagle "secret service" stocks.

People have been carrying guns in their pockets ever since firearms became small enough to fit there.

Wild Bill Hickok carried one or more derringers in his pockets to back up his famous pair of 36-caliber cap 'n ball Navy Colts. Wyatt Earp testified under oath *in re* the deaths of Frank McLaury, William Clanton, and Thomas McLaury that he began the OK Corral shootout with his hand on the butt of a Colt Single Action Army 45 revolver in the pocket of his overcoat. Colt's in-house gun shark J.H. Fitzgerald made up a pair of heavy frame New Service 45 revolvers with stubbed barrels, and wore a pair of them in leather-lined side pockets in his trousers. He made up one of those guns for Col. Rex Applegate, who packed one in a hip pocket when he bodyguarded Franklin D. Roosevelt. Legendary Border Patrol gunslick Bill Jordan was

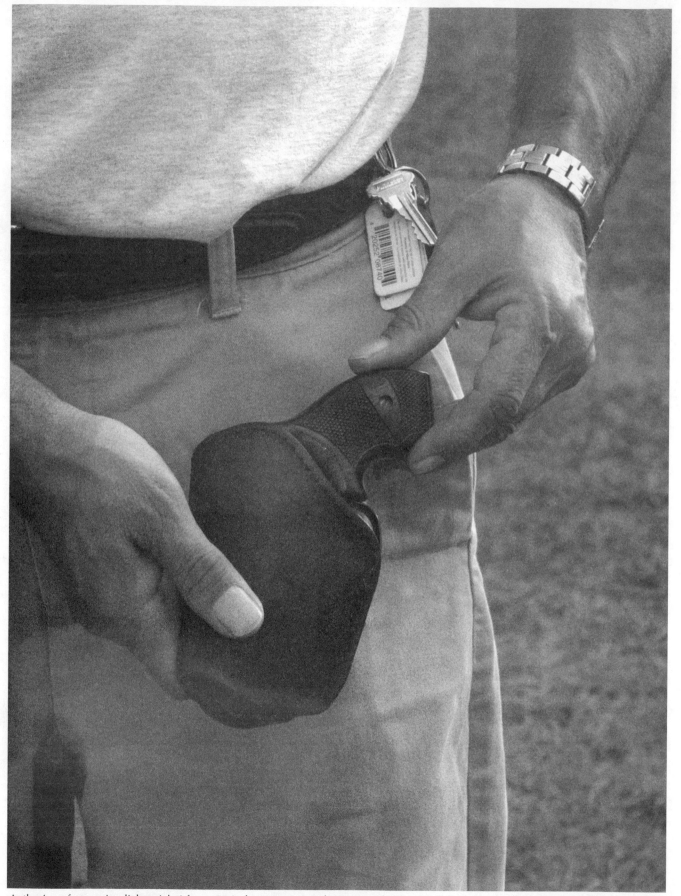

Author's preference is a lightweight J-frame 38 in front trouser pocket on non-dominant hand side, for backup, so either hand can access a weapon.

partial to a bobbed-hammer Smith & Wesson Model 37 Airweight Chief Special 38 in a hip pocket for backup and sometimes off-duty wear. On duty or off, famed NYPD Stakeout Squad gunfighter Jim Cirillo carried a hammer-shrouded 38 Colt Cobra snubby in a trouser pocket.

Today, in the 21st Century, we don't have the baggy pants of the Depression Years that allowed "Fitz" to carry a big-frame 45 in each pocket. But, thanks to the caprices of the fashion world, we have billowy Dockers-style trousers and BDUs. We have light, powerful handguns only dreamt of in Fitzgerald's time. And, perhaps most important, we have the finest pocket holsters that have ever existed.

The Pocket Itself

In the olden days, the pocket *was* the holster. The history of the Old West tells us that Luke Short carried his Colt Thunderer double-action 41 in a leather-lined hip pocket, and used that combination to outdraw and kill a gunman deemed much more dangerous than he,

"Long-Haired Jim" Courtright. Famed lawman Dallas Stoudenmire carried a pair of short-barrel Smith & Wesson single action, top-break 44s in special pants, whose hip pockets he had likewise had lined with leather by an obliging tailor.

Today, the leather-lined pocket has gone the way of the dodo bird. However, reinforced pockets designed expressly for handguns remain. A company called Betz started the trend to jackets with hidden, built-in holsters. A Betz coat can carry a full-size service auto inside next to the breast. It's drawn in a fashion similar to what you'd use with a shoulder holster. The Royal Robbins 5.11 Tactical vest has built-in gun pockets of similar style. Our nation's largest sheriff's department, comprised of several thousand uniformed deputies, orders all their uniform jackets with a special inside pocket of this kind, cut for the J-frame S&W snubnose 38 most of their sworn personnel carry for backup. Concealed Carry Clothiers has reinforced side pockets for small handguns in their line of vests made especially for CCW carriers.

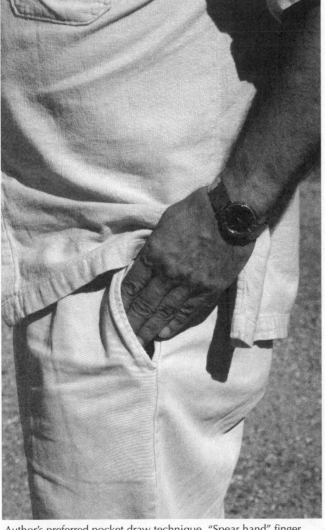

Author's preferred pocket draw technique. "Spear hand" finger configuration slides hand rapidly into pocket...

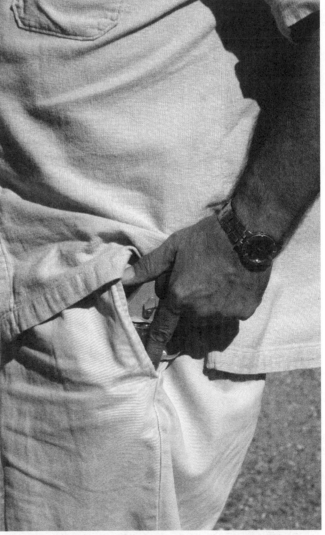

...to allow for tight pockets and spurred hammers, thumb takes this position. It dramatically reduces hand's thickness profile, thus reducing chances of a snag. It also turns the thumb into a hammer shroud for conventional-hammer revolvers...

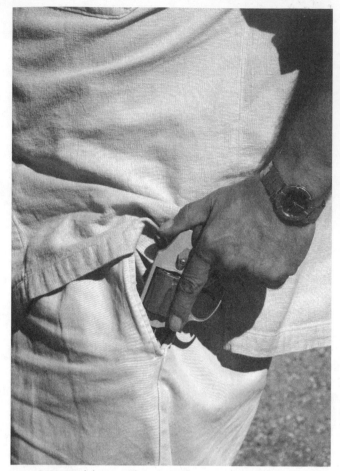

...as S&W Model 342 with LaserGrips emerges, note that trigger finger is still straight on frame, completely clear of trigger and trigger guard ...

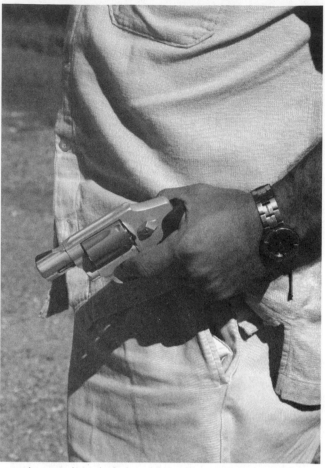

...and as gun clears the holster and begins to rock up toward threat, finger only now enters trigger guard, and *then only* if purpose of draw is to immediately fire instead of taking threat at gunpoint.

Nor have pants pockets been neglected. For decades, the troopers of a certain state have been issued two handguns, one full size and one small. The full-size gun, of course, went in a uniform belt holster. The smaller was carried in a side trouser pocket: mandatory, no exceptions. The pants were ordered with one reinforced pocket from the uniform manufacturer. Over the years, many a trooper in that state was saved by this little pants pocket hideout. Sometimes, it happened when someone got the primary gun away and the trooper had to resort to "Plan B." Sometimes, it was just easier to approach a stopped car with the hand inconspicuously in the pocket and wrapped around the little 38. When danger threatened, this made for a lightning fast draw and return of fire. Over the years that department went from the 38 Special as a primary service revolver, to the 357 Magnum, to the 9mm auto, to their currently issued 40-caliber service automatic. The backup has stayed pretty much the same: a small-frame Smith & Wesson revolver with short barrel. The current issue is the Model 640-1 "hammerless" 357 Magnum, loaded with +P+ Hydra-Shok 38 Special ammunition.

"Civilians" have not been neglected. Blackie Collins created special jeans for pistol-packers, appropriately called Toters. Both hip pockets and both side pockets are specially reinforced for carrying handguns. Since this is the very same Blackie Collins who first became famous as a knife designer, there's also a special quick-access pocket for a tactical folder.

Pocket Holsters

Even by the time of the Old West gunfighters, it had become apparent that regular pockets by themselves weren't enough to sustain the carrying of a defensive handgun. The pistol's weight, and sometimes its sharp edges, would tear through pocket linings. A small handgun could change its orientation due to body movement through the day, and perhaps turn upside down in the pocket. The shape of the gun was likely to "print" through the fabric, betraying the "concealed" element of concealed carry.

The first pocket holsters were simply leather squares or rectangles with gun pouches sewn on, sometimes crudely. In modern times, the art and design of the pocket holster have been refined dramatically. In addition to leather, we now see them crafted of Kydex, nylon, and assorted other synthetics. Greg Kramer popularized a leather model with a flat Kydex square on the outside, which broke up the outline of the gun. With tight pants, someone might be able to see that you had something in your pocket, but they wouldn't be able to tell that it was a firearm.

There are numerous fine pocket holsters available today. Manufacturers of same include Jerry Ahern, Lou Alessi, Gene DeSantis, Galco, Greg Kramer, Ky-Tac, Mach-2, Bob Mika, Milt Sparks, Mitch Rosen, Thad Rybka, Safariland, Uncle Mike's, and more. I've used most of the above, with good success.

Personal favorites, for my own specific needs, have come down to three. With a snub-nose J-frame revolver, I've had the best luck with the Safariland. Designed by Bill Rogers, it's made of synthetic Porvair on the inside and *faux* suede on the outside. The outer surface makes it stick to the pocket lining and yield the gun instead of coming out with it, no matter what the angle of draw; the smooth Porvair on the inside reduces friction and speeds the draw. Unfortunately, it seems to be made *only* for J-frame snubs at this writing. (Seems to wear hell out of the gun's finish, too.)

For the baby Glock, I use either the Mach-2 or the Ky-Tac. Both are made of Kydex and are so close in design and function that they're hard to tell apart. An almost curlicue flange at the top catches the upper edge of the pocket as you clear the square-shaped auto pistol, and a similar protrusion at the rear of the holster catches the bottom edge if you prefer to draw horizontally out of the pocket.

For most anything else – for instance, the neat little Kahr PM9 polymer-framed 9mm, a favorite pocket auto, or the 380 size Colt Pocket Nine – I prefer Greg Kramer's classic pocket rig. Mike Dillon, who makes a point of putting only the best of everything in his Blue Press catalog, lists the Kramer pocket holster in those pages. It's a hell of an endorsement, and when you work with a Kramer pocket rig, an understandable one.

Drawing From the Pocket

Starting with your hands well away from the gun, you'll probably find drawing from the pocket faster than from, say, an ankle holster, but it'll never be as fast as getting it out of a good hip scabbard. The reason is, your hand is surrounded (and, in tight clothing, distinctly hampered) by fabric as it makes its way to the gun.

The hand needs to be flat as it enters the pocket. Fingers should be stiff and straight, in the configuration of a martial artist's "spear hand."

Once the hand is in the pocket, middle finger and ring finger (and little finger, if the grip frame is long enough) wrap around the stocks. Keep the trigger finger stiff and straight. If the gun snags on the draw and the finger is on the trigger, there's a good chance you'll shoot yourself in the leg. The finger shouldn't enter the trigger guard until the gun is not only up and out, but on target, and not until you have made the decision to fire the weapon.

Don't let the trigger finger press tightly against the pocket holster. If you do, it will come out with the gun, rendering you unable to shoot.

With a revolver, put the thumb on the hammer or where a hammer would be. First, if you have a spur-hammer revolver, the thumb will now act as a hammer shroud and keep it from snagging on the draw. Second, and for many most important, this streamlines the shape of the drawing hand, which is why you should do it even if your revolver's hammer is bobbed or shrouded.

A simple exercise you can do right now, even if you're reading this in an office or airport, will show you why. Put your empty hand in your side trouser pocket. Make a fist. Now try to pull the fist out. Did it snag? Well, guess what: this is the configuration your hand will be in if the thumb is curled down around a handgun's grips, and it's going to snag then, too. Now, put the hand in the pocket again. Make a fist if you want, but put the thumb up as if it was on a revolver's hammer. Do the draw again. Snaked right out of the pocket, didn't it? OK – you've got it.

This is one reason revolvers seem to be so much faster than autos when drawing from a pocket. To get the thumb up on the hammer area or the back of the slide, which is much farther back on an auto pistol than on a revolver, you have to compromise your grasp on the handgun.

You may have to tailor your draw to the type of holster you're using. If it was designed to rock to the back to escape the pocket, with the holster catching on the bottom edge of the pocket opening, you'll have to master a draw which brings the handgun out in that direction. If its "catch flange" is at the front of the holster, it wants to catch at the top edge of the pocket. This means you draw the gun straight upward until it is well out of the pocket, then perform the same rock and lock movement you would when drawing from a hip scabbard. That is, rock the muzzle upward and lock it on the target in front of you as you bring the gun up into firing position. It's now on target if you have to fire sooner than you wanted to because the threat is closing in on you rapidly.

Most of us use the side trouser pocket for handgun carry. It's fast and secure. In the hip pocket, a gun can be uncomfortable when you sit down and is more likely to be pushed out of the pocket by pressure against the surface on which you sit. Still, some shooters prefer that location.

My friend Jim Jacobe, the ace firearms instructor from Oregon, found that the hip pocket better suited his personal range of movement. Finding no commercial pocket holster that would work from that location instead of the side pants pocket, he had a leather shop make one up to his specifications. The supple leather of that custom holster holds his S&W Model 442 very comfortably, and he's lightning fast with it.

You may have to tailor your draw to the type of holster you're using.

The Weasel in Your Pocket

Jeff Cooper and Ray Chapman taught pistolcraft. They are both big, strong men. I'm little and weak, so I concentrate on weaselcraft. In a world where action beats reaction, and where the bad guy gets to be the actor and you and I get stuck having to react, I want all the little tricks of the trade on our side that I can get.

As noted early on, getting into your pocket and withdrawing your gun can take longer than drawing from a conventional hip holster. However, when the gun is in your pocket and danger threatens, nothing says you have to start with your hands clear of your body in an IPSC "ready" position. A hand on your hip-holstered firearm might be tactically unsound, but you can slip a hand into your pocket and look perfectly casual.

The gun is now in your hand. That changes everything.

There are two basic steps to drawing a gun, access and presentation. Access is getting your hand wrapped around the blaster. That's the tough part, the fine motor skill part. Presentation is simply ripping it out of the holster and bringing it on target. That's raw gross motor skill, which is a whole lot easier – and a whole lot faster.

Back in the 2002 *Complete Book of Handguns* from Harris publications, (still available from Police Bookshelf, 800-624-9049, www.ayoob.com) I set out to test this method for speed. I began with my non-dominant left hand in my side trouser pocket, wrapped around the Crimson Trace LaserGrips of my Smith & Wesson Model 442 Airweight. I was standing as I would on patrol beside a stopped sedan, with the target in about the same position and at about the same distance as a seated driver. When the PACT timer went off, I drew and fired "from the hip," the time stopping when the 38 Special round blasted into the silhouette. Five runs took 0.76, 0.62, 0.66, 0.65, and 0.54 seconds, which averaged to 0.65 of one second. That included reaction time, which for me on that day averaged 0.21 of one second. This means that the actual draw and fire time alone averaged 0.44 of a second.

In other words, the simple weasel trick of sneaking my hand onto the pocketed 38 before hand had given me sub-half-second draw and fire capability.

Firing Through the Pocket

For the same article, which was titled "The Savvy Fast Draw," I was able to enhance react-and-fire speed still more by using an old street trick. The same revolver was in the hand inside a jacket pocket, and already pointed at the target, which was just barely within punching distance. On the signal, the 38 was simply fired through the coat pocket.

The times recorded for five runs were 0.50, 0.46, 0.48, 0.54, and 0.49 seconds. Average time rounded off to 0.49 of one second. Taking out reaction time, the actual shooting was taking only a quarter of a second, the time it took to get the index finger off the frame and onto the trigger.

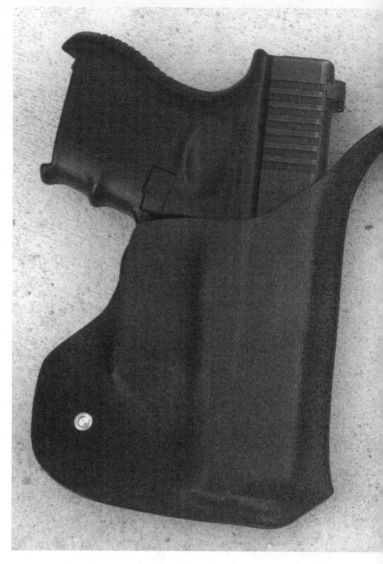

Obviously, you want to practice with a jacket that you don't plan to wear any more, since the muzzle blast will tear it apart on the first shot. Most of your practice, just for the sake of practicality, will have to be dry fire. Still, you want to do it live fire a few times to be sure that you're on target, since this is point shooting in the truest sense, with no visual index of gun on target possible. It's strictly a close range (as in, within arm's reach) proposition.

Take particular care if you are heavy through the midriff, since barrel cylinder gap gas blast from a revolver can cut through fabric and injure a protruding abdomen. It goes without saying that this technique should not be practiced live fire by pregnant women. If the garment in question is an anorak or heavy winter sweatshirt with a pocket that goes across the belly, make sure that there is enough room to get the gun muzzle pointed straight away from you before firing.

Conventional wisdom tells us that a revolver is the way to go for shooting through a pocket, since pocket lining can snag the slide or block an ejecting casing, jamming the pistol. It is also possible for a revolver with an unshrouded hammer to snag, even

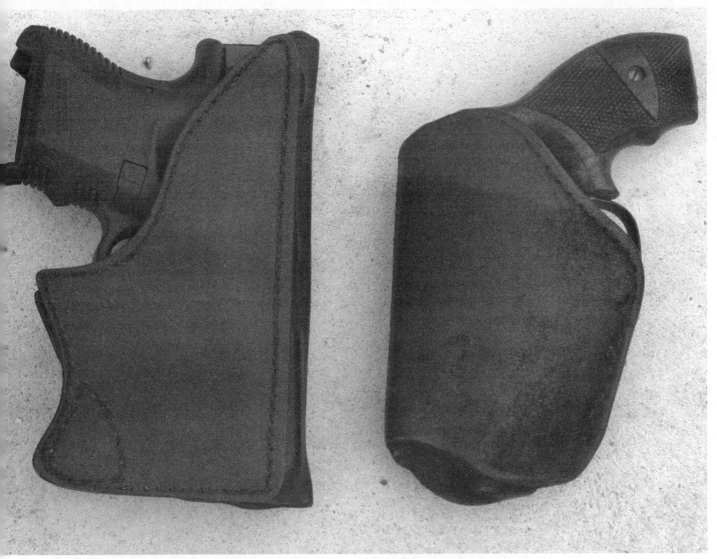

Three of the best pants pocket holsters, in the author's opinion. Left, Ky-Tac ambidextrous with Glock 27 40. Center, right-hand Greg Kramer with 357 Glock 33. Right, left-hand Safariland pocket holster with Eagle-gripped S&W Model 442.

if the hammer spur has been bobbed off. A fold of clothing can get caught between the hammer face and the frame, causing a misfire and even jamming the wheelgun enough to prevent another shot.

Now, I hasten to add that we tried this recently at Lethal Force Institute's new CQB (Close Quarter Battle) class, at the Firearms Academy of Seattle range in Onalaska, Washinton. Three of the participants used autos for firing through coat pockets. The guns represented were the Kel-Tec P32 and the North American Arms Guardian. All three specimens went five shots for five tries without a malfunction. The shooters did notice that it was distracting to have trapped, hot casings burning their hands and wrists inside the pockets.

Do fifteen shots without a malfunction mean that it's a good idea to try to shoot an auto pistol through a coat pocket? No! Damon Runyan is credited with saying, "The race is not always to the swift, nor the battle always to the strong…but that's still the way you should bet." Something similar is going on here. The auto pistol may not *always* foul and jam after firing

through clothing…but that's still the way you should bet. Consider the shooting through pockets thing to be the province of the shrouded-hammer revolver, a'la the Smith & Wesson Bodyguard or Centennial.

I've heard folks talk about clothing catching fire if a gun is fired through coat pockets. I suppose it could happen with old blackpowder guns. With modern smokeless powder ammunition, I've run students through live-fire shoot-through-pocket drills and done it a good bit myself. While you can feel a flash of heat when the gun goes off, I've never yet seen a garment catch fire. I suppose, however, that there might be some particularly flammable coat fabric out there that could prove me wrong. (*Please* don't try this after spilling gasoline on yourself at the service station pump…)

Finally, remember to shoot through only the pockets of outer garments like coats, and remember that the garment needs to fit loosely for this to work. Trying to shoot through a pants pocket, or through the pocket of a tightly fitting jacket, can lead to you shooting yourself instead of the bad guy.

Breast pocket draw, using hidden gun/wallet pocket behind breast pocket of Woolrich Elite shirt designed by Fernando Coelho, now CEO of EoTac tactical apparel. Movement pattern is like drawing from a shoulder holster; thumb is on hammer area for reasons stated elsewhere.

Summary

Pocket carry has been proven effective since handguns became small enough to fit into pockets. For the most part, you want the gun to be in a pocket holster. Practice regularly. Remember that firing through the pocket is a special purpose emergency tactic; as a rule, you'll want to draw and visually index the weapon on target before firing. Always carry a gun that cannot go off when dropped. Guns have been known to fall out of pockets, and pants or jackets with guns still in them have been known to be taken off and tossed, landing on a hard surface.

With common sense and careful practice, a compact handgun in the pocket can be a life-saver.

ANKLE HOLSTERS

Gould & Goodrich ankle holster shown w/baby Glock.

I had the privilege of knowing the late George C. Nonte, Jr. The man knew his guns, and he had broad connections with others in the industry and in the field who knew their guns, and he funneled that knowledge into his work. In his last book – *Revolver Guide*, published posthumously by Stoeger – George told the following tale that highlights the wisdom of carrying a spare gun south of one's body's own middle border.

"Many uniformed officers consider a belly gun as much a part of their equipment as a nightstick or cuffs. And, if the truth be known, the belly gun is not always employed in the singular. An example of the plural might well be a Texas Ranger known to me, who got just a wee bit careless or unlucky one day when entering a building after a felon. Somehow the black-hat got the drop on him and relieved him of his main six-gun.

Here's author's namesake method of drawing from ankle holster while standing…

…non-gun hand reaches down to grasp trouser leg. It's important to grasp ABOVE the knee…

Eventually an opportunity presented itself, and the Ranger whipped out his belly gun and ventilated his unfriendly assailant.

"Later he was asked somewhat jokingly, 'What would you have done if he had found your hideout gun, too?' His response was not entirely unexpected, but might be just a slight shock to those who've never had to depend upon a gun for their lives – 'Well,' he said, 'I'd probably have shot him with this one,' and slipped yet another two-inch 38 out of his boot top."

There's a lot of lore and wisdom in those couple of short paragraphs by the late Brother Nonte. Note that the boot top was the Ranger's choice for his snub-nose 38. It is safe to assume that horsemen prepared for trouble have been stuffing handguns down in their boot tops since the time of the earliest match-lock pistols. The spot was *there*…it was handy to a man astride a horse…and it kept belt space free for more equipment, including another handgun.

Why are ankle holsters popular today, when we're more likely to ride the family automobile (or a Police Interceptor) than something with hooves? For much the same reasons. The spot is *there*…it's handy to a seated individual…and it keeps belt space free for more equipment, including another handgun.

...gun hand side leg steps out wide as free hand pulls trouser leg up as high as possible. Knees flex and shooter begins to drop into deep crouch, further shortening gun hand's reach to ankle holster...

...gun hand contacts pistol, thumb breaking safety strap of Gould & Goodrich ankle rig...

The rise of the ankle holster can be tracked through the history of 19th, 20th, and 21st Century America. 1934: Eugene Cunningham saw publication of his book *Triggernometry*, a study of the guns, gear, and gunfighters of the Old West. He noted that despite the movie image of big six-shooters swinging openly on hips, many Western towns prohibited the carrying of guns, and a man who wanted to be armed needed deep concealment. Said Cunningham, "The hide-outs were various. A man rammed his six-gun into the leg of his boot – just in case something came up, in which he'd want to gain what was lost in the deal by what he could do on the draw."

1960: In his classic book *Handgunner's Guide*, Chic Gaylord wrote, "To be effective, the undercover holster should carry the gun in a position on the body that cannot be detected by the 'bump frisk' often employed by hoodlums or their girl fiends. Shoulder holsters and belt holsters are too easily detected by a few pseudo-amorous passes. The holster's position should also enable its wearer to reach the gun with reasonable speed."

Added Gaylord, "The best of all undercover holsters is the ankle holster. Guns the size of the Chief Special or the Detective Special are easily and effectively hidden in this manner. It is an extremely comfortable holster even after as much as eighteen straight hours of wear. You can draw a gun from this rig while seated

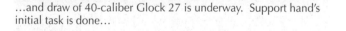

…and draw of 40-caliber Glock 27 is underway. Support hand's initial task is done…

…and shooter can now fire one-handed for all expedient speed…

in a car or in a tavern far faster than from any other type of holster. When seated at a table, the gun can be drawn and held at ready with no one the wiser in case of impending danger. Its ready accessibility counts heavily when you are wearing an overcoat; and when standing you can draw it nearly as fast as from a belt holster. Many a New York City police officer uses this rig while on duty in uniform. When jumped by a mob of hoodlums and knocked to the ground, he can draw his gun faster than from a belt holster. One of the advantages of this holster is that the officer can wear jeans and a skivvy shirt without fear of being 'made.'"

1986: In the second edition of *Blue Steel and Gunleather* by John Bianchi, it is observed that ankle holsters "have grown enormously in demand in recent years. Many off-duty police carry a gun under the trouser leg, usually a small-frame, hideout piece. The handgun is well concealed in the lower body extremities, but it is not readily accessible, even from a seated position. Practice in drawing the gun with this system improves the efficiency for the draw and fire. It is recommended primarily as a second gun carry for both uniform and plainclothes situations."

At this writing, ankle holsters remain popular…and the guns carried there have gotten bigger. I can think at the moment of two state patrols who issue their troopers "baby Glock" pistols with ankle holsters, and

… or remain in low cover crouch with two-hand grasp…

… or, if time permits and no low cover is available anyway, rise to preferred two-hand shooting stance.

expect them to be carried daily as backup when in uniform. One such agency issues the troopers Glock 39 pistols in caliber 45 GAP, to back up the full-size Glock 37 pistols in the same caliber that ride in their uniform holsters. That agency's issue backup holster is currently an ankle rig with thumb-break retainer by Gould & Goodrich. The other agency had been issuing 380 automatics with ankle holsters for years, but was not happy with their reliability. The department adopted Glock 27 pistols, caliber 40 S&W, and issued them with ankle rigs, the brand of which escapes me at the moment. The little 40 Glocks worked out so well that when that department's heavy 10mm Smith & Wesson service pistols were due to be replaced,

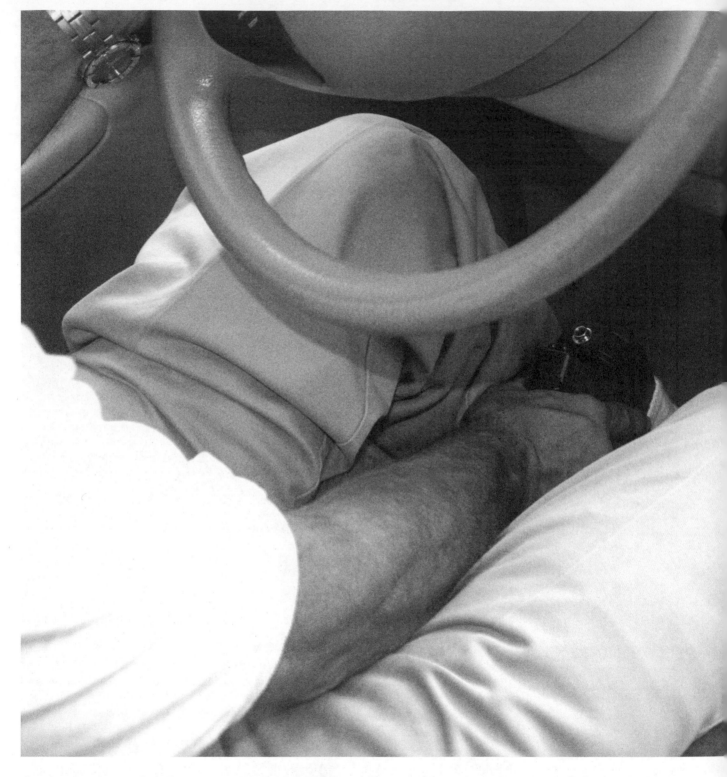

the department traded them in on Glock 35 pistols with 5.3-inch barrels. The latter guns' 15-round 40 magazines will work in the G27 subcompact model, just as the full-length magazines of a G37 will work in the chopped and channeled version, the G39. In either case, a trooper whose primary Glock is snatched, inaccessible, or shot out of his hand still has another Glock in the same caliber, and two spare magazines on his duty belt, with which to continue the fight.

One reason for the rising popularity of the ankle holster can be summed up in a single word: Velcro. When I was a kid, ankle holsters were available but uncommon. One company, Legace, made one with little straps and buckles. If your ankle diameter wasn't *exactly* right for one tongue and loop combination of that set-up – and if it was uncomfortable for you to put it on one notch loose and pad the inner circumference by wearing an extra sock – it just wasn't going to work for you. Too tight restricted circulation unmercifully, and too loose was almost as painful, with the chafing

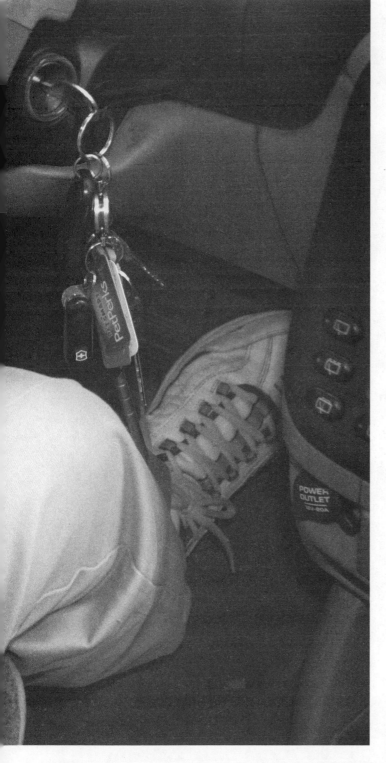

Ankle holster is ideal for seated practitioner, as here in driver's seat.

be adjusted for pretty much perfect fit. Along about the '70s. a lot of thought went into a rig called the Milwaukee Legster. Velcro secured the regular ankle rig in the usual location, but a strap ran up from it to another Velcro'd strap that encircled the leg between the knee and the calf muscle. This gave a suspension effect that helped hold the rig in place to keep it from shifting around.

That feature was widely copied. It turned out that end users loved or hated the calf strap, with no middle ground at all. The reason, I discovered, was anatomical. The guys who liked them worked out and ran a lot, or were naturally muscular, and had bulging calves. This allowed them to secure the upper strap comfortably, without fear of it slipping down, and without having to wrap it so tightly that it interfered with circulation.

I was in the other camp. With scrawny bird-like legs, the upper strap would work its way down over the calf by the end of the day and start bunching down around the ankle if I didn't pull it up, like an old man whose garters were slipping. If I secured the upper strap tightly enough to keep that from happening, it was *so* tight, I soon felt my lower leg "going to sleep." Ankle holsters are *extremely* "individual needs intensive."

As you read the comments on ankle rigs by four masters of the topic who cover multiple generations – Cunningham, Gaylord, Nonte, and Bianchi – notice some advice they have in common. Cunningham and Gaylord make it clear that the only time it's a good idea to carry the primary gun here is when, for reasons of a tactical or lifestyle nature, you *can't* carry your primary handgun in a more accessible place. Note that Nonte and Bianchi emphasize its use for *backup* as opposed to primary handguns. Hmmm…a consensus emerges: it is not a great idea to carry the only gun you have, strapped to what is probably the part of your body that is farthest from your gun hand.

The Rationale of the Ankle Holster

Gaylord's passage above typifies why his one and only book was like pemmican: thin, but meaty and full of nutrients. In those short paragraphs, Gaylord explained the ankle rig's many advantages. It's *great* for accessibility when seated, as he noted, and more important in our time than in Gaylord's because of mandatory seatbelt laws. A person strapped into a car seat will often have difficulty reaching a handgun in the usual location, the strong-side hip area.

When you are down on your back, with a bad guy on top of you, your body weight is no longer pressing down on the legs, and your balance is no longer dependent on having two feet solidly on the ground. Your back is bearing your weight, and now it's a piece of cake to snap your foot toward your hand and your hand toward your ankle, making for an *extremely* fast ankle holster draw.

that occurred as the sloppy-fitting rig bounced all over the place with every step you took, not to mention problems with concealment.

I recall seeing one ankle holster of the period – I forget the brand – that secured with lacings and grommets, like a shoe. Trouble with that was the same as with shoelaces: they could become untied. There was also the problem of a lace dangling below a trouser cuff giving away the hidden holster.

Velcro changed all that. It allowed the holster to

Many years ago, I wrote an article for *Combat Handguns* magazine that extolled the virtues of the ankle holster for backup carry. It included cases like the officer in the Miami area who was caught off-guard by two vicious armed robbers who disarmed him of his duty weapon at gunpoint. They ordered him to his knees and prepared to execute him. Stalling for time, he begged, "Wait! Let me pray first." The two thugs looked at each other and laughed mockingly.

The cop had the last laugh, though. As they turned to look at each other to mock what they thought was a helpless victim, the kneeling cop reached back to his ankle and came up with a blazing Smith & Wesson Model 60. He wiped the laughter off with a 38 Special hollowpoint fired into each of their sneering faces.

That story and others like it apparently resonated with some of the readers. Several folks got back to me to say the article had convinced them to carry ankle guns for backup.

And two of those folks told me it had saved their lives.

One was a cop down south. He had noticed that the department issue gun/holster combination, a Smith & Wesson Model 686 in a Safariland Level III retention holster, did not allow him to draw when he was seat-belted behind the steering wheel of his cruiser. The rearward rock required to clear that particular piece of leather could not be accomplished, because the butt of his service revolver was already pressed against the rear of the seat. After reading the article, he went out and bought an ankle rig and a Colt Agent lightweight 38 Special revolver with two-inch barrel.

He got into the habit of dropping his hand to his inside lower leg and taking a drawing grasp when any

Ankle draw is ideally suited to supine "downed defender." Here, unimpeded by body weight, "holster leg" begins to flex upward as gun hand begins its reach…

…moving toward each other, hand and ankle meet and draw begins…

...reciprocal movement reverses at this stage of supine ankle draw, with gun hand pulling back and holster-leg pushing forward and down to separate gun and holster...

...and holster-leg pushes itself down and clear of muzzle as practitioner prepares to fire upward in self-defense. Hardware here is "baby Glock" in 40, Gould & Goodrich ankle holster.

stranger approached his patrol car to talk to him through the driver's window. None ever spotted the casually dropped arm, or his ready-to-draw status.

The night came when a furtive-looking man in an overcoat incongruous with the warm weather approached his parked cruiser at a rapid pace. The officer put his hand on the ankle rig. He was starting to say "Can I help you?" when the man swept the coat open and swung up a sawed-off bolt-action shotgun.

The cop's alertness had saved him. He saw it coming and he jerked his head back, almost out of the line of fire. As the sawed-off shotgun (a .410 and not a 12 gauge, thank God) went off in his face, he had pulled his head back enough to save the eyes and the brain, but the blast shattered his jaw, blew away several teeth, and badly lacerated his tongue. Reflexively, he jerked the 38 from the ankle holster at the same time.

The would-be cop-killer tried to bolt another shell into the chamber to finish the job.

He never made it. The cop's backup Colt was barking now, and five of the six hollowpoints he fired buried themselves into the attacker's body. The attempted murderer went down for the count before he could fire again.

The officer lost some of his sense of smell and taste, and some hearing on the left side. His face was scarred, but plastic surgery reconstructed his jaw. Last I knew, he was back to work on full duty. The ankle gun – and his alertness, and his plan – had saved his life.

Another who read that article was an African-American security professional who worked in plainclothes in a large pharmacy in upstate New York. His carry gun was a Smith & Wesson Model 10 38 Special in a shoulder holster, and after reading that

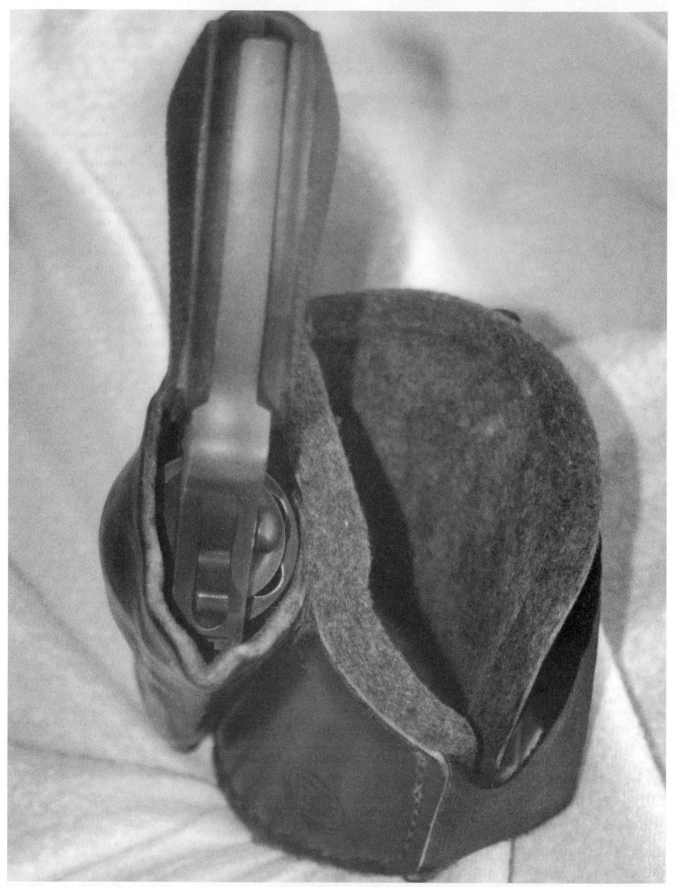

Snub-nose revolver and ankle holster are a timeless combination. This is lightweight Colt Agent 38 Spl. in ankle rig made by DeSantis for Personal Protection Systems, tightly boned for friction fit and maximum speed with silent, surreptitious draw. All-wool felt lining drinks up sweat.

particular issue of *Combat Handguns* he supplemented it with a five-shot Charter Arms Undercover snub-nose 38 Special in a Bianchi ankle holster. Part of his duties included the mission euphemistically known as "loss prevention," and the day came one winter when he spotted a large Caucasian male shoplifting African-American oriented cosmetics and hair care products. Noting the "booster's" odd choice of merchandise to steal, he followed him past the checkout counters and discreetly accosted him in the foyer of the store just before he could exit.

What the security man could not have known at the time was that he was dealing with a total whack job. The suspect was a white supremacist who tended to establish relationships with women of subnormal intellect, always choosing black women as if he was acting out some sick fantasy of being a slave-master. He kept his victims at his home in a state of virtual bondage. It was later theorized that he stole things for them because he didn't think black people were worth spending money on.

And now, a black male authority figure was about to "arrest" him. The man went nuts.

He violently attacked the security man, a slightly built fellow much smaller than himself. The fight carried out into the slushy winter street, and the powerful offender literally "ripped his arm out of the socket," causing a separation of the right shoulder that tore out the rotator cuff. His dominant arm disabled, the guard was knocked down, and in the struggle for his service revolver that followed, the Smith & Wesson went skittering out into the wet street.

The big white guy jumped up. Leaving his opponent supine and battered on the sidewalk, the supremacist ran into the street reaching for the revolver. As he bent to pick it up he screamed, "I got your gun and you're dead meat now, Nigger!"

This turns out to be a really stupid thing to say to a black man who carries a second gun.

By the time the attacker was coming up with the six-shot S&W, the good guy already had the Charter Arms out of the ankle rig and trained on him. There was nothing left to do. He shot the assailant in the head. The bullet killed him instantly, saving the life of the security professional and perhaps, the lives of five or so witnesses the nut case would have been able to murder after he had slain the security man.

There was another case that I didn't come into until after the shooting. I was hired as an expert witness for the involved officer in the lawsuit that evolved from the justified homicide. The defendant was a California Highway Patrolman, who supplemented his standard Smith & Wesson service sidearm with a Smith & Wesson Model 36 Chiefs Special 38 snub in a Bianchi ankle holster. He pulled over a lone motorist for an open container violation after seeing him drive his pickup truck while sipping from a can of Coors

Light. As he searched the truck subsequent to the stop, the driver sneaked his hand into the bed of the pickup and came up with a deadly, 28-ounce framing hammer.

He swung it at the officer, hitting him so hard he broke his neck. As the officer staggered back, the man hammered him again, center chest, apparently trying to rupture the heart. The officer's concealed body armor, complete with steel trauma plate, saved him from death but the force of that blow knocked him backwards. As he felt himself losing his balance and about to pass out, he drew his duty gun and opened fire. Then everything went black.

The highway patrolman awoke flat on his back, and realized that his dropped gun was between him and the offender, who was on his hands and knees shaking his head like a mad bull. The offender glared at him with a look of baleful hatred, and reached for the dropped Smith & Wesson. The state policeman realized that the bad guy could reach the gun before he could.

But fortunately, he had another.

His hand flashed to his ankle, and he came up shooting with the stubby backup gun. Five shots, five hits, and the suspect went down. This time he didn't get back up. He died in the hospital of a total of nine gunshot wounds. The highway patrolman was forced to retire as a result of his injuries. The gun in the ankle holster saved his life.

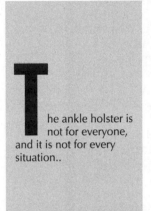

he ankle holster is not for everyone, and it is not for every situation..

Contraindications

The ankle holster is not for everyone, and it is not for every situation. I totally agree with Nonte and Bianchi that its best role is for *backup* guns, and that it's not a good choice for carrying the primary defensive handgun. It is simply too far away from the reaching hand. It will be very difficult to reach an ankle holster while grappling with a standing man, and it's not terribly easy to draw from even while standing *still*.

Remember that article I mentioned a few paragraphs back, which convinced at least two readers to acquire the ankle holsters that wound up saving their lives? Well, another reader had what he considered a more negative experience, and wrote an angry letter to the editor that got published. I don't have it in front of me, and therefore can't quote it verbatim, but basically, it went like this:

"Ayoob and his damn ankle holsters! After I read his article I decided to start carrying my gun on my ankle. It could have got me killed!"

He continued, "There I was, walking down the street when four black guys came at me very swiftly. I tried to reach my gun. I couldn't. I bent over to get my gun and I couldn't get the pants cuff up in time! They went on past me, and…"

You caught it, huh? "They went on past me…"

You know, I don't mind folks criticizing what I write, but I wish they'd *read* it first. It would save angst on both sides.

First, I had never said that he should carry his one and only defensive firearm strapped around his ankle, about as far from his reach as a standing man can possibly get. I suggested it for *backup,* not for primary. And I still feel the same way.

Second, though, and probably much more important in this case, his inability to draw his gun probably prevented a tragedy. Alarmed by a group of young black men moving rapidly toward him, he had presumed himself to be under attack. Instead of moving off mid-line of the perceived assault, he stood his ground to go for his gun...and then the young men rushed past him. Obviously, he had not been the target of anything except his own paranoia and, some would say, his own preconditioned racial prejudice. The circumstances being what they were, thank God he *didn't* get his gun out of his ankle holster "in time."

I know what he's talkin' about, though. Back in the '70s, I was in a large middle American metropolis on a hot summer day when a Colt Detective Special in an ankle holster seemed to be "enough." As I waited for the elevator at my hotel – a nice one, but on the edge of a rough part of the city – I noticed two young white guys scoping me out. I made eye contact and they both looked away, which is never a good sign.

We all got on the elevator. No attack. So far, so good, because I realized I didn't have a snowball's chance in hell of getting my hand to my ankle from a standing position if these two jumped me in those close confines. As the door opened at my floor, one said a hokey "Well, see ya later" to the other.

I got off the elevator and headed toward my room, noticing out of the corner of my eye that one of them had stepped off a moment behind me and was following me. I reached the corner of the corridor where I had to turn, and looked over my shoulder. The one behind me broke eye contact. Not good. I kept going forward, and realized he was closing the gap.

If there's anything harder to do with an ankle holster than to draw from standing with it, it's trying to draw from *running* with it. A couple of doors ahead, I saw someone else's hotel room door open, with the maid's cleaning cart just inside the doorway. As the one behind me closed the gap, I took a quick couple of steps to the door, and then a fast side-step inside, shoving the cart between me and the open door – not much cover against gunfire, but a useful short-term obstacle against contact assault. As I did so, my right hand went immediately to my left ankle. Entering the room, I'd done a quick visual, and saw no one there.

Colt lightweight Agent 38 snub in this DeSantis holster served author as backup for many years.

The man following me moved jerkily, taken aback by the sudden evasive action. He tried to charge into the bedroom after me, saw me on the other side of the cart…and also saw a blue steel Colt Detective Special. His eyes widened, and he turned toward the direction whence he had come. I saw him raise his palm and move it forward down the hall, in a gesture that said, "Go back!" Then he began running down the hall.

I pulled the cart clear and stepped to the doorway. Sure enough, the guy's accomplice who'd said "See ya later" was planning to see him – and me – sooner, because he had gotten off after all and had been moving behind the first. He was now between him and the corner. The other gestured frantically, said something to him that I couldn't hear, but which made his eyes go wide. He turned and they both disappeared, sprinting toward the elevator.

I silently thanked the absent maid who had left the door open and the cart there. I snapped the Colt 38 back into the ankle holster and went on my way, making a mental note, "Lesson Learned: Ankle holsters for backup *ONLY* from now on!"

For some practitioners, the ankle rig is not the best choice even for backup. We geezers with arthritis find that a leg holster can "grate" on the ankle more than it did when we were younger. Phlebitis, varicose veins, and other circulatory problems can make the constriction of the ankle holster a bad thing. Women by and large have more delicate calves and ankles (and, fashion-wise, higher pant cuffs) than men, and I've found damn few women who like ankle rigs.

Once again, we're dealing with highly individualized needs and decisions. I also know people who've been wearing ankle holsters literally for decades and are perfectly comfortable with them.

Oh, yeah…ankle-deep mud and knee-deep snow don't go well with ankle holsters. Neither do summer shorts.

Comfort Factors

If you've ever worn a pistol at the 3 o'clock position on the belt, right on the hip-bone, you've probably noticed some chafing. The stiff leather, weighted with a steel gun full of lead bullets, is pressing against a bone that has little but skin to shield it. Well, that's going on *big* time down at the old ankle bone when wearing a leg holster.

Most who've carried them for some time concur that the holster and the leg strap should be *soft* and *wide,* and that there should be some sort of *cushion* between the holster and the skin. Unless you have legs like the Incredible Hulk or are carrying a tiny mouse gun, you also probably want a carry that puts the muzzle angled back and the grip angled forward, to minimize bulge.

That Bianchi ankle holster the New York security pro and the California Highway Patrol officer found perfectly comfortable for all-day wear just didn't work for me. John Bianchi and his design team were famous for their good quality "hard" holster leather, and they brought the concept to this ankle rig. The holster was closed at the bottom, which extended its length slightly and created a blunt edge on the bottom where the relatively heavy leather was stitched together. (The closed bottom kept snow or mud from plugging the gun barrel if the wearer stepped into same.) The back of the rig was amply lined with soft, friendly sheepskin, the purpose being comfort. For the guard and the state policeman, and for a great many other people, it worked. It was comfortable. For them.

Not for me. I loved that finely-made holster, but I just couldn't bond with it. A calf-strap might have pulled it up high enough to make it work for me, but calf straps don't work for me either, as noted earlier. This left the hard bottom edge by the gun's muzzle digging mercilessly into my ankle bone with every step. I finally had to retire the holster, and go with something else.

Another couple of makers did open bottom ankle rigs, superbly crafted of the finest leather, and backed with so much sheepskin that it felt as if I had strapped a pillow to my ankle. Comfort factor was great. Unfortunately, the cushioning was so heavy that it also *looked* as if I had strapped a pillow to my ankle. The darn things bulged too much for my legs. They didn't conceal well, and I finally had to give up on them, too.

What worked best for me personally was the type of ankle rig that was backed with all-wool felt. The felt lining just seems to soak up sweat without leaving the ankle damp, clammy, and chafed. My first such holster was made of synthetic leather by a nameless manufacturer in the early 1970s. It was a prototype that went out to several police equipment dealers.

What worked best for me personally was the type of ankle rig that was backed with all-wool felt..

STREET TIP: When wearing an ankle holster and crossing your legs, keep the foot of gun-side leg on the ground. Here, Glock 40 is not obvious…

…but here, with wrong leg crossed, ankle holstered handgun becomes glaringly apparent.

One was my old friend at Scientific Detection Devices, Dick Marple, who passed this sample along to me to "beta test." I loved it, and kept it. The company went out of business – out of the ankle holster business, anyway – and I kept that orphaned, nameless sample until the stitching started to give way many years later. It was great.

I'm partial to the Alessi ankle rig among today's crop. The Renegade holster has earned many fans: flexible, fast, silent, and *very* comfortable. Its only downside is that it wears out sooner than some high quality leather holsters. Being a cheap old guy, I've never trusted myself to throw away things that are starting to wear out. With clothing, that just keeps you off the "best-dressed" list. With defensive gear, it can get you killed. But if you have more self-discipline in that regard than I, the Renegade may be the perfect ankle rig for you. Galco's Ankle Glove is another very popular holster, with a very well-deserved reputation for comfort and function. The Safariland has also won a lot of fans. I like the Gould & Goodrich ankle rig (I remove the modular calf strap) with thumb break that was developed for a Southern state police agency for their baby Glocks.

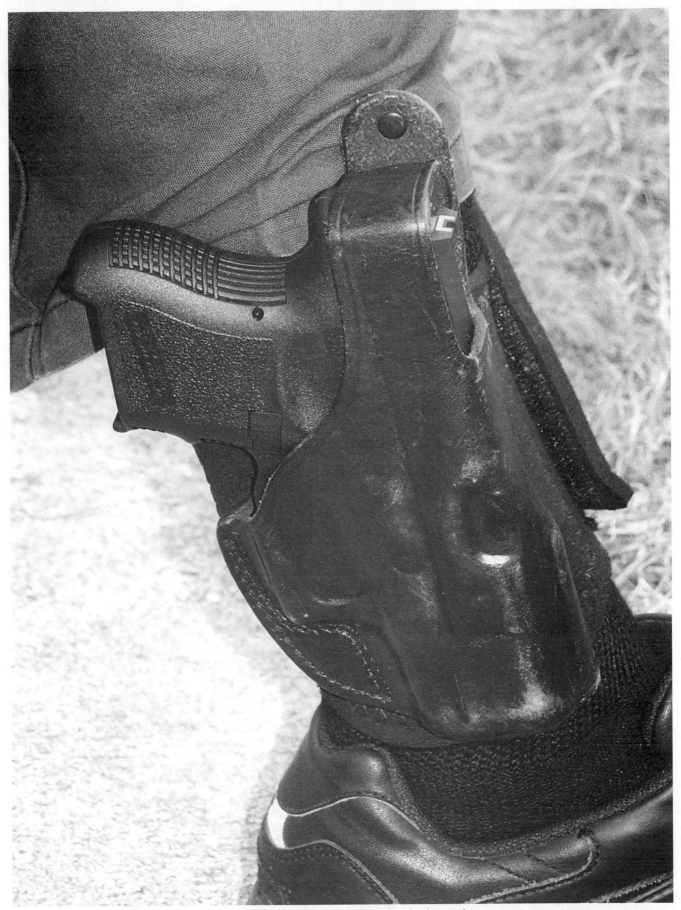

Glock 39 subcompact 45 GAP in Gould & Goodrich ankle holster is daily backup for this southern state trooper.

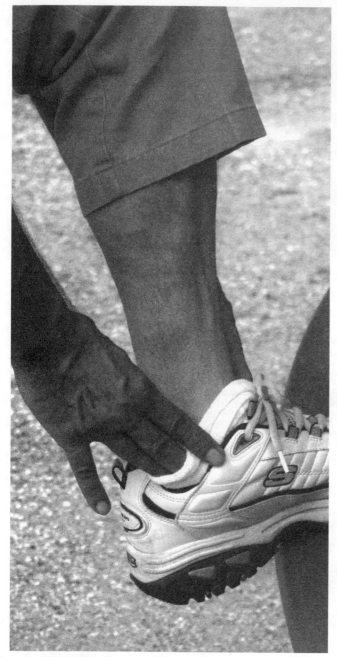

Here's how to put on an ankle holster for maximum concealment. First, roll sock down (thin white cotton sock can optionally be worn underneath if wearer is allergenic)…

…now, empty holster is strapped on snugly (tip from Richie Rosenthal, NYPD retired)…

Clothing and Gun Considerations

Some of the fashion contraindications to ankle rigs are obvious. They won't work with shorts. They won't work with a lady's Capri or Toreador style pants. Some other contraindications are less obvious, though.

The "barrel" of the lower pant leg needs to be relatively wide, both to conceal the ankle holster and to make it readily available when you need to draw. The straight-cut leg of the pants that come with the classic American men's "sack suit" work fine with ankle holsters, as a couple of generations of lawyers and executives who wear that "uniform" can attest. So do the pants of most Class A police uniforms.

Fatigue or "combat" uniforms may or may not work. BDU (Battle Dress Uniform) pants tend to be cut with very loose legs and cuffs. Good so far. However, if the pant legs are going to be tucked and bloused into high-top combat-style boots, there will be no place for an ankle rig. If you're going to untuck the cuffs with pants like these, that's fine. You can even wear them with boots. Gould & Goodrich is one company that offers a "boot holster" that works like an ankle rig, but is designed to go around large-circumference combat boots, and even has grommets for the boot lacings to go through. If the pant legs are wide enough, these can work great with boots. Some concealed carry practitioners have gone to the extent of sewing

…only then is loaded baby Glock carefully inserted in holster, with finger off trigger…

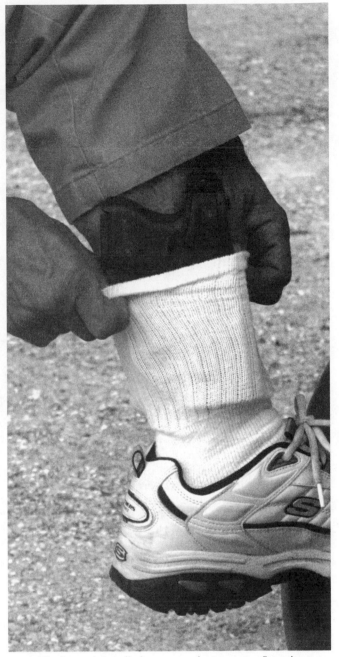

…and finally, sock is pulled up over to better camouflage the hardware. Rig is by G&G, latter tip is from the late, great Chic Gaylord.

additional lengths of elastic and Velcro onto regular ankle holsters so they can go around a boot.

However, if you're going to do this with BDU pants, *remove the string ties at the cuff!* Designed to keep the pant legs in place when bloused into high top boots, the string ties serve no purpose at all when the boots are inside the pant leg. However, those loose "strings" *can get caught inside the trigger guard as you are putting the pistol into the ankle rig! Your hand is likely to reflexively keep pushing…and it is now pushing the trigger against the obstacle. This can lead to shooting yourself in the ankle or foot by accident!* If you're going to carry this way, *remove the string ties from the cuffs of the pants!* You're doing it for

the same reason we remove the string closures from warm-up jackets and windbreakers and sweatshirts when we carry guns at belt level: they can get into the trigger guard and lead to an accidental discharge.

Going to casual wear, if you're wearing an ankle holster you want your jeans or cords to have, minimum, "boot cut" cuffs. The bell-bottoms of the '70s (now back in style in some quarters and known as "flares") are even better. This gives lots of room so the pants cuff can be brought up more quickly and smoothly, and that extra room makes it less likely that the "handle" or any other part of the gun will snag the fabric and interrupt a fast, life-saving draw. Gun guy and knife designer Blackie Collins came out

If you're going to carry in an ankle holster, practice drawing and shooting that way! Here a line of Georgia State Troopers qualify with their backup mini-Glocks, all drawn from G&G ankle rigs.

with Toters jeans, expressly designed for carrying guns. They're loose in the waist for IWB, side and hip pockets are set up expressly for pocket guns and pocket holsters...and the cuffs are loose enough to work just fine with most ankle holsters.

Loosely cut pleated pants of the style popularized by Dockers are great for concealed carry. The slightly billowed legs do a great job of hiding small handguns in pocket holsters, and the loose cuffs work extremely well with ankle rigs.

You'll occasionally see pants with legs slit up a few inches from the cuffs, held closed by zippers or Velcro. I for one don't care for them. Having to open this slit adds another fine-motor movement that greatly slows the draw, and ankle holster draw is slow enough as it is. Zippers, and particularly Velcro, make a distinctive sound when opened. This blows the surreptitious draw of the kind that saved the officer's life in the Miami area incident described above. And, as we all know, zippers can stick and "jam." I wouldn't trust either of these trouser cuff designs for ankle carry.

One gun-specific piece of clothing worthy of note in this regard is the series of BDUs by Woolrich in their Elite series, and by some other makers, which have Velcro-closed cargo pockets not only at the thighs, but low at the calves. Smokers often use them for cigarette packs. A friend of mine on the Woolrich Elite beta testing team discovered that they could also carry very comfortably, at least for him, a tiny Kel-Tec P32 pistol. This particular backup gun may only be a 32 auto, but it weighs well under ten ounces – less than the famously tiny Baby Browning 25 auto – and is wafer-thin. He finds it doesn't bump against his leg, and it carries above the ankle bone. It's on the outside of the leg, not the inside, and the user has to rip open a Velcro flap to get at it. It's not my choice, but for a very small gun, it's one more option and a legitimate variation of "ankle carry."

Let me share a couple of tricks to enhance comfort with ankle holsters. I was still a kid in public school when I read Chic Gaylord's *Handgunner's Guide* and saw his trick of pulling the outer sock up over the ankle holster. Good trick then; good trick now. When the trouser cuff comes up as you sit down, others in the restaurant or at the board meeting don't see the bottom edge of a boned and sculptured holster or, God help us, the muzzle of the gun. What they see is a bunched up, baggy sock. Might get you a warning citation from the Fashion Police, but won't draw the attention of the Gun Police.

As soon as I started packing in an ankle rig, I took advantage of Gaylord's wisdom. I discovered that depending on the type of male hosiery, the socks wear out two to four times faster than normal, or worse, depending how "fat" the package of the ankle-holstered gun may be. I learned with a handgun that had a conventional hammer spur or with adjustable

sights to not let the top edge of the sock come anywhere near that point. What mid-20th century gun expert Paul B. Weston called the "Fish-Hook" effect of the hammer spur, or the sharp edge of an upraised rear sight, can catch on the top edge of the sock and snag, dangerously and perhaps even lethally stalling your draw. (Once the sock is rolled down to the proper point, I never found them to creep back up. Worn socks tend to creep down, sort of like the abdomens of guys my age.) One officer survival manual got this

concept mixed up a bit, and illustrated the principle with an executive-length sock pulled entirely up over the semi-auto pistol they depicted in an ankle holster, hiding the whole gun butt and grip frame under the sock. A classic case of "people unclear on the concept."

Some folks are allergic to wool, and might otherwise have hypersensitive skin in the ankle area that makes it unworkable for them to wear an ankle holster against bare skin. In that case "neutral"

or hypoallergenic white cotton socks can be worn under the ankle holster, between the rig and the skin, and the regular sock then pulled up over the ankle-holstered pistol.

I learned another useful ankle holster trick from Richie Rosenthal, an NYPD veteran who at one time worked at that department's excellent FTU (Firearms Training Unit) and went on, if memory serves, to become a chief of police in Massachusetts. Rich made the point that to get the most perfect, secure, snug fit

If ankle gun works the same as primary holster gun, all the better. Each Georgia State Patrol trooper is issued a full-size Glock 37 and subcompact Glock 39, both chambered for 45 GAP.

of holster to ankle, one should leave the ankle holster *empty* to start. Put it on and adjust it until it feels just right. *Now* insert the loaded handgun, and *voila:* you have a much more secure and stable fit of the whole gun and rig. Pulling the sock up over it for added discretion won't change anything. Thanks, Rich.

Some handguns work a *lot* better than others in ankle holsters. In one of his movies – I think it was *Kindergarten Cop,* but I'm an old guy working on memory here – the director had Arnold Schwarzenegger carrying a full-size Beretta 92 pistol in an ankle holster. Now, there are a good many cops

and a good many more soldiers and Marines who have carried that pistol in an exposed duty holster, and found it a little large for even *that* application. In an *ankle holster,* there just ain't no way, even for someone Schwarzenegger's size.

A couple of other Hollywood paradigms come to mind. In one of the *Naked Gun* police spoofs, a senior detective is seen struggling desperately like Houdini trying to escape a cocoon of ropes, trying to get his revolver out of an ankle holster. Gotta laugh. That's probably just what it feels like trying to get the wrong gun out of the wrong ankle holster hidden under the

Ankle holster works very well from kneeling, provided that holster leg is UP and it's the OTHER leg that's in knee contact with ground.

Detonics. Only when a scene required the gun to show or to come into action did Johnson actually strap that gun on. Not to put too fine a point on it, he actually stood and extended his arms while the aide slipped the shoulder harness on for him, like a butler helping the master slip into his dinner jacket.

More proof that in the real world, you can't walk around concealing a large auto pistol under a tightly fitted Armani suit, *or* a chunky 45 auto in an ankle rig under tight, "trim-fit" jeans. "Only in Hollywood…"

Unless you're a huge person with huge, baggy pants, you'll need a compact gun for ankle work. I know some cops who've carried Glock 19, Glock 23, Glock 30, and Glock 29 pistols in ankle holsters. They're all big guys with legs like trees. Average size people will need smaller guns.

Most small pocket autos do not thrive in ankle holster carry. The ankle rig holds the gun literally only a few inches above the ground. Every step you take is kicking up dust and dirt from the sidewalk and even mud and muck from bare ground. Anyone who has carried an ankle holster for any length of time has noticed that after just a day, protectively pulled-up socks notwithstanding, the gun is covered with a fine film of dust and grit. The longer that goes on, the more crap builds up *on* it and starts getting *into* it. I've seen the hammer-slots of shrouded revolvers, Colt snubbies with Colt or Waller hammer shrouds, and the S&W Bodyguard series and the analogous Taurus model, literally filled with "dust bunnies."

The interesting thing is, double-action revolvers always seem to work, even when they're covered with dust. Small, tightly fitted "pocket pistols" of the Walther PPK type, and virtually every 25 auto I've worked with, have such tightly fitted parts that they're prone to choking on that dust and grit once the shooting starts and the slide has to cycle. I've run across cases of ankle-holstered 380s jamming that way, from Florida to California, when the chips were down.

I can count on my fingers the small autos with "mil-spec" fitting that will survive that sort of abuse and still work. The baby Glocks, the Kahrs, and the Kel-Tecs come to mind.

wrong kind of trousers.

On the *Miami Vice* TV series, shot on location in Miami, Don Johnson as lead character carried a big autoloader (10mm Bren Ten or S&W 45, depending on the season) and a Detonics Combat Master subcompact 1911 45 in a nylon ankle holster. He also wore snug jeans or tight Armani suits. How did he conceal that hardware under that garb?

Turns out he didn't. One scriptwriter for the show was one of my graduates, and so was technical advisor Bob Hoelscher, an ace veteran of the Metro-Dade police department. I wound up visiting the set with my family while the crew was filming an episode on location in Miami. We noticed that one member of the crew seemed to have the sole, specific task of holding the shoulder-holstered duty auto and the ankle-holstered

Two ankle holsters, three options. 1) use holster at top, with calf strap. 2) use same holster and lose calf strap. 3) "boot holster" at left goes *outside* patrol boot but still under trouser cuff; note grommets for boot laces. Both by G&G, shown w/baby Glocks.

It's a good idea to avoid "rubber" grips on ankle-holstered handguns. Their tacky surface will tend to bind with the inner fabric of the trouser leg, slowing or even stalling the draw.

Lighter is better for ankle holsters. Comfort is obviously one big reason for that statement, but a less obvious reason is security. When running, jumping, rolling on the ground or otherwise performing strenuous activity, if the ankle rig is an open top design (or if its safety strap has come undone), the heavier gun is more likely to come out of the holster "by itself." The heavier gun develops more momentum with all that bouncing. It will take proportionally more violent movement to dislodge a lighter gun. An AirLite Titanium or Scandium J-frame snub is less likely to bounce out of an unsecured ankle rig than an aluminum-framed Airweight, and the Airweight in turn will be more likely to stay in place in the same holster under the same circumstances than a still heavier, all steel version of the same revolver.

Gould & Goodrich ankle holster. Note optional, modular calf strap, and soft sheepskin lining to cushion sensitive ankle-bone.

Bottom Line

Good news is that the ankle rig can be a life-saver in terms of backup, especially if you find yourself down on your back or in a seated position when you need to draw. Bad news is it's uncomfortable, tough to reach from a standing position, and particularly demanding of certain clothing styles and of a holster style adapted to the individual wearer.

NON-TRADITIONAL
CARRY METHODS

odel 640-1 S&W 357 Magnum, with Magna-Port recoil reduction treatment. Note Barami Hip-Grip, which serves revolver inside waistband without a holster.

There are certain non-traditional methods of concealed carry that are, for good or ill, in wide use. They bear discussion for that reason alone. The first point of discussion needs to be this: *every single one of them is based on convenience at the expense of serious practicality.*

One of these is so-called "Mexican carry," the gun simply shoved into the waistband without benefit of holster. The term is not pejorative. It arose long ago among gun people, in *homage* to proud Mexican men of the 19th and early 20th centuries. Beset by tyrants who stripped them of liberties, including

Guardian Leather Portfolio looks like a lawyer's briefcase, but contains a hidden bullet-resistant panel…

…and hidden compartment on edge gives access to an excellent CCW pistol, this aluminum frame SIG-Sauer P220 45.

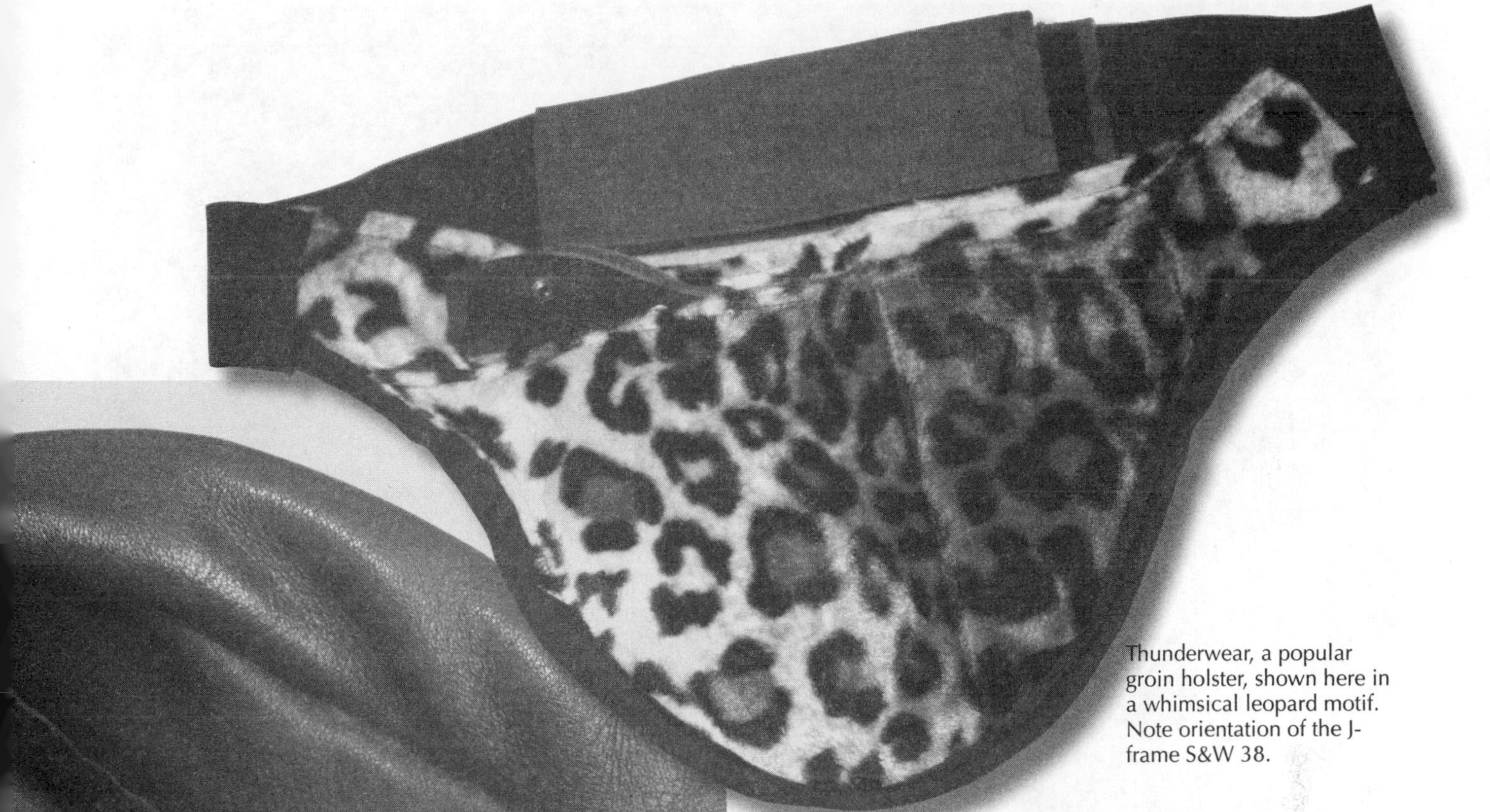

Thunderwear, a popular groin holster, shown here in a whimsical leopard motif. Note orientation of the J-frame S&W 38.

the right to carry guns if they were not part of the political elite, these defiant citizens chose to carry as an expression of "willful civil disobedience." They needed to be able to ditch the gun to be retrieved later if they were about to have contact with *Federales,* and since a holster could not be so quickly ditched and would be *prima facie* evidence of resistance to tyrants' law, the holster was dispensed with.

This turns out to work reasonably well with a flat-sided automatic, like the 1911 38 Super that was so popular in Mexico, the 45-caliber version having been banned as a "government-only caliber." However, the gun can come loose with strenuous activity, and can slip out when lying down for a siesta. There is no retention against a snatch, of course. It also tends to get gun oil all over the clothing.

"Improved Mexican carry," as it were, would be an attachment on the gun that keeps it from at least slipping down the pants leg. The Barami Hip Grip for revolvers and the Brown & Pharr belt clip for the 1911 serve this purpose. They'll keep the gun from sliding *down,* but won't necessarily keep it from sliding up and out. The protruding edge of a Crimson Trace LaserGrip on an auto pistol will have this same effect to some degree.

Personally, I would "go Mex" *only* for very short periods. Getting up to answer the door at 3 AM if I didn't have a holster. Putting the gun away after drawing from a belly-band in public. A short trip to or from an airport with a borrowed gun, mine being already stowed in luggage. It's best treated as a brief expedient, not regular carry. And it should *never* be done with a Glock, S&W M&P auto, or other

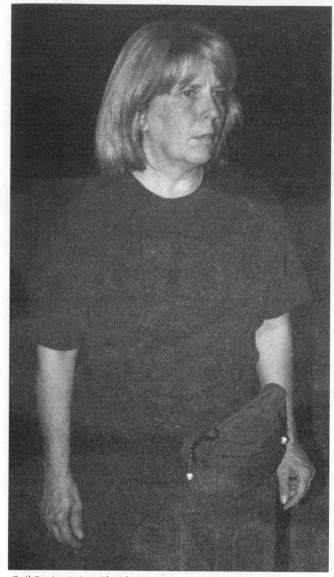

Gail Pepin, 2-time Florida/Georgia regional IDPA woman champion, demonstrates fanny pack draw with Safe Direction product...

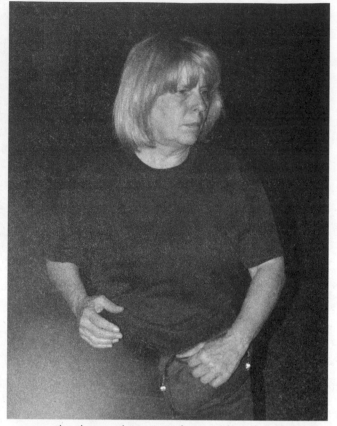

...support hand grasps drawstring release, and gun-hand-side hip comes back to angle weapon toward threat, as right hand...

... brings up the Kahr 40 cross-draw, free hand rises into blocking position and out of way of gun muzzle...

semiautomatic that needs only a short pull of the trigger to fire. The manufacturers agree. I would make an exception for the HK P7 squeeze-cocker so long as the grip lever was not depressed when putting the gun in place, and for the XD pistol if inserted with thumb on back of slide to keep the grip safety from being pressed during "holsterless holstering." Otherwise, I would stay with an auto whose manual safety was engaged, or which had a long and heavy double-action trigger pull design, or a pistol carried Israeli-style with empty chamber.

Off-Body Carry

The purse, the "man-purse," the briefcase and the short-lived "dayplanner portfolio that hides a gun" were all designed for convenience. A slowed access to the weapon was traded for greater physical comfort and wardrobe flexibility, in return for having a gun around us *somewhere*. In most situations, if safety and

...and comes up in classic Weaver stance, a natural posture for any type of cross draw.

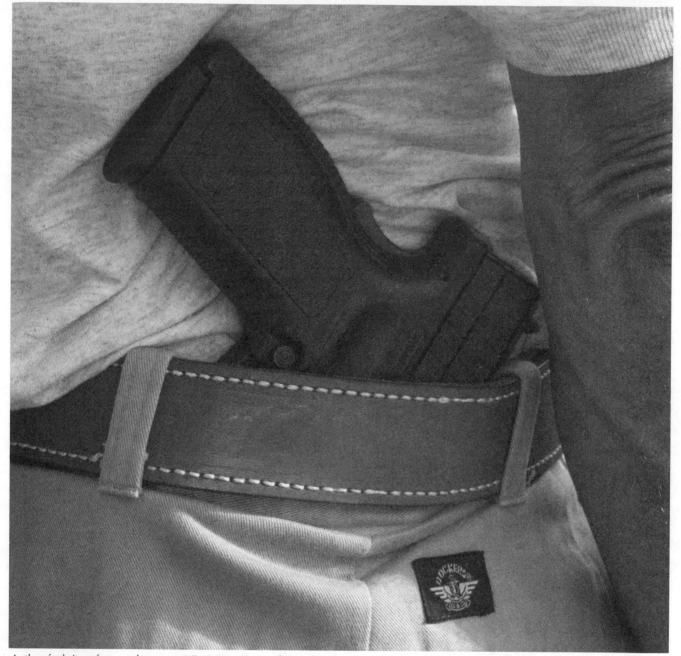

Author feels its safe enough to carry XD45 "Mexican style," so long as grip safety is not depressed. He still does not recommend the practice, however.

confidence and peace of mind are the goals, this is not a fair trade.

Purses get *snatched*. Briefcases get *stolen*. Neither is always within reach when we need what they contain. And how many times have we had to go back and get a purse or attaché case we left behind in another's home or office, or some public place? One time while in South Africa, I saw a man sentenced to prison for criminal negligence because he had left his gun purse in a restaurant, and it had been stolen by the time he noticed it missing and went back for it. In Florida, where Unified Sportsmen of Florida have rigidly kept track of all offenses involving concealed carry permit holders, the miniscule number of arrests seem to mostly involve people who forgot the gun

was in their attaché case or purse when they went through a metal detector into a secured area such as airport or courthouse. When the gun is not on us to remind us of its presence, it is all too easy to forget that it is there. This can lead to huge and devastating consequences.

If you accept the trade-offs and still want this stuff, the best "gun purses" I've personally seen are the ones from Coronado and Galco. The best carry case I've seen is the Guardian Leather Portfolio, which resembles a fine lawyer's briefcase with shoulder strap, but carries a bullet-resistant panel and hidden quick-access gun pouch. It's no trick to learn to draw the handgun to a one-hand stance as the free hand sweeps the ballistic-reinforced Portfolio up against the

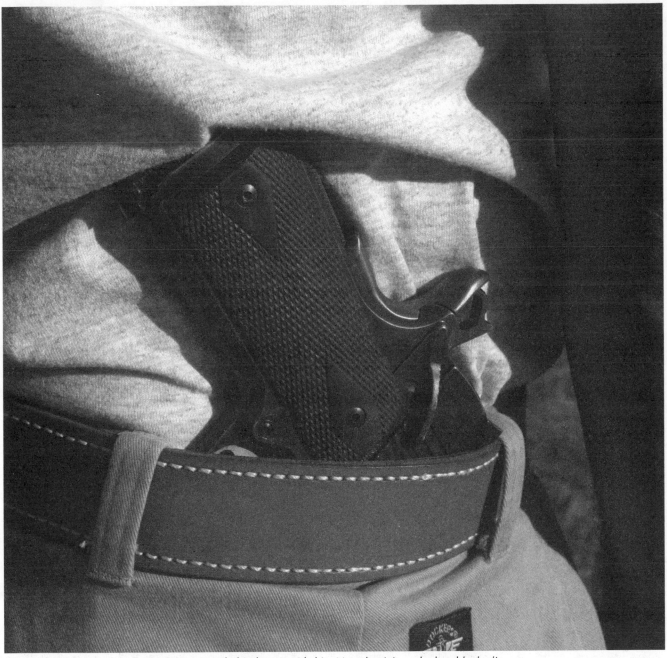

Kimber Classic 45 in "classic" Mexican carry behind strong side hip. Note that it is cocked and *locked!*

front of your torso. Blackhawk recently introduced a similar model in plain black nylon, though you may have to find your own ballistic insert for it. I've found them useful for court…just remember to take the gun out before you hit the security checkpoint!

Fanny Packs

Ever since Gene DeSantis created the first firearms-specific fanny pack, the Gunny Sack, these things have been hugely popular. They can be carried off-body with the strap slung over the shoulder, but have the added advantage of securing on the body in their normal intended fashion. Gun folks like to sew Nike or Nikon labels to the front, and order them in bright pastel colors, to distract from any "gun" image.

(Interestingly, joggers always ask pistol packers where to buy cool black nylon fanny packs like ours, that won't show the dirt. The grass is always greener…) The fanny pack can be easily unbuckled and left in the car when going into the post office, hospital, or other "gun-free zone."

Downsides? Thieves assume fanny packs contain wallets, so they're prime targets for theft when off your body, and even for snatching when strapped on. As with purses, having your gun in the thing the assailant is likely to grab first is not a good start to the fight. Moreover, they're slow to draw from, needing one hand to rip the thing open while the other goes for the gun, and *achingly* slow if that free hand is tied up warding off a knife-wielding opponent. Still, they're better than no gun at all. Practice, practice, practice. Centerline of the body is the best place to carry, I've found, and regular cross draw techniques are the way to draw to a fighting stance from the fanny pack. DeSantis has been making these longer than anyone else, and it shows: I've seen none better.

Barami Hip-Grip has been popular for decades. Here, on petite gun shop manager Ashley Reichard, the grip is about all you can see (and a black shirt would camouflage it nicely) …

However, I've become partial to the well-made Safe Direction from Steve Camp. Its back panel is bullet-resistant Kevlar, giving the lower abdomen some protection in a fight. More to the point, though, the whole Safe Direction line is designed to give you something to point at (the proverbial "safe direction") when routinely loading, unloading, and dry-firing handguns. Just make sure it's not strapped on your body during *these* proceedings.

Groin Holsters

Hiding below the belt and above the pubes under your pants, rigs like Thunderwear and Smart Carry resemble thin fanny packs worn between the underwear and the trousers. I've found them uncomfortable, and particularly awkward in men's rooms. To get at the gun, the drawing hand knifes down the inside of the front of the pants, preferably aided by a support hand that pulls the front of the waistband out away from the body. Personally, I find these holsters give me the creeps, but a lot of knowledgeable people with dress codes that make their option "this or nothing" have found such groin holsters an acceptable trade-off. Thunderwear and Smart Carry are both well made, and well designed for their purpose

Bottom line? A conventional holster is generally a better bet than any of the above. However, my situation may not be your situation. The above options do sacrifice practicality for convenience, but sometimes, convenience *is* practicality.

…but in fact it's a Model 640-1 S&W 357 Magnum, with Magna-Port recoil reduction treatment and an action job by her famous dad, Denny.

Chapter 13

CONCEALING LARGER HANDGUNS

With some thought applied to holsters and wardrobe, the good guy with the larger gun can improve survival potential and save money at the same time!

F

Four-inch barrel 41-frame Colt Python 357 Magnum rides in Ayoob Rear Guard holster rendered in sharkskin. Securing the gun inside the waistband enhances concealment.

With more fine, powerful, very small and light handguns than ever, why would someone want to wear a full-size service pistol concealed? There are several good answers to that question.

For many, the reason is commonality of training. Let's say you're a military person who will be issued an M9 pistol in combat, and you've cared enough about your skill at arms to purchase your own identical Beretta 92 pistol for practice. Or, you're a police officer who has been issued a full-size Beretta, Colt, Glock, HK USP, Ruger, SIG, or S&W service pistol. Your employer has not only paid for the

Top, Ruger Redhawk .44 Magnum; below, Ruger GP100 .357. The GP is a pretty big gun, and the Redhawk is relatively *huge,* but with the right gear the committed user can effectively carry each concealed.

gun and ammo and magazines, but has paid you to train with that particular gun until you can use it to the best of your ability.

Certainly, you can buy a smaller version of your duty pistol for concealment and transfer much of that skill. A Mini-Cougar from Beretta, any of several subcompact 1911s, the baby Glock, the USP Compact, or the flat little P239 from SIG or Model 4040 from S&W will share a high degree of "commonality of training" with their companion models of full size service weapons. However, if you carry the service pistol itself, you have 100 percent commonality of

training with on-duty and off-duty carry since you're using the same pistol for both purposes.

Money is an issue. That chopped and channeled mini-1911, baby Glock, or whatever will cost you several hundred dollars. For well under $100, you can purchase a suitable concealment holster that lets you discreetly wear off-duty the pistol you already have for on-duty carry.

This is why the topic of the cop using the issue gun off duty versus buying his own off duty weapon can be a controversial one. There are two sides. At this point in my life, I buy and carry my own, and use the "company

Author wins Florida Sunshine Games championship using the big GP100 for Stock Service Revolver class. He wore the same gun concealed to and from the event. It's all about the right holsters and clothes. Holster is Kydex by Blade-Tech.

L-frame Smith & Wesson, here the Model 686 in 357 Magnum tuned for maximum performance by Scott Mulkerin and including night sights. With proper holster, and acclimated tolerance of weight, this gun can be carried daily in plainclothes.

guns" only when working for the PD. This is because I travel a lot, and if I'm involved in a self-defense incident in another jurisdiction, I don't want a money-hungry plaintiff's lawyer thinking my use of a department gun could tie in the department, and its community's tax base, for a deep-pockets lawsuit. Having dealt with several such sharks, I'd rather keep that blood out of the water. At the same time, I remember being a young cop, not making much money, and a quality personal handgun being a significant expense that could cut into family needs. Each officer has to weigh and balance and make his or her own choice in the matter. The important thing is to carry *some* high quality handgun of adequate power off duty.

For some, the difference in performance between the small gun and the big one is dramatic. Back in the days when cops all wore revolvers, it was a four-inch gun or larger for uniform wear and typically a small-frame model with a two-inch barrel for plainclothes. Many an officer who qualified just fine with the full-size six-gun simply couldn't make the grade with the snubby; it was that much more difficult to shoot well.

There is less performance difference between the full size and subcompact police service "automatics" of today than there was between the revolvers that preceded them. Still, though, there are some advantages to the bigger guns. A friend of mine works for the FBI and was given the choice of the full-size Glock 22 or the compact Glock 23, both firing the same 40 S&W duty loads. He appreciated the greater concealability

of the G23 under the suit he wears to work, but he still chose the bigger G22 for one reason: he shoots it just a little bit better than he does its little brother. If he has to pay more attention to his wardrobe and holster selection to gain absolute maximum combat shooting performance, he figures it's a cheap price to pay for an edge that could someday save his life.

I know what he means. I am fond of the 40-caliber Glock in both the full-size G22 configuration and the miniature G27 format. The little one, of course, is much easier to conceal. From the bench at 25 yards, the little one is actually a little bit more accurate than the big one. It'll put five 155-grain Winchester Silvertips into an inch and a half at that distance, and its big brother will seldom do better than two inches even with the load it likes best, the Black Hills EXP 165-grain JHP. But the big gun handles better when the speed and the pressure are on. The toughest qualification approved by my state, known as Course Five, comprises 36 rounds from three to twenty-five yards in time frames as fast as two shots in three seconds from the leather. In qualification mode on the B27 target, where anything inside the competition 8-ring is worth five out of five points, I can score 180 out of 180 possible with either. But when it goes to the tighter rings of competition scoring, I'll be in the 355 out of 360 range with the full-size Glock 22, but will only score around 345 with the subcompact Glock 27. Because performance edge is as important to me as it is to my FBI buddy, I, like him, am more likely to carry the Glock 22.

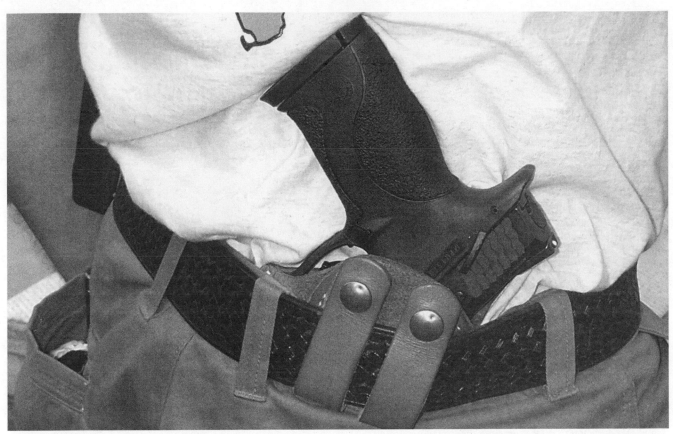

Inside-the-waistband holsters are a boon to those who carry large frame pistols. This full-size Smith & Wesson Military & Police 45 is its owner's daily concealed carry gun.

The full-size pistol has another performance edge: the longer barrel generates more pressure from the burning powder within, increasing muzzle velocity. This is particularly important with some rounds, like the 45 ACP, whose velocity falls off dramatically as the barrel is shortened. It can sometimes mean the difference of whether or not the hollow-point bullet you've fired opens up as intended.

For cops, there's another good reason to carry that full-size issue gun. If an officer is involved in a shooting, that expensive pistol can become "evidence" for a period of years until the last civil lawsuit arising from the incident is wrapped up. Even when you get it back, it may be rusty from bloodstains left *in situ* for evidentiary purposes, and its finish may have been ruined by the fingerprinting process. If the expensive gun is going to be lost to you for a period ranging from weeks to years and come back messed up, many cops' reasoning goes, let it be the department's expensive gun instead of your own. Once it is taken for evidence, unless you are indicted or something, they have to issue you a replacement anyway.

So, it may be a performance factor or an economy factor or both that brings you to the decision to use a full-size handgun for concealed carry. Whatever the reason, there are two critical areas you'll have to address in concealing a larger handgun: the holster, and the wardrobe.

Concealment Holsters for Big Guns

No question about it, *inside-the-waistband* is the best place for that beast to be if you want to hide it under a minimum of clothing. The concealing garment can rise as high as the lower edge of the belt without revealing the holstered gun, and the fabric of the trousers breaks up the line of the holstered gun when you are seen in silhouette.

There is no more proven inside-the-waistband (IWB) holster than the Summer Special, created by Bruce Nelson and popularized by Milt Sparks. Both of these great holstermakers are gone now, but their work lives on. With a rough-out cut, on the theory that having the rough side of the leather toward the body stabilizes the holster and having the smooth grain side toward the gun speeds the draw, these rigs remain the choice of many gun connoisseurs today. I have several, including one for the N-frame Smith & Wesson which has concealed my 44 Magnum under an untucked bush shirt or jacket in the streets of Johannesburg and Pretoria, and in cities in Europe, without drawing undue notice nor causing undue discomfort.

However, one downside to a rough-out holster is that when you perspire heavily, it is more likely that the sweat will permeate the leather and get to the gun. This can discolor the holster and, worse, rust your finely blued sidearm brown. Milt Sparks himself tacitly recognized this problem, I think, when he

Four-inch barrel 41-frame Colt Python 357 Magnum rides in Ayoob Rear Guard holster rendered in sharkskin. Author has carried big S&W 44 Magnums concealed the same way in U.S., South Africa, and Europe. Securing the gun inside the waistband enhances concealment.

encouraged his young protégé Tony Kanaley to design his Executive Companion holster. With the grain outside in the conventional manner, this model seems to protect the pistol better than rough-out designs, and with no perceptible interference with drawing speed or smoothness. The Executive Companion also rides a bit lower than its predecessor, and I for one find that it conceals a bit better as a result.

Most interpretations of the IWB design have the belt loops at the same point as the gun, causing a little more bulge when the holstered gun is snapped in place. Makers such as Derry Gallagher, and Milt Sparks with the latter's Versa-Max, offer IWB holsters cut with the belt loops fore and aft of the holster body, making for more discreet carry. This also helps to stabilize the holstered gun on the belt, on a principle a bit like Pontiac's old "Wide-Track" concept. The two IWB holsters I designed each tackled that problem a bit differently. When Ted Blocker and I designed the LFI Concealment Rig for his holster company back in the '80s, we went with a Velcro tab instead of belt loops or clips. This mated with Velcro lining in the accompanying dress gun belt. The primary accessory, an IWB magazine pouch, attached the same way. This resulted in minimum bulge, with the added bonus that the wearer could adjust to the exact height and cant angle he liked, and then press the belt down on the Velcro to stabilize the holster solidly in place.

In the '90s, Mitch Rosen asked me to design an IWB for full-size fighting handguns. I made it with a belt loop at the rear of the holster, where it wouldn't add to gun bulge and where it would lever the gun forward in an FBI cant, preventing the common problem of the weight of the ammo in a loaded semiautomatic's butt dragging the pistol rearward to bulgingly "print" through the clothing. Because of this design feature, I called it the Rear Guard. Mitch introduced it as the Ayoob Rear Guard, or ARG. Today he calls it the American Rear Guard.

There are so many makers of good IWB holsters on the market, that careful shopping will allow you to "mix and match" the features you seek. For instance, the well-made Galco NSA combines the rough-out design of Bruce Nelson's original Summer Special with the rear-mounted belt loop of the Ayoob Rear Guard.

A feature many like is a built-up surface toward the body, to shield the flesh from the gun and vice versa. Sweat contains salt and causes rust. Particularly on individuals with a bit of a spare tire, hard gun edges can dig into the side unmercifully. An integral shield prevents this. You can get it on Sparks leather IWBs, and on Kydex IWBs by SideArmor and other makers.

Another approach to IWB is the so-called *tuckable* holster. The first of these was Rosen's Workman, named after the original designer, Dave Workman. What makes it "tuckable" is a layer of leather in a V-shape connecting the belt loop to the holster body. Inside that deep "V" nestles the shirt-tail of a tucked in shirt. With the shirt very slightly "bloused" over the handgun, the concealed pistol disappears. Workman and Rosen recommend it primarily for small autos and snub revolvers, and suggest it for nothing larger than a baby Glock. However, if the body shape and the dress code allow it, a full-size 45 auto can be concealed there. Milt Sparks and Elmer MacEvoy's Leather Arsenal are two companies that make convertible IWB holsters that turn into tuckables and can hide even a Colt Government Model under a tucked dress shirt.

Of course, the most "tuckable" IWB option of all is the *belly-band*. It was designed by John Bianchi, who appeared in *Gun World* magazine with a prototype circa 1960. Before he could put it in production, a firm named MMGR in Brooklyn came out with a copy. It was an instant hit. Today, the belly-band is produced by numerous makers in numerous styles, but basically comprises a four-inch wide band of elastic with one or more gun pouches. It is designed to be worn "over the underwear but under the overwear." Carried on the strong-side hip, it is drawn from in the same fashion as a tuckable, by using the free hand to pull up the shirt in the movement known as the "Hackathorn Rip" and then making a conventional draw with the dominant hand. A small handgun on the order of a two-inch 38 can be worn to the side of the belly button for an even faster draw, but any larger handgun will tend to dig into the thigh or groin when you sit or bend.

Selling for as little as $15 for the cheapest, the belly-band is unquestionably the most economical method of carrying a large pistol hidden, and also one of the most effective. With little more than elastic around it, there is no added leather or Kydex to bulge around the gun. However, there is always a price to pay. In almost every model, it is extremely slow and awkward to reholster a drawn gun in a belly-band. This severely hampers critical drawing practice, and can be a tactical problem after you have drawn your gun to hold a criminal at bay, and uniformed police are arriving who may not recognize you as a good guy with that big handgun in your fist.

My own favorite of all the many belly-bands I've used, from the original MMGR on up, is the Bianchi Ranger. Superbly made, it also doubles as a money belt and has other hidden pouches for credit cards, ID, etc.

Outside the Belt

Some people just can't bear IWBs. They've bought their pants to fit their waist, not to fit their waist circumference *and* a large-frame holstered pistol. Others have a low waist (read: small butt) and find the front end of a full-size handgun can pinch the buttocks or the back of their thigh when they sit down. Still others may have a "spare tire" that rolls over a gun

inside the waistband and inhibits quick draw.

If an outside-the-belt scabbard is chosen, remember that you'll need a longer garment to keep it covered. To hold it tight to your body and minimize "print," you'll want belt attachments both fore and aft. This concept was pioneered back in the 1970s by Roy Baker with his Pancake holster. That rig is no more, but the "pancake" influence has become generic throughout this part of the holster industry.

My own favorites in this style include the Lou Alessi's CQC, designed by my friend and colleague Dave Spaulding, a long time career cop who worked a lot of narcotics and liked having a big automatic where he could reach it quickly in plain clothes. Snapping on and off the belt with sturdy fasteners, it is extremely handy and very well made. Another is the Ted Blocker DA-1 (with thumb-break safety strap) and DA-2 (open top) series. These scabbards have a ring of leather in the front belt loop. Slip it down, and the holster rides on the strong side hip with the FBI style forward tilt that many of us prefer for concealment; slip that loop upward, and the loops are now set to hold the holster vertical (neutral cant), a position favored by some tall men for strong side carry, and the best way to put the holster on the belt for a cross draw. Mike Dillon makes a nice scabbard that I like for double action, on-safe autos because the leather doesn't cover the slide-mounted safety catch, and I can get to it early in the draw. Strong Leather's Piece-Keeper is another of my favorites in this genre. It uses Roy Baker's original three-slot belt cuts to give you forward tilt, neutral cant or cross draw options, and has the added feature of a trick thumb-break safety strap which makes it act as a concealable retention holster. I've often used mine to conceal my once-department issue Ruger P90 45 auto, by no means a small pistol.

Clothing Factors

If you think you can conceal a big pistol inside a tight-fitting Armani wardrobe, your reality check just bounced. For an inside-the-waistband holster or belly-band, you want about two inches more in the waist than what you'd normally wear. You wear a size 44 sport jacket in regular sleeve length? You won't be able to button it over a full-size gun in a hip holster without a giant bulge unless you go to a size 46, keeping the same sleeve length of course.

The finest belly-band or tuckable won't hide your blaster under a fishnet shirt. That's an obvious example, though; more to the point, it won't hide well under a thin fabric cotton dress shirt, no matter how finely made the garment. You want a solid weave fabric with a crisp surface. A little bit of starch won't hurt. Vertical stripes will help break up the shape of a concealed handgun under a tucked shirt of any kind.

If you think you can conceal a big pistol inside a tight-fitting Armani wardrobe, your reality check just bounced.

With a longer sight radius, a larger frame that gives the hand more to grasp, and more mass to absorb recoil, full-size service handguns are easier to shoot fast and straight than subcompacts. Here author takes First Master, Custom Defense Pistol Division, at 2007 Pennsylvania State IDPA Championships. He's wearing uniform rig, but the same gun conceals well in any of several holsters. Note that the Ruger 45 is back on target with spent casing from the first shot no more than three inches out of the ejection port.

Untucked shirts – tee shirts, polo shirts, golf shirts – will conceal a full-size combat handgun inside your waistband if they are *(a)* solid fabric, preferably of darker color or patterned; *(b)* straight cut, that is, without any taper toward the waist; and, most important, *at least one size larger than you normally wear.* This will give you the concealing fabric drape that you'll need.

Hawaiian shirts, bowling shirts, Cuban-style *guyebarra* shirts, and square-hem safari shirts are all superb for gun concealment. Just make sure you don't get them in gauzy fabrics, and make sure they're one size large…and that they fit into a wardrobe image that you're comfortable with.

Other Options

Well, let's see. There's the glove box or the desk drawer…but will you be close enough to either location to reach the gun in time when danger threatens? There's the fanny pack…but the heavier the gun, the more pressure the belt strap will put on your lumbar region, and fanny packs are slow in any case. Shoulder rigs? They only conceal under more substantial outer garments for the most part, at least with really big pistols and revolvers. Purses, attaché cases, and even day planners with hidden gun compartments are one answer. Remember, however, that with this "off-body carry" you can accidentally leave the gun in the wrong place, or have it knocked out of your hand at the opening of a surprise encounter.

Of course, there are tweed coats and photographers' vests. Hell, for that matter you can go Gothic and conceal your 50 AE Desert Eagle under a Dracula cape or a big black trenchcoat. The fact is, though, that hiding a gun under a big garment is so easy it doesn't really require you to read a book for advice. Hiding a gun big enough to fight your best with – the best you can do with a handgun, anyway – under something like a tucked in shirt or summer casual wear? *That's* a challenge.

But it's a challenge that the advice above will allow you to meet.

IMPROVING YOUR DRAW FROM CONCEALMENT

There is a lot of bad advice out there about drawing techniques.

Here are practical tips for drawing faster and smoother from beneath concealment.

More Americans than ever can now legally carry their handguns concealed. However, not very many of them have as much training and practice in bringing them into action from concealment as some of us would like to see. Even in law enforcement, it is common for plainclothes officers, and cops qualifying with their off duty weapons, to draw from exposed holsters when firing for the record on training days. In NRA's training programs for civilians, the shooter always starts with the pistol or revolver in low ready. If by definition the gun is carried concealed, it is an absolutely critical skill to be able to draw it swiftly, smoothly, and safely from hiding.

There is a lot of bad advice out there on drawing techniques. Some that I've seen demonstrated are nothing less than hazardous. Others are, at best, less efficient than they could be. Let's look at ways of bringing the concealed handgun to bear from the most common carry locations.

First, a few general points, geared primarily to safety.

Do your initial practice with a dummy gun or unloaded gun. It's the equivalent of a student pilot learning on a simulator before taking an actual aircraft aloft. The student should be well practiced and confident in the draw before it is attempted with a loaded gun.

*Always keep the finger completely outside the trigger guard until the gun is drawn and on target, **and the decision to fire immediately has been made!*** Strict adherence to this rule would probably do more to reduce accidental shootings than any other one thing.

Holster as carefully as you draw, with the finger outside the trigger guard and the handgun on safe or decocked. Today, most good quality holsters have covered trigger guards. This industry-wide design change has done much to reduce instances of individuals shooting themselves accidentally as they draw. However, we are seeing too many cases of people shooting themselves while holstering. If the finger is left on the trigger, the portion of the holster that covers the guard interdicts the finger and holds it against the trigger, forcing the trigger back as the holstering movement continues.

Always practice drawing with the gun in a safe direction, bringing it to bear on something that can function as a backstop should the gun accidentally discharge. This is one more "safety net for training." I recommend that those who own body armor use the vest set against a wall or on a chair for this purpose. The Better Bilt Safe Direction unit is expressly designed for this sort of thing.

Strong Side Hip, Open-Front Garment

The most popular carry position among savvy pistol-packers seems to be on the strong-side hip, concealed by an open-front upper body garment. There are many trick techniques for getting at the gun in this location, but many of them don't work if you're seated, up against the wall, or otherwise positioned where the garment can't be swung out behind the holster to clear a path for the reaching hand. I designed the following technique to solve those problems.

Let the gun hand come in and touch the torso at

The most popular carry position among savvy pistol-packers seems to be on the strong-side hip, concealed by an open-front upper body garment.

the centerline with all four fingertips, and then – maintaining fingertip contact with your torso – sweep the hand back to the gun. The bottom edge of the hand will not only clear the coat or vest or whatever under the adverse circumstances described above, but will hold it back out of the way long enough to gain a grasp of the grip-frame if something happens to slow the draw.

Once your hand gets there, grasp the handgun firmly with all fingers but the index, which should be straight outside the holster. The web of the hand should be at the highest possible point on the grip frame. The thumb will at this point release the safety strap if one is in place. Keeping the elbow joint pointed to the rear (so the long bones of your arm will be in line with the direction in which you'll be applying force), clear the gun from the holster with a "rock and lock" movement that levers the muzzle up toward the target as soon as possible. Now, drive the gun forward toward the target.

Throughout the draw so far, the support hand has been at midline of the body. For a combat draw, I prefer the fingertips of the support hand to be pointed forward, which gives the arm more leverage to resist a grab by a close-range opponent. Now, as the gun is coming forward, the support hand takes its position on the firing hand. Be certain that the muzzle of the handgun is well ahead of the support hand before this part of the operation is put into effect.

You now flow into your stance of choice. A double-action auto carried on safe can be thumbed into the "fire" position anywhere during this procedure, but a cocked and locked single-action auto should remain on safe, with the thumb in position on the manual safety, until the decision to fire is made. Only when that decision is made should the trigger finger enter the guard; it should have been "in register" throughout the draw, that is, with the pad or tip of the trigger finger touching the frame above the trigger guard.

Strong-Side Hip, Closed-Front Garment

If the gun is under a buttoned or pullover shirt, a pullover sweater, an anorak or similar garment, it will be more difficult to access. All the same basic rules are in play, you just have to work a little harder.

If both hands are free, grasp the garment at its hem in front of the holster with the free hand, and jerk it upward as high toward the gun arm's shoulder as you can. You may not have enough play in the garment to get the hem that high, but if you try for the shoulder you will probably at least clear the holster area enough for a clean draw. The gun hand now draws exactly the same as it would with the holster in the same strong side position. As the gun comes clear, rock the muzzle on target. The support hand will come in from above and behind the gun, safely clear of the muzzle. This two-handed technique was popularized by my old friend Ken Hackathorn.

Unfortunately, you won't always have both hands free for this purpose, so of necessity you want to devote about half of your practice drawing from under closed-front garments to the following one-handed technique. Extend the gun hand's thumb toward the body and let it track up the seam of the trousers, or along the common peroneal nerve, toward the gun. This will allow the thumb to lift the garment enough to gain the proper drawing grasp. From there, the draw is the same as above, with one difference: to gain more clearance, I bend my knee slightly on the gun hand side and drop the hip, pulling the gun down and out from under any remaining fabric to prevent it from snagging.

Let me tell you how practice ingrains a technique. Early in 2005, I took a busman's holiday and attended one of my friend and colleague Chuck Taylor's excellent shooting classes as a student. When I was drawing my Glock 17 from under my open-front Royal Robbins 5.11 Concealment Vest, Chuck asked me, "Why do you bend your right knee when you draw?" I was stumped; I didn't even know I'd been doing it. It took me a day to figure out that what I was doing was born of decades of practice in drawing my off-duty gun, usually a 4-inch barrel service revolver or 5-inch barrel combat auto, from under the un-tucked polo or tee shirt that normally concealed it off duty in hot weather. The practice had – harmlessly, it turns out – transferred itself to my regular concealed draw from under an open-front garment.

Shoulder Holster/Cross Draw

Any carry in which the gun is on the side of the body opposite the dominant hand, either butt forward or suspended horizontally or upside down, is some variation of what is called a cross draw. The term "cross draw" is normally applied to a gun holstered on the belt in a butt forward position, but the popular shoulder holster is a variation of cross draw. So is the common practice of attaching a small handgun's holster to the straps on concealed body armor, carrying the gun beneath the armpit on the non-dominant side.

First, if circumstances permit, edge the non-dominant side of the body toward the target. This will minimize a close-range opponent's ability to "jam" or "stall" your draw. It will also minimize the dangerous, inefficient muzzle swing that has caused so many training courses and police departments to ban cross draw holsters.

To keep the muzzle from crossing the non-dominant arm, swing that arm up with the elbow forward and high. It is a movement similar to running your fingers through your hair. It also raises the elbow to

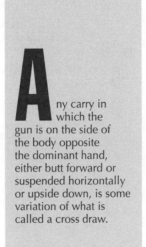

A ny carry in which the gun is on the side of the body opposite the dominant hand, either butt forward or suspended horizontally or upside down, is some variation of what is called a cross draw.

a blocking position, refined by master police trainer Kerry Najiola, which can help protect you during a close-range assault.

Reach inside the concealing garment with what a martial artist would call a "knife hand" or "spear hand," with all the fingers pointed straight toward the holster. This slims the profile of the reaching hand and allows it to get to the concealed weapon faster.

As with the straight draw, the hand contacts the gun with the web as high as possible on the back strap, middle through little fingers firmly grasping the frame, and trigger finger straight outside the holster. The thumb releases any necessary safety straps.

Now, pull the gun straight out across the midriff if drawing from the belt, or across the chest if drawing from a shoulder rig. If the body has been properly edged toward the target at the start of the draw, the muzzle should already be in the direction of the target. A straight thrust of the arm toward the target puts you into your stance. Once the muzzle is safely forward, the non-dominant hand drops down and assumes its position in support of the firing hand. Trigger and safety are manipulated as described earlier, with trigger guard kept empty until the decision to fire immediately has been made.

Pocket Holster

All but the most tightly tailored police uniform pants and suit pants will allow a small, light handgun to conceal in a side trouser pocket. So will currently fashionable "pleated pants" of the Dockers style, and cargo pants. In jeans, only a "relaxed fit" cut is likely to be practical for this sort of carry.

Always carry your pocket gun in a pocket holster! This will *(a)* keep its safety catch, if it has one, from being wiped into the "fire" position inadvertently; *(b)* keep the gun oriented properly for a quick draw; *(c)* keep the muzzle from wearing a hole through the pocket, and *(d)* keep the distinctive shape of the pistol from "printing" against the fabric and revealing the fact that you are armed. Do not allow anything else to occupy the same pocket as the gun. Ahern, Alessi, Kramer, Ky-Tac, Mach-2, Mika, Rosen, Safariland, Sparks, and Uncle Mike's are just a few of the pocket holsters that have proven popular.

The "spear hand" is once again technique of choice for beginning the draw. It slims the silhouette of the hand as much as is possible, and speeds your access to the gun. As with the techniques presented earlier, you want the web of the hand high on the grip tang, and the lower three fingers on the hand (or middle finger and ring finger, if the gun's frame is that small) to take a firm and immediate grasp. With a revolver, I put my thumb on the hammer area even if it's a "hammerless" to reduce the hand's profile and minimize chances of a snag coming out of the pocket. This often is not possible with a small auto while maintaining a firm grasp, due to the auto's different shape.

You want to be sure that the trigger finger is *outside the pocket holster*. This keeps it from entering the trigger guard prematurely. Do not press the trigger finger against the pocket holster, or it can trap the holster to the gun and cause both to be drawn together.

The angle at which you draw may be dependent on the pocket holster you've chosen and the cut of the pocket. With a square pocket, you'll have to draw straight up, and with a steeply cut "slash pocket," you may have to pull the gun rearward as you draw. Similarly, some pocket holsters are designed to catch on the pocket's lower edge and separate from the pistol, while others need to catch on the top edge. Adjust your angle of draw accordingly.

As soon as the gun is out of the pocket and completely clear, thrust it muzzle-forward straight toward the target. As before, don't allow the support hand to come in to do its job until the muzzle is safely forward and past it. Also as before, do not let the trigger finger enter the guard until the decision to fire has been made.

Ankle Holster

Remember that you need generously cut pant-legs to make this carry work. The old bell-bottoms were ideal for ankle carry, as are today's "flares." The straight-cut legs of the standard American "men's sack suit" work with it, and so do the similarly-cut legs of most police uniform trousers and BDUs. In jeans or cords, the ankle holster will generally only be compatible with "boot-cut" cuffs.

There may have been more bad drawing techniques taught with ankle holsters than with any other type of carry. Standing on one leg like a stork isn't going to work in a reactive situation. Hell, do even *storks* defend themselves this way? Though the ankle rig is extremely accessible while seated or down on your back, it's the most awkward of draws when standing. That's why I developed the following technique several years ago.

Carry the pistol on the inside of the leg opposite your gun hand, butt to the rear. The movement begins by grabbing a fistful of trouser material on the holster-side leg with your non-dominant hand and pulling it up as far as you can. This is important because once the knee bends, it will hold fabric below it taut and you'll have to push the cuff up from the bottom instead of the much easier expedient of pulling it up from the top.

As the material begins to slide up, scoot your gun hand-side leg out to the side, keeping the sole flat to the ground. Now bend deeply at the knees, trying to bring your buttocks down to about knee height. Essentially, you are sliding into a martial artist's horse stance. With the torso bent sharply forward, the dominant hand now has plenty of reach to take its grasp of the ankle-holstered defensive handgun. The gun hand should sweep up from below, with the thumb pointed up, so it can catch any residual pants cuff material and shove it up and out of the way.

As always, make the initial hand contact with the web high on the backstrap and all fingers but the trigger finger grasping firmly, using the thumb to break the safety strap if one is present. Pull the gun up, and as soon as the muzzle clears the holster bring it up to the target. If time permits, bring your support hand into play as before. If there is time, you can stand back up into your preferred firing position, or drop to kneeling on the non-holster leg if you're behind low cover. The horse stance position, which I call the "cover crouch" or "speed crouch," is a remarkably strong firing posture, if a somewhat uncomfortable one.

Final Advice

Always stick with the safety advice given in the opening portion of this article. Remember that you'll never get so fast and so smooth that you don't need to drill on the movements: the more you train, the faster and smoother you'll get. The less you train, the rustier, slower, and clumsier you'll get. How do I know this, you ask? (Sigh.) Trust me. I know this...

Remember that safety is the over-riding concern in this sort of training. You never get so good that you can drop your guard. The old adage that "familiarity breeds contempt" is absolutely true. After 23 years of accident-free training at Lethal Force Institute, we finally experienced a self-inflicted gunshot wound at a class in the summer of 2004. The student involved was an instructor herself, and quite competent. She simply went too fast, and in a "familiarity breeds contempt" moment, allowed her finger to remain on the trigger of her loaded 10mm auto as she inserted it into the holster. The resultant accidental discharge sent a 150-grain bullet down the outer edge of her leg at some 1300 feet per second. Fortunately, it was a superficial wound, but she'll be the first to tell you that it's an experience you don't want to share.

Train wisely. Train carefully. If you do, the above techniques should serve you well.

Good luck!

THE BACKUP CCW

With powerful handguns as small and light as this 13.3-ounce S&W Military & Police Model 340 357, there's little excuse NOT to carry a backup.

The backup gun is a second handgun, normally carried concealed, used as a supplement to a primary handgun that may be carried openly or concealed, depending on the circumstances. It has a long history among lawfully armed men and women. Originally a law enforcement practice, the carrying of backup has spread to ordinary American men and women who are licensed to carry loaded handguns concealed in public.

One only has to cruise the "gun boards" on the Internet to notice how many private citizens who carry are either considering the wear of a second weapon routinely, or are already committed to the practice. It has been said that in America, private citizens model their sporting rifle purchases based on what the military is using, and their defensive handgun purchases on what their police are using. The rise of the bolt-action rifle in popularity among hunters and target shooters followed the adoption of the Krag-Jorgensen in the late 19th century and the Springfield in the early 20th…semiautomatic hunting rifles such as the Remington Model 742 and Winchester Model 100 became popular among a generation of Americans who returned from fighting WWII and the Korean conflict with semiautomatic Garands…and today, the single most popular model represented in new rifle sales seems to be the AR-15, the semiautomatic version of the M-16 that has been our nation's primary military rifle since the Vietnam conflict..

Similarly, the dominance of the revolver among private citizens followed the adoption by the Texas Rangers of the Walker Colt before the middle of the 19th century. For most of the 20th century, the double-action revolver in 38 Special, followed in popularity by the same type of gun in 357 Magnum, was virtually the standard law enforcement weapon *and* the most popular home defense/concealed carry firearm among "civilians." As the police went to semiautomatics, so did the law-abiding public. At this writing, the high tech auto pistol typified by the Glock is the most common type of police duty handgun, and likewise one of the biggest sellers in the commercial handgun market.

This being the case, it is not surprising that the law officers' taste for a second handgun carried on the person, has been acquired by the armed citizens of the same population.

A *sweet* backup gun! This Colt Pocket Nine is the size of a Walther PPK 380 and considerably lighter, yet it just put five rounds of Winchester SXT full-power 9mm into approximately two inches at 25 yards. Sadly discontinued, it is worth haunting gun shops to find second-hand.

The Rationale of Backup

There are several good reasons to carry a second handgun for defensive purposes. None are the exclusive province of law enforcement. Let's examine them in detail.

The primary gun may be taken away. In Kentucky, an armed criminal caught a uniformed policeman off guard and took away his Smith & Wesson 10mm service pistol. The lawman was able to access his concealed Walther PPK 380, a backup gun issued to him by his department, and empty it into his attacker. The criminal died; the officer lived.

The primary gun may be unusable because it is the object of a struggle. In Ohio not long ago, a police officer found himself in a desperate battle for survival as his opponent struggled to take away his department issue Glock 22 pistol. Fortunately, the department had had the foresight to issue every officer a Glock 27, a subcompact version of the duty pistol, as backup. In the last instant before the suspect gained control of his service weapon, the officer was able to draw his backup G27 and fire a shot into his would-be murderer's head, killing the assailant and saving his own life.

The primary gun may be empty. Drawing a second, loaded weapon is often faster than reloading the first when it runs dry. In Michigan, a woman and her husband were working in the store they owned and operated together when they were hit by multiple armed robbers. The felons shot and wounded the husband early in the encounter. The wife drew a double-action revolver and shot back. Her gun ran dry, and she grabbed a second revolver with which she continued to return fire. That sustained fire allowed her to win the gunfight, saving her life and that of her husband, who survived his wounds. Their attackers were not so lucky.

The primary gun may malfunction. In the South recently, a police officer died with a jammed pistol in his hand. Witnesses said he was struggling with his choked semiautomatic when his opponent, a criminal armed with two double action revolvers, shot him to death. The officer's pistol, a popular brand famous for its reliability, had jammed part way through its 15-round magazine. The quick drawing and firing of a second weapon might have saved the officer's life.

The primary gun may be struck by an opponent's bullet and rendered inoperable. This scenario is not so far-fetched as it may sound. Law enforcement training in this country was profoundly affected by a 1986 gun battle on the edge of Miami where two FBI agents were killed and five more wounded by two heavily armed criminals who were ultimately killed

Sometimes it's easier, and even more efficient, to carry two small handguns of adequate power instead of one large one. *Left*: 20 ounce Model 640-1 above, 15 ounce Model 442 below, both J-frame 5-shots by Smith & Wesson. *Right*: 22 ounce all steel Kahr MK9 above, 14 ounce polymer frame MK9 below, both 7-shot 9mms.

at the scene. Two of the seven agents who returned fire resorted to their backup handguns during that firefight, and the agent who put the final, fatal bullets into the criminals did so with his Smith & Wesson revolver after his Remington shotgun ran out of ammo. (Bad guys also resort to backup guns. One of the two cop-killers in that encounter fired rounds from a stolen Mini-14 Ruger rifle, his own Dan Wesson 357 Magnum revolver, and his partner in crime's S&W 357 before he was finally killed.)

In that encounter, one agent's Smith & Wesson 9mm auto pistol was struck by a 223 bullet and rendered inoperable. That particular agent did not carry a backup gun, and was helpless to defend himself when the suspect with the Mini-14 walked up on him and shot him to death. Twenty years later, in April of 2006, the same phenomenon was observed in a Seattle gunfight. A city cop's Glock 22 service pistol put a 40-caliber bullet into the cylinder face of a criminal's Colt Officer's Model Match 38 Special, rendering it inoperable. In that instance, the criminal fortunately did not have a second gun, and was neutralized by police fire.

The primary gun may not be as readily accessible as the backup. In New York some years ago, an off duty cop in winter was carrying his primary handgun under two coats, and his backup Colt Detective Special snub-nose 38 in his overcoat pocket. Set upon by two armed robbers, he knew he would not be able to dig under his clothing and draw his duty weapon before being shot by the drawn gun held to his head. On the pretext of reaching for a wallet in his overcoat pocket, he got his hand on his backup Colt, then slapped the gunman's pistol aside with his free hand as he drew and fired. His bullet went through the gunman's brain, killing him instantly; the accomplice fled, and was later taken into custody. The officer was uninjured, saved by his backup handgun.

In the Carolinas, a man with a hidden weapon approached a parked police car and opened fire at the officer through the driver's window, wounding him. Seat-belted in place, the officer was unable to reach the service handgun locked in a security holster at his hip, but *was* able to access the Colt Agent backup gun strapped to his ankle. He drew from the ankle holster and returned fire, neutralizing his assailant.

He survived his wound and returned to full duty, saved by his backup gun.

The primary gun can arm only one good person at a time. With a backup gun, the user can arm a second competent "good guy or gal" who did not bring their own firearm to the emergency. In California, a police officer facing a complex problem involving armed suspects was offered assistance by a private citizen he knew to be trustworthy with firearms, but who was not licensed to be armed. He "deputized" the citizen, arming the man with the Smith & Wesson Chiefs Special snub-nose 38 the officer carried in an ankle holster. The situation came to a satisfactory conclusion.

In New York, two detectives had a reporter along in their unmarked car when they had occasion to go after a particularly dangerous armed robber they had been seeking. Knowing the reporter to be an ex-cop, one detective handed him his backup gun, a Colt Detective Special. When they made the confrontation, the suspect was facing three drawn guns. His own choice of weapons was a sawed-off double barrel shotgun. Few criminals are too stupid to realize that they can't possibly neutralize three armed good guys with a two-shot weapon without being shot himself.

This one chose to surrender without violence or bloodshed, and served a long term in prison.

We've just seen no fewer than seven very good reasons why a person who has a need to carry a gun might see a need to carry two of them. Any one of those situations could face an armed citizen *or* a police officer on any given day.

"Gentlemen, Choose Your Weapons"

There are several different approaches to the selection of backup guns. Predictable danger, wardrobe, training and familiarity already ingrained, and other situational factors will determine what might be the best approach on any given occasion.

On "heavy days" – i.e., high-risk situations – a pair of full-size fighting handguns makes sense. There is lots of historical precedent for this. On the Western Frontier, gun-wise lawmen from Wild Bill Hickok to Wyatt Earp carried a brace of sixguns. That is, a matched pair. Hickok wore twin Navy Colt .36 caliber cap-n'-ball revolvers, and allegedly "freshened" them daily by firing each charge in each chamber every morning in a short practice session, and then reloading with fresh powder, ball, and caps. Earp wore a pair of Colt Single Action Army revolvers, caliber 45 Colt.

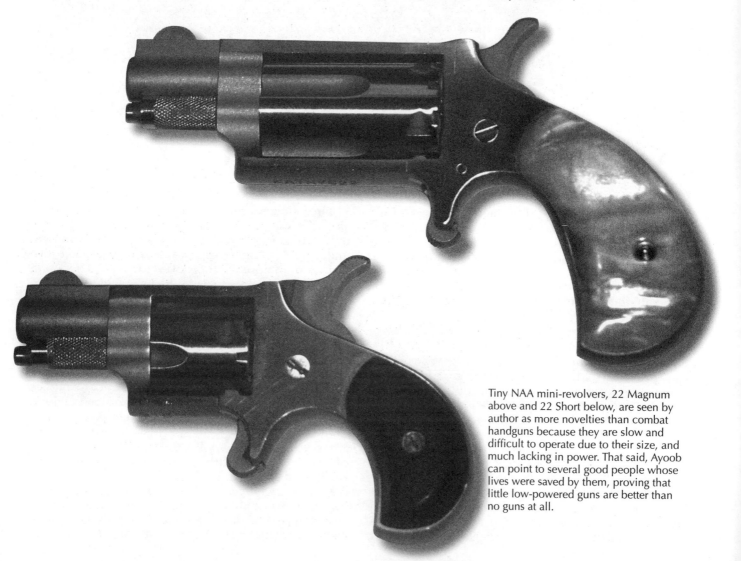

Tiny NAA mini-revolvers, 22 Magnum above and 22 Short below, are seen by author as more novelties than combat handguns because they are slow and difficult to operate due to their size, and much lacking in power. That said, Ayoob can point to several good people whose lives were saved by them, proving that little low-powered guns are better than no guns at all.

SIG P226R 16-shot 9mm, above, backed up by 5-shot 38 Special S&W Model 442, below.

Similar practices were seen in more modern times. On the night he and his team took down John Dillinger, FBI Agent Melvin Purvis was said to have been carrying a pair of Smith & Wesson Military & Police 38 Specials. That significantly outgunned the Colt Pocket Model 380 Dillinger was carrying, though it is believed that a 45 ACP bullet from the Colt Government Model of another agent was what actually killed FBI's "Most Wanted" fugitive that night in Chicago.

Decades later the most famous member of the NYPD Stakeout Squad, Jim Cirillo, went to work each day with essentially the same gear carried by Purvis, though by then that particular Smith & Wesson was known as the Model 10. Each of Jim's was a four-inch, with a heavy barrel on the strong-side hip and a tapered barrel version worn cross-draw as backup. Jim actually had one more backup gun on each occasion, a Colt Cobra 38 with a hammer shroud and two-inch barrel, carried in a pocket, and usually had a 14-inch barrel Ithaca 12-gauge shotgun handy to start things off.

Because most days *aren't* heavy days, a much more common paradigm has long been the full-size, serious-caliber "combat handgun" as primary weapon, with a smaller and sometimes less powerful handgun for backup. Generations of cops have used tiny 25 autos for backup. While they are better than nothing, these guns are infamous for their poor stopping power, and being very tiny, they also tend to be difficult to manipulate under stress. Long before that, it was popular for lawmen to carry a six-shooter as primary, and a two-shot derringer as secondary. The derringer, fortunately, has pretty much passed from the scene.

Today, tiny 32 autos like the Seecamp, the North American Arms Guardian, and the irresistibly slim and light Kel-Tec P32 have found their way into backup position on the bodies of many police officers and armed citizens alike. In common with their predecessors, they are better than nothing, but they are also feeble in terms of the power they can put out. It is significant that when police departments issue backup guns, they normally look for something more powerful.

The New York City Police Department, for example, has long encouraged backup guns, but they allow only two calibers: 38 Special in a revolver, and 9mm Parabellum in a semiautomatic. This is the result of long institutional experience encompassing a great many gunfights, and it embodies common sense.

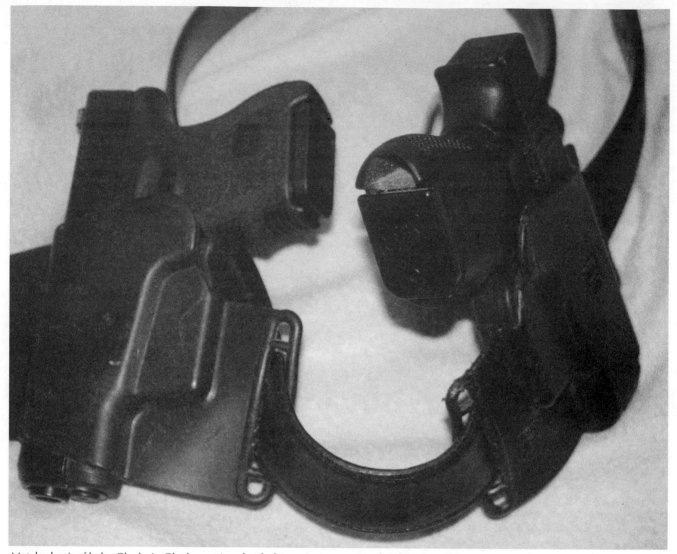

Matched pair of baby Glocks in Glock sport/combat holsters. A gun worn each side, mirror image, saves pocket space and puts one available readily to either hand. Balance on hips is perfect and natural. Author thinks of it as carrying a spare magazine with another pistol wrapped around it.

As this is written, there are at least five state police agencies that issue backup handguns to all their troopers. Two of them consider commonality important issuing Glock pistols in two sizes and the same caliber. One agency issues the standard size Glock 37 and "baby" size Glock 39, both in 45 GAP. The other issues the 5.3-inch barrel Glock 35 and the 3.6-inch barrel Glock 27, both in 40 S&W. If the primary weapon is lost, snatched away, or damaged, the trooper still has a spare pistol and two spare magazines to fight with, because the smaller Glock will take the larger Glock's magazines in the same caliber. Similarly, the G26 subcompact will accept the magazines of the compact G19 or full size G17 in caliber 9x19, and the subcompact 357-caliber G33 will work with the same-caliber magazines of the compact G32 or the full size G31.

The other two state police agencies in question take a different route. One has issued the Beretta 380 for the backup role, while equipping its uniformed personnel with full size Beretta 9mm and 40 pistols over the years. With a recent switch to the Glock for duty, that department may soon be trading its 380s for baby Glocks in a more potent caliber. Another agency has issued snub-nose S&W revolvers for decades as backup, the current gun being the Model 640-1 in 357 and loaded with 38 Special +P+, complementing a SIG P226 duty weapon in 40 S&W. Within the last couple of years, a fifth state police department has bought S&W 38 Special Airweights for all troopers, in addition to their standard issue 357 SIG pistols.

Each person in the private sector must make his or her own decision. Certainly, the ability to interchange spare ammunition between the backup gun and the primary is a real "plus." For many decades, cops carried their spare 38 Special ammo loose in pouches or loops, and were encouraged to get a smaller 38 Special for backup for just this reason. Indeed, they were taught that if they carried a Colt as primary they should carry a Colt as backup, and ditto with Smith & Wesson, because the cylinders would rotate in the same direction and open the same way.

In the 1970s, revolvers still held sway in police work, but speed loaders became accepted duty gear. It was discovered that the speed loader sized to fit a K-frame Smith & Wesson service revolver would fit perfectly in a six-shot D-frame Colt backup gun. The hot set-up became a four-inch or six-inch Smith 38 or 357 in the uniform holster, and a two-inch Colt as backup gun, with the speed loaders filled with hot 38 Special ammo that could be fired from either revolver.

Today, with autoloaders so hugely popular, commonality is still a factor, but not always. Certainly, Glock interchangeability makes huge sense. Someone carrying a double-stack S&W 9mm of conventional size can carry a Kel-Tec P11 for backup, secure in the knowledge that the 14.5 ounce 9mm Kel-Tec will accept the magazines of a Smith & Wesson 5906 or 6906 in the same caliber. If the full-size or Commander-size 1911 is chosen for primary, a subcompact such as the Colt Defender can work with full-length magazines in the same caliber in an emergency, but those longer mags can over-travel and lock up the gun when slammed into a full-size 1911 that's at slide-lock.

Many backup gun users have decided to do without ammo interchangeability in the name of convenience, concealment, or faster tactical access. Some just don't happen to have a primary gun that's magazine-compatible with a smaller one for interchangeability. For instance, this writer's department issues the Ruger P345 as a duty pistol, and this 45 auto does not have a subcompact version available. Accordingly, each officer is issued a Ruger SP101 357 Magnum snubnose revolver for backup, and most carry a Bianchi Speed Strip with spare 357 rounds somewhere on their person while at work.

"Civilians" and police officers alike have found that while autos might be a better choice as primary weapons, revolvers may be preferable as backup because of faster access out of pockets due to their rounded grip-frames, or better resistance to dust and grit when carried in ankle holsters. Another advantage of the small revolver for backup comes in one of the applications mentioned earlier in this article, the use of the backup to arm another competent good guy or gal. You may not have time to explain to that person how your auto works or why they need to keep their weak side thumb out from behind the slide when you hand them your backup auto. However, anyone competent to wield a gun in a crisis situation will be competent to handle a double action only revolver when there is no time to explain the "manual of arms."

Where to Carry the Backup

Mirror image on the belt is how Hickok and Earp each carried their backup six-guns, with one accessible to each hand. However, neither man worried much about concealment of two full-size revolvers, and both made it a point to practice intensively firing with each hand. That is essential in this type of carry.

Strong side plus cross draw is quite popular. This is how Cirillo carried sidearms on the NYPD Stakeout Squad. The second gun in a cross-draw makes it readily accessible to the dominant hand, and also positions it where the weak hand can reach it in an emergency.

A shoulder holster is a form of cross-draw. Many cops (and armed citizens) over the years have packed their "second" in a shoulder rig. (In years past, it is believed, Earp's friend and contemporary Dr. John "Doc" Holiday wore one Colt single action on his hip and another in a primitive shoulder holster of the period. John Wesley Hardin, perhaps the deadliest gunman of the Old Frontier, fashioned a leather vest that held a pair of revolvers in semi-shoulder holster position.)

Pocket carry is extremely popular for backup guns.

A holster strapped to a concealed ballistic vest under the weak arm is a variation of the shoulder holster draw. It is extremely popular with uniformed police, but of course, only works if one happens to be wearing body armor. LAPD SWAT operators are issued two Kimber 1911 45 autos apiece. One is worn on a tactical thigh holster on the strong side, the other, attached to the heavy body armor in the chest area for a semi-shoulder holster type of access. This carry has also proven popular with some of our armed forces personnel in Iraq and Afghanistan at this writing.

Ankle holsters are long-time traditional favorites for backup. They are out of the way of the often already crowded gun belt. While slow to reach from a standing position, the ankle rig is ideal for a person seated behind a counter or seated behind the wheel of a car. When you are down on your back, your legs are no longer supporting your body weight and you can quickly flex your knee and snap your ankle up toward your reaching hand. The ankle holster is also fairly accessible to either hand, an important consideration in backup gun placement because there is always a likelihood of your gun hand or arm being injured and disabled in the course of a fight.

Bear in mind that ankle rigs take some time to get used to. They also require full-cut pants cuffs. Police uniform pants work well with ankle holsters, as do straight-cut suit pants and cargo pants. Sports slacks and jeans will require "boot cut cuffs" if they're going to give you access to an ankle holster. This type of rig works best with smaller handguns; a compact Glock or equivalent is about the largest that most people can effectively carry in an ankle holster.

Pocket carry is extremely popular for backup guns. Tactically, it allows you to put your hand in your pocket in a "hinky" situation and already have the gun discreetly in hand if lethal danger suddenly threatens. Many backup gun users place the pocket gun on their weak side, leaving the strong hand free to carry out its trained reflex to the primary handgun. Whenever carrying in a pocket, *be sure to use a pocket holster!* This will: always hold the gun in the same position for faster access; break up the gun's outline and prevent you from being "made" as someone who is armed; speed the draw under any conditions; and prevent sharp edges on the gun (such as the front sight on a J-frame snub-nose revolver) from wearing holes in your clothing.

Off-body placement is an often ignored but sometimes practical location for backup guns. This was how the lady in the mom-and-pop store mentioned earlier accessed both the revolvers she used to gun down the armed robbers who opened fire on her and her husband. Lance Thomas, the famous Los Angeles Rolex repairman who survived multiple gunfights with armed robbers and killed several opponents, kept a loaded handgun discreetly concealed about every three feet along his side of the counter and workbench in his small shop. He was always able to grab a gun – or *another* gun, when he shot the first one empty – in time to win every single one of his gunfights. A spare handgun secreted in the map pocket of the driver's door of your car may be easier and more discreet to reach to than the primary gun in your hip scabbard or shoulder holster, when you have to draw on a carjacker or a kidnapper who is already in the car with you. While not always recommended by experts, discreet off-body placement of concealed handguns has doubtless saved the lives of multiple good people in certain situations.

The Bottom Line

Now you know why street-wise gun expert Phil Engeldrum once wrote, "If you need to carry a gun, you probably need to carry two of them."

Georgia State Patrol issues each trooper a mated pair of Glocks in 45 GAP. Left, the service-size G37; right, the subcompact G39.

The choices are yours. What to carry, where to carry, and whether to carry it at all.

If you do choose to go the backup gun route, remember the following.

The backup gun should be simple to operate under extreme stress. That's the only time you'll be reaching for it. That simplicity will also serve well if you must hand your backup to another person, with no time to explain how to use it.

The backup gun is literally a last resort, and therefore should be powerful enough to stop a fight. This is why most experts shy away from small-caliber handguns as backup weapons.

Because the backup gun *is* likely to be a last resort in a life-or-death situation, it must be absolutely reliable.

If you carry backup, you need to train with it. Practice getting it out and into action. Practice shooting it, particularly with the "weak" hand if you carry it on the non-dominant side. If you don't groove in the movements and techniques now, they won't be there when everything goes auto-pilot in a life-threatening crisis.

Backup handguns have saved the lives of a great many cops, and would have saved more had they been present. They can do the same for law-abiding citizens who legally carry concealed handguns to protect themselves and those within the mantle of their protection.

Chapter 16

OPEN CARRY:
TWO SIDES OF A COMPLICATED ISSUE

This Bianchi
Evader requires
middle finger of drawing
hand to hit a paddle to
unlock this Glock 22.

In days of old, Americans often carried handguns openly in public. Not because they were police or anything, but because *(a)* it was their right, and *(b)* in certain parts of a young frontier nation, it was expected of them.

This Bianchi Evader requires middle finger of drawing hand to hit a paddle to unlock this Glock 22.

Among those of us who are advocates for the civil rights of gun owners, there are some who think the time is ripe for a return to this concept...and there are those who not only don't feel a need to resurrect the old paradigm, but believe it might actually be counter-productive to our side of the Second Amendment battle.

As with most intense debates, there are sound arguments on both sides of the issue.

The Pro-Open Carry Platform

The arguments in favor of private citizens carrying loaded handguns exposed to plain sight in public seem to break down as follows:

Crime deterrence. This philosophy holds that criminals who were thinking of robbing this convenience store or that bank will abort their mission when they see a gun on the hip of a citizen. On a more personal level, they argue, it will tend to deter criminals who have targeted specific individuals for crimes against the person, such as mugging or rape, in lonely places deliberately selected by the predator for being remote from police assistance.

Good public relations for gun owners. The theory advanced by advocates of open carry is that when the public gets used to seeing their neighbors and other good people carrying guns in plain sight, they'll lose their fear of firearms and become more amenable to supporting gun owners' rights.

Convenience. Particularly in warm places, it is often uncomfortable to wear a concealing garment. The plain hip holster worn exposed is simply more

The importance of "dressing to the gun" in open carry. In ordinary indoor lighting, author does not readily appear to be armed…

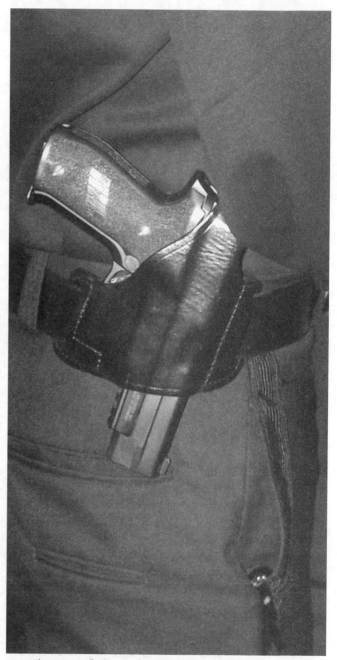

…until camera's flash reveals black SIG P226 in black thumb-break Blocker holster/belt set, normally somewhat camouflaged against dark gray pants and black shirt.

comfortable and convenient than a belly-band, a shoulder rig, or an inside the waistband holster, before you even consider the potential discomfort of an additional piece of clothing to hide a gun.

The exercise of rights. This argument comes with a powerful sound bite: "A right that is not exercised will wither away."

The Concealed-Rather-Than-Open Carry Platform

These arguments come, not from anti-gun groups or other opponents of civil rights, but from armed American citizens who are neither uniformed security professionals nor police officers, but simply don't like the idea of carrying their guns out in the open before the eyes of the general public.

Open carry invites disarming. Those who prefer to carry their guns concealed point to all the police officers who have been killed with their own weapons. They prefer to keep their guns hidden on their person, where only they know where they are.

Open carry sacrifices the advantage of surprise. Concealed carry advocates point out that the decades-old archives of the Armed Citizen columns in the National Rifle Association's *American Rifleman* magazine show countless cases of armed citizens who only won their armed encounters because they were

Most folks in this pastry shop won't spot the fact that one is wearing a gun openly, its black finish blending in with black LFI Concealment Rig and black clothing.

able to draw from concealment and take their criminal opponents by surprise, an advantage that would have been lost if the assailants could have seen beforehand that they were armed.

Open carry makes enemies for the pro-gun movement, instead of friends. The vast majority of the American public does not carry guns openly on city streets and do not see others that they know to be law-abiding private citizens do so. Therefore, says this argument, they are frightened when they observe guns worn openly by people not readily identified as those they are "socialized" to seeing armed, such as armed guards and police officers, and are therefore frightened when they see ordinary folks with guns on their hips.

Open carry advocates are just show-offs crying for attention. This is probably the least effective argument for concealed as opposed to open carry.

Personal Experiences

For those of us who go armed, open versus concealed carry is an intensely personal issue. It is only fair to the reader that they know the personal experiences of anyone addressing that issue, since such personal experiences can create preconditioned bias or prejudice. Any opinion must be seen in the light of the person doing the opining.

This writer has been carrying concealed since the age of 12. In a time and place where a permit was only required to carry a *concealed and loaded handgun in public,* and in which the chief of police of the city in question had told my father and me that it was perfectly legal for my young self to carry loaded and concealed inside our family-owned place of business so long as I didn't step out on the sidewalk so armed, it gave me an early start on the concept. I have "open-carried" as a sworn, part-time police officer for thirty-

Author STRONGLY recommends some type of security holster to those who feel they must practice open carry. This carbon fiber Blackhawk SERPA with proprietary trigger-finger lock release mechanism is carried by a state police trainer in casual clothes. Pistol is baby Glock.

some years, which doesn't really count except for the "deterrence" argument on one side and the "exposed to disarming attempts" argument on the other, but have also open-carried in plainclothes from Arizona to North Carolina on city streets.

And, in those capacities, I have seen things that support both sides.

In Arizona, a friend and I were in a convenience store between Prescott and Paulden on the way to Gunsite Training Center. My friend came from a state that then had no provision for private citizens to carry a handgun in any fashion, and was luxuriating in his ability under Arizona law to carry his custom Colt 45 auto in an exposed holster. I was a few steps away when I saw a man walk in, do a double take when he spotted the gun, and deliver a "target stare" to the loaded pistol. Almost in exaggerated pantomime, he mugged an expression of outrage and pointed at the pistol, making eye contact with others in the store that indicated his outrage. And then, that man moved in behind my friend, reaching out for the holstered pistol.

I stepped between them, glaring at the interloper. He stopped, looked at me, obviously decided that whatever was going to happen wasn't worth it, and walked away with an angry look on his face. I don't *think* he was going to try to shoot anyone with my friend's gun, but he was obviously going to grab it and do some show-off thing, which could have led to a struggle for a loaded gun in a crowded convenience store, with an obviously high potential for tragedy. Score one for the case against wearing an exposed handgun in public.

Yet, in North Carolina, I had an exposed pistol on my hip when I walked out of a store and saw a very aggressive panhandler approach an apparently unarmed and unprepared citizen, who fled on foot. The panhandler then turned toward me, walking toward me rapidly with a hostile expression on his face. I turned to face him in an interview stance…and he saw the weapon on my hip.

It stopped him in his tracks, without a word or a touch from me. He looked back and forth between my eyes and my sidearm, then shook his head and made a gesture that said he didn't want to fight, and turned around and walked away. Score one for the deterrent effect claimed by the advocates of open carry.

Been there, experienced both sides, and realize that each side as some solid points. Now, with that out of the way, let's look at the issue argument by argument.

Analyzing the Arguments Over Open Carry

Crime deterrence? There's no doubt in my mind that openly carried firearms have prevented crime. The trouble is, whether you're talking capital punishment or open carry, deterrence is something that is impossible to empirically measure and quantify. All we have is anecdotal evidence. The Virginia Citizens' Defense League (VCDL) is an extremely effective gun owners' civil rights group, and has taken the promotion of open carry (legal in their state) as one of their causes to promote. One of their members was recently in a bank, openly wearing a pistol, when he observed a man acting suspiciously like a robber. The man saw the VCDL member's pistol; his eyes widened; and he backed off and left. Bank employees later confirmed the armed citizen's impression that the man was definitely about to attempt a bank robbery, and was scared off by the sight of a good guy with a gun. No arrest was sought since the man had made no overt act, but I for one am comfortable scoring that as a point for the pro-open carry argument.

What about the vulnerability to disarming attempts? The concealed weapon is no guarantee against gun snatches: many plainclothes officers have been disarmed of their concealed weapons. The "out of sight/out of mind" thing works both ways, and those whose weapons are exposed can at least hopefully be presumed to be more alert to disarming attempts. Any fight that degenerates into a wrestling match can find the opponent's arms going around the good guy's body, feeling his gun, and attempting to snatch it from under the concealing garments.

That said, though, the long history of police being disarmed and murdered with their own guns shows that a definite danger comes with carrying an exposed handgun. Advocates of open carry cry, often stridently, "Show me a case where it was a private citizen instead of a cop who was disarmed because the criminal could see his open-carried gun!"

OK.

I'll show you two.

Both occurred in Indiana, to gun shop owners who carried handguns openly exposed in hip holsters. In the first case, the criminal pretended to be a customer and asked the shop owner for an item on a counter behind him. When the shopkeeper turned to reach for the product, the suspect ripped the dealer's Colt 45 auto from its open-top scabbard, and tried to shoot him with it. Fortunately, the Gold Cup Colt was on-safe, and efforts to pull the trigger failed. The owner was able to grab a second gun and open fire, driving the assailant off.

In the second instance, gunmen entered the store with weapons drawn and took the owner, off-guard, at gunpoint. They may well have "cased" the place before and already known that he was armed. They took his HK P7 out of the holster. Attempting to shoot him with his own gun, they failed because the one with the P7 didn't know how to operate its unique squeeze-cocking

> There's no doubt in my mind that openly carried firearms have prevented crime.

lever. This bought the shop owner time to grab a hidden 357 Magnum. Final score: two dead bad guys, one live good guy, but no points at all for the open carry deterrence argument and two strong cases in point against letting the other guy see beforehand that you have a gun, and letting him see where it is.

Are some open-carry advocates really just show-offs crying out for attention? "Look at me, look at me, I'm ba-a-ad?" Well, I think a *few* of them are, and you only have to read some of their posts on this or that Internet gun forum to realize that it's true. However, I think it's *only* a few. I know a lot of folks from VCDL, for example, and I honestly don't think that's what's motivating them. As noted earlier, the "show-off" accusation is probably the argument against open carry that carries the least weight.

Where the "show-off" element comes in most heavily, I personally believe, is in the negative behavior that open carry brings out in certain strangers who observe it. Remember the guy in the Arizona convenience store? He saw, I suspect, a man who held a power he didn't have, and felt an atavistic (and really stupid) need to show that he was bigger and stronger than the man with the gun. On an Internet forum, a practitioner of open carry told of the time he was having an ice cream in a restaurant with a lady when a belligerent stranger went ballistic (no pun intended). The man started screaming, "What the (expletive deleted) are you carrying that (expletive deleted) gun for in here?!?" The incident ended without physical harm to anyone, but that sort of thing does not exactly promote pro-gun feelings among the general public.

What about the "exercise of rights" argument? It is indeed persuasive to say that something unexercised will atrophy. However, the argument does not necessarily stand the twin tests of history and logic, at least insofar as open carry.

The state of New Hampshire has had "shall-issue" concealed carry licensing since the first quarter of the 20th century. It has also had open carry legal on the books the whole time. In more than half a century of living in that state, I only *once* saw a man walking on city streets with an open-carried handgun and no police badge clipped to the belt alongside it. Guys in hunter's garb with hunting licenses clipped to their shirts, and a Ruger Super Blackhawk or Smith & Wesson Model 29 hunting revolver strapped to their belts, in a rural diner during the pre-dawn hours during deer season? Sure…and no one looked twice. But that was a totally different thing. They were literally "in costume," readily identified as someone with both a right and a good reason to have a gun on. But, say, a Glock worn openly in a large bookstore in the state's

Author's favorite exposed-in-the-station plainclothes holster for his then-department issue Ruger P90 45 was this Strong Piece-Keeper. Baker-like triple "pancake" slots allowed optional carry angles…

most populous city? One fellow did so – one of my graduates, actually, who respectfully disagreed with my comments in class about "discretion" – and found himself grabbed and thrown "into the position" by uniformed police officers responding to a frightened citizen's desperate 9-1-1 call that amounted to "man with a gun, there now!" He raised a ruckus about being treated so when merely "exercising his rights," and fortunately was not arrested for disturbing the peace (a genuine possibility under the prevailing law). It's still safe to say that the incident didn't win any new friends for the gun rights movement.

With almost no one exercising their right to carry concealed in NH, the right still exists. So do a huge number of concealed carry permits, in the hands of residents and non-residents who exercise that privilege constantly, and who keep their handguns discreetly concealed when out and about in public. Therefore, I have to question the "rights unexercised will wither away" argument, as strong as it sounds on the surface.

I will make one suggestion, though. I have lost count of the number of people who practice open carry who say that when asked why they do so will reply, "Because I can!"

I will most strongly suggest, *throw away that particular argument!*

"Because I can" is an answer that carries a very negative connotation. Any cop can tell you of the drunk wife-beaters who, when asked "Why did you do that?" as the handcuffs went on, sneered back, "Because I can!" Any parent who has ever upbraided a young bully who was pushing around a smaller child and asked him why he did it can remember hearing, "Because I can!" Those are near-universal human experiences. When *you* are asked by someone who has had such an experience, "Why do you carry that gun like that?" and you reply "Because I can," you will almost certainly be perceived as the same sort of bullying dirt-bag they previously heard utter the same words to defiantly attempt to excuse inexcusable behavior.

May I submit that you would be far better off to say, "I am an advocate of gun owners' civil rights, and as a good citizen I carry this to remind other people that they have the right to protect themselves to the same degree," or words to that effect. Some open carry advocates, including some members of VCDL, even carry cards with such messages to hand out to people who ask. If you are going to open carry, I don't think that's a bad idea at all, so long as the wording of the explanation is neutral. Hint: don't let the message include the word "sheeple" to describe anyone who *doesn't* carry a loaded gun in plain sight in public.

Winning Hearts and Minds

One point where the open carry folks butt heads directly with the concealed carry folks is the issue of making friends for the Second Amendment among members of the public who are sitting on the fence in terms of gun issues. In an adult lifetime of active advocacy for "gun rights" causes, I have met many former fence-sitters, and even some "antis," who came over to our side of the debate because they were influenced in a positive way by someone in their life whom they respected and whom, they found out to their surprise, carried a gun for personal protection. However, I have not yet met even one person who changed their opinion to our side of the issue because they saw that person carrying a loaded gun exposed in a place open to the general public.

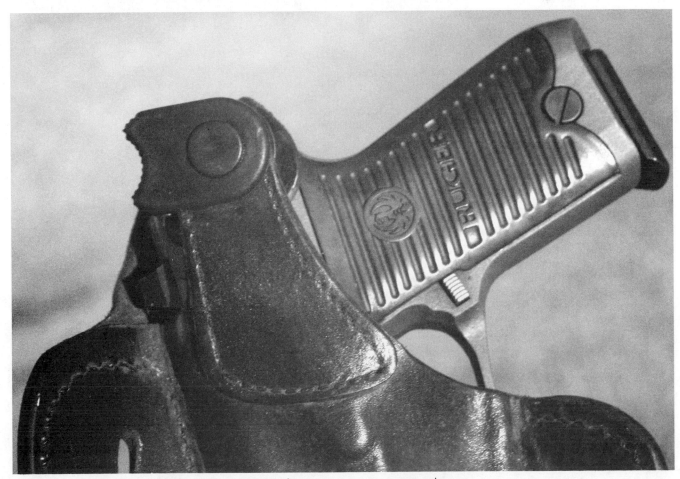

...and the proprietary Piece-Keeper thumb snap required two separate movements to release.

On the other hand, we've seen whole communities frightened by ostentatious displays of people carrying guns in what those observers perceived to be a "show of force." Remember the Black Panthers, marching armed in California? It's safe to say that this action won no converts to the rights of African-Americans from previously uncommitted citizens and voters. It is probably safe to say that the same will be true insofar as an arguably "ostentatious" display of what much of the public sees as only "the power to kill"?

The weak fear the strong. The helpless fear the armed. Fear breeds hatred. Think about it: fear is the key ingredient to hate. That which we call hate, absent fear, would be merely contempt. One benchmark of our lives, of our empowerment, is when we realize that those we once hated we merely hold in contempt. Many of those people out there in the vast public aren't where you are yet. They still fear armed people they don't see wearing the badges they've come to associate with the guns that society told them will protect them.

When fear equals hate, oppressed minorities such as, oh, gun owners probably should not be creating fear among those who may one day vote in a

A good choice for open carry *or* concealed, this Bianchi Evader requires middle finger of drawing hand to hit a paddle to unlock this Glock 22.

Bottom Line

Elsewhere in this publication, you'll read about security holsters suitable for daily carry that make good sense for anyone who carries a gun openly in public. Such holsters have long since become the rule more than the exception among the cops and uniformed security personnel who have carried exposed handguns in public for lo, these many years, and we would be foolish to discount the wisdom they have learned so hard at the cost of so much preventable pain and death. Open carry can be done, *in jurisdictions where it is expressly legal,* of course. We just need to ask ourselves whether, in the balance of competing harms and needs, the practice does not pass the point of diminishing returns.

Suppose one is in a jurisdiction where it *not* possible to legally carry concealed, but *is* legal to carry a loaded, *exposed* handgun? I can only say, "been there, done that." I can remember when North Carolina issued carry permits only to residents, and had no provision for non-resident permits, but did allow open carry. When I was in NC at that time, my choice was to be able to protect myself with an openly carried handgun, and risk upsetting some people, or to go unarmed.

I chose open carry. I never regretted that decision. I was amazed at how many people never even noticed that I was carrying a full-size 357 Magnum revolver or 9mm or 40- or 45-caliber semiautomatic pistol. (No, I *won't* use the word "sheeple" … I won't … I *won't* …) But, the fact is, I almost certainly did alarm or upset a very few people.

I would not have bothered those folks if there was no reason to carry exposed. But there *was* a reason, and under those circumstances – carry your gun openly, or go unarmed – my assessment of the doctrine of competing harms told me to carry my gun openly, and I did.

Things are different now. I drove through North Carolina last week. For some time, NC has had reciprocity with Florida, and my Florida concealed carry permit authorized me to keep my 9mm SIG discreetly concealed under my photographer's vest and my Smith & Wesson Airweight 38 just as discreetly concealed in my trouser pocket. And no one was startled or alarmed. "No 'sheeple' were frightened in the course of the trip."

And that, it seemed to me, was the best of all worlds.

But it's just one guy's opinion. Each of us has to make our own decision on the complicated issue of open carry versus concealed carry. Let me leave you, though, with a final thought: if we have made the decision to responsibly carry loaded guns to protect ourselves and those who count on us to keep them safe, we are not enemies on this matter. We are allies in agreement on a fundamental issue of human rights, and are merely debating the fine points.

Camo-finished Glock in camo holster. With camo pants and shirt, author wonders, what would be both legal and practical interpretations of "concealment"?

referendum to determine whether or not they will be allowed to even *own* handguns. Such referenda have gone to the polls in California and Massachusetts during the lifetimes of many of us. The potential for open carry to create fear that in turn creates hatred should not be discounted.

Many, many decades ago there was an arbiter of etiquette named Beatrice Tanner Campbell. She was the "Miss Manners" of her day. She wrote a classic line: "I don't care where people make love, so long as they don't do it in the street and frighten the horses."

The wisdom holds true. Think about it for a moment. When we are out and about in public carrying a loaded gun, we literally *are* "doing it in the street."

It follows that we have an obligation to "not frighten the horses."

Insofar as the issue of "winning hearts and minds," it's hard to look at things realistically and not come down on the side that says flaunting guns in public among strangers may not be the best way to "win friends and influence people."

MAKING OPEN CARRY SAFER

If you choose to carry an exposed handgun in public where the law allows, can you "keep yourself safe" even more safely? This writer says you can, and shows you how.

A number of jurisdictions allow law-abiding private citizens to carry loaded handguns, *exposed,* in public. This chapter will focus on two specific elements of open carry, which have been called into discussion by those in the gun owners' rights movement who think carrying concealed is a better idea.

Those two particular elements are *discretion,* and *handgun security* against snatch attempts. By discretion, we mean a method of carry that, while exposing the gun, does not call attention to it. You don't want to "frighten the horses." You don't necessarily want any criminal in sight to realize that if he blindsides you with an ambush from behind, your firearm is his for the taking. Unless you're a show-off screaming silently for attention, you want as few people as possible to notice the exposed handgun.

Handgun security against snatch attempts is something cops came to terms with long ago. Any officer will tell you, "In any conflict where someone is within arm's reach of you, they have a gun within their arm's reach: *your* gun." Since open carry allows a present or potential antagonist to see that you do have that gun, you want it to be held in something that will not yield it up to the first clutching hand.

Discreet Appearance

I learned early that "protective coloring" extends to the visibly armed citizen as surely as it does to the beasts of the forests, the denizens of the sea, and the fowl of the air. For polar bears, protective coloration is "white on white." The reflective surfaces of metal are such that a chrome-plated, pearl-handled gun may actually be *more* conspicuous against a white shirt with white slacks. However, a matte black gun and

Not the right way to do it. In coffee shop, author is standing with back to customers, point-and-shoot SIG 9mm in unsecured open-top holster, arms folded. Open to a gun snatch? *Ya think?*

Open carrying in a Starbucks, Ayoob keeps his gun side toward the counter, a reasonably secure posture.

holster almost disappear against black clothing.

Some years ago, in North Carolina, I arrived to teach a deadly force class and was told that, cop or not – even though I was officially on police business and teaching in a police academy setting – I could not carry concealed as an out-of-state policeman unless I was extraditing a felon. I asked about non-resident carry permits or permit reciprocity: no dice. I asked if there were any avenues at all. "Sure," said one indigenous cop, "just carry it exposed in the holster. We have 'open carry' here."

I do not care for the "frighten the horses" effect of open carry. However, I also do not care to be unarmed and, therefore, all but helpless against the armed. Suddenly, open carry was looking more attractive. In fact, I took to it like a duck to water. (Well, maybe like a reluctant duck that didn't like water very much.)

The handgun I was carrying that week was a blue steel Colt Python 357 Magnum revolver, with black Pachmayr grips. I wore it most of the time in an inside-the-waistband holster I had designed for Mitch Rosen, the Ayoob Rear Guard (ARG). Even with most of the mass of the weapon obscured from view by the inside-the-waistband design, the weapon was clearly visible against the royal blue trainers' shirt generally worn by my school's staff.

While on that trip, I had to do a film for a trial that showed how rapidly a certain suspect could have disarmed and shot the officer who had been forced to kill him to keep that from happening. On the day of the filming, I happened to be wearing a black polo shirt and black BDU pants. A photographer was taking stills while the cinematographer was shooting the video.

Later, in court, I had occasion to closely examine not only the videotape, but also the giant blow-ups of the stills that were introduced as evidence. A couple of people in the courtroom told me that they'd hadn't realized that I was armed, even though the big 41-framed revolver was toward the cameras and in plain sight. I asked a few other folks, showing them the pictures, and most when subsequently asked hadn't noticed that I was wearing the big six-gun.

Hmmm…interesting.

I thereafter made it a point to bring black or very dark gray gun, holster, shirts, and trousers whenever it looked as if I would have to "open carry." The gorgeous, high polish Royal Blue of the Python had not reflected enough to show up in the pictures or the video, but that was only because the ARG holster hadn't exposed much of its sideplate. Later experience with flat black Glock pistols, and a Kimber with a flat gray/black finish that resembles Parkerizing, showed me that these finishes blended beautifully with black holsters and belts, and black clothing.

The holstered guns were still in plain sight. They

could be spotted by someone looking for them. But they did not draw the eye.

One evening I found myself stopping on the way home from the range at a supermarket that must have had a hundred people in it. I was open-carrying the dark Kimber 45 cocked and locked in a black basketweave Gordon Davis thumb-break holster on a matching Bianchi dress gun belt, with black polo and black BDUs. The old "one of a hundred people will notice" prediction absolutely came true. The only person who showed indication of having spotted the big military auto pistol was a little girl, and that was probably because she was only a couple of feet away from me in the aisle, and her height put her at eye level to the gun.

I saw the little tyke's eyes widen in alarm, and watched as she urgently grabbed her dad's sleeve and began tugging. When he looked down, she wordlessly but vigorously pointed at the 45. I had made a point to wear my police badge clipped in front of the scabbard, and her dad spotted it at the same time he saw the pistol.

"Aw, it's OK, honey," I heard him tell her gently. "He's a *po*-lice."

So far, so good. There are some dads out there who might be macho enough to feel a need to impress their kids if those kids were alarmed by what the father perceived as an ostentatious display of a deadly weapon. In this case, there was no problem. And the lesson is, black gun in black holster against black clothing draws very little attention from those who *aren't* at eye level with the handgun.

As noted earlier, an inside the-waistband holster buries much of the gun in the lower body's clothing. The gun is still exposed *per se*, and therefore still openly carried. In a jurisdiction where the given person is legal to carry openly but not concealed, that's an important distinction to bear in mind.

In theory, one could resort to genuine camouflage. Several manufacturers have produced pistols and revolvers with camouflage finishes, including recognized patterns such as Woodland. I've often wondered about getting one of those, and a matching camo set of belt and fabric holster, and wearing it outside pants and shirt in the same camo pattern. Would it conceal as well as black on black on black on black? Probably. Maybe better.

I haven't tried it yet. The reason is, while a camouflage thing is going with the black on black, the color black is not considered camouflage per se. A regular camouflage pattern most certainly would be. One definition of "camouflage" is "concealment." If a camo gun was openly carried in a camo holster against camo clothing, all matching, could a creative anti-gun prosecutor convince a grand jury to indict for concealed carry, if the latter was against the law in that time and place? Almost certainly.

Now, whether that case would be decided against the armed citizen at trial would be something else again. It would make a fascinating test case. Since my mother did not raise me to be a test case, I've never undertaken the experiment to find out. If y'all want

to do so, feel free, and let me know in care of the publisher how it worked for you. However, neither the publisher nor I will take any responsibility for what happens. And, yes, my tongue is *slightly* in my cheek as I write this…

The Security Factor

Will criminals attack an obviously armed person just to get his gun? Sure. It has happened. I know a guy who was a young cop out West who was walking foot patrol when the lights suddenly went out. He groggily regained consciousness to discover that he had a massive headache and an empty holster. A two-by-four was lying nearby. The department determined that an unknown, never-caught malefactor had come up behind the officer stealthily, smashed him in the back of the head with a board, and taken his custom Smith & Wesson and sauntered away from the cop's unconscious form. The officer recovered from the blow, and his assailant did not choose to execute him as he lay helpless. He was lucky. And he knows it.

"Gosh, look at the tall buildings." At a friend's request, Ayoob open carries in Phoenix area. SIG-Sauer pistol is at right hip. Black clothing, belt and holster make black gun less conspicuous. Note that forearm remains near pistol to forestall snatch attempt.

More recently – this past winter, as I write this in the summer of 2007 – a perpetrator in New York City decided the best way to pay off his debts was to commit a string of robberies, and he determined he'd need a gun for that. Where to get a gun? He came up behind a uniformed rookie cop and smashed him in the head with a baseball bat. When the cop fell to the pavement, his attacker beat him about the head some more with the bat, then managed to get his 16-shot 9mm out of the duty holster. The suspect was captured shortly thereafter by other officers, and he confessed, which is how we know not only what he did, but why. The officer was seriously injured and possibly permanently impaired when last heard from.

So, yes, there have indeed been cases of people who attacked those visibly carrying guns for no other purpose than to get the guns. In is not an everyday thing, but it is something to worry about. The private citizen around other people unknown to him, with an exposed gun clearly visible, runs the same risk.

"Out of Sight, Out of Mind": A Two-Way Street

Concealed carry advocates are often heard to say, "Concealed means concealed! If they don't know it's there, they can't grab it away from you!"

I'm afraid it isn't quite so simple.

First, *the assailant may know where your concealed gun is before the assault begins.* This can come about in any of several ways.

Perhaps the assailant *knows you carry a gun, and even knows where you carry it.* This in turn can come from several directions. The attacker could be an estranged former significant other. He could be the disgruntled former employee you had to fire, and he hates you for it and wants revenge. He might be your son-in-law, whom you found out was abusing your daughter and who has seen you with a gun and wants to hurt *you* to punish *her.*

Perhaps the attacker is a stranger, who didn't decide to attack you until your concealed handgun inadvertently became exposed, and he saw it. In many areas, a $500 handgun is worth $1,000 on the black market. Guns and prescription drugs are about the only two things crooks can steal from you and re-sell for more than their intrinsic value, instead of fencing for dimes on the dollars. Did you or a friend ever unintentionally expose a concealed handgun to one another? If that happens in front of the wrong person, you could be targeted in a disarming attempt.

And perhaps the gun becomes visible or palpable in the course of a fight that has not yet reached deadly force proportions. Watch armed men in plainclothes punching or grabbing each other, and you'll see coats sweeping back, shirts being pulled loose, pants cuffs coming up...things that will expose hip holsters, shoulder holsters, and ankle holsters. A common wrestling maneuver in a streetfight is to grab the other man around the waist with your arms. If the antagonist does that to you, he'll almost certainly feel your holstered gun, and now the struggle for your weapon is on.

There is also the absolute fact that in concealed handgun carry, *"out of sight, out of mind" goes in both directions.* That is, the person who is perhaps falsely confident that no one will spot his gun, is less motivated to be alert to a grab for that gun.

I guess what I'm saying here is that, concealed *or* open carry, recognizing beforehand that you might experience a gun-snatch attempt is a wise thing. It follows that it is equally wise to plan ahead to defeat that attempted gun grab.

Proven Retention Strategies

Handgun retention is the corollary science to handgun disarming, and it encompasses both a hardware side and a software side. Let's look at the hardware first.

Security holsters have been available for some time that will ride on a conventional dress gun belt and don't require a police officer's or security guard's big, heavy utility belt. The most popular of the breed these days seems to be the Blackhawk SERPA. This synthetic rig has a discreet trigger-finger panel that is biomechanically natural for the wearer's draw angle, but not for the hand of an unauthorized person coming in on it from an angle other than straight above...and your own gun arm and shoulder are blocking his access to that particular angle. I know a lot of cops are now wearing the SERPA when they do open carry in plainclothes on investigative duties, or in the not-readily-recognizable permutations of the various "administrative uniforms."

Strong Holster Company has long made their Piece-Keeper, which uses a special thumb-break design to require a double release movement before the draw can begin. Bianchi has a wide line of holsters with "level two" retention. Safariland has produced a whole series of holsters with hidden releases, or niche locks that require the gun to be pulled in a certain specific direction before it will come out. All have great promise for low-profile open carry, and for that matter, these holsters are concealable.

I would strongly recommend a thumb-break safety strap as a bare minimum of security for anyone openly carrying a loaded handgun in public.

Mechanical safeties are another good thing in these circumstances. History has shown us again and again – with cops, armed citizens, and security professionals alike – that when a bad guy gets a gun away from a good guy and tries to shoot him with it, he often takes several seconds to figure out how to make the gun work. Those seconds have often been the difference between life and death.

Unless you're a show-off screaming silently for attention, you want as few people as possible to notice the exposed handgun.

Are these hardware fixes desirable even for those trained in handgun retention? Yes. When my older daughter briefly open-carried in Arizona, she had an on-safe Beretta 92 in a Strong Piece-Keeper holster, and appreciated the peace of mind that combination gave her. (She also quickly grew tired of people staring at her, pointing, and mouthing "The little girl has a gun!") My kids learned handgun retention early – this daughter was the youngest instructor ever certified to teach the Lindell Handgun Retention System by the National Law Enforcement Training Center – but remember the cops I mentioned earlier who were cold-cocked before they had a chance to defend their guns. For situations like that, hardware that is "proprietary to the user" can be a lifesaver.

The *software* fix is every bit as important. When I first discovered I had to carry open or not at all in North Carolina, I was carrying a point-and-pull revolver in an open top holster. I was damn glad that I was an instructor of long standing in Lindell weapon retention. The same was true more recently, when I posed for some photos walking around the greater Phoenix area open-carrying a rig I had intended to carry concealed: a point-and-shoot SIG P226 in an open top LFI Concealment Rig by Ted Blocker. Since the gun-grab may come after you've already drawn and off-safed, being able to successfully grapple with the grabber and peel him off the gun is an essential skill in any case.

Bottom Line

Some carry openly to make a statement about gun owners' civil rights. I can sympathize with that. Some few do so to make a spectacle of themselves. No sympathy here. Either will experience the word "make" in another context: they will be "made" as someone carrying a deadly weapon in public.

The more the gun can "hide in plain sight" through discreet selection of the color of gun finish, stocks, holster, and surrounding clothing, the less trouble the exposed handgun will cause instead of quell.

The more difficult the gun is for an unauthorized user to get out of its holster, and the more difficult it is for an unauthorized person who gains control of it to activate, the better. These are not just political correctness issues. When you look at the number of people who have been killed with their own or their partners' weapons in the history of law enforcement and professional security, you can see just how significant the risk is that we are talking about. Only a fool would ignore it.

Open carry may not be this writer's choice, but for many of our brothers and sisters, it is the only legal way they can be armed in public to protect themselves and their loved ones. Whether or not we choose to

Safariland 0701 is an excellent, and concealable, security holster. It works on a similar principle to same company's famous SS-III snatch resistant duty holster...

...and delivers "Level II security," meaning it requires two movements before this Glock 17 can start out of the holster.

exercise it, we want to keep the right of open carry. The above advice is offered in the hope of doing so with maximum safety for ourselves and others.

WARDROBE FACTORS

The clothing you wear is obviously going to be critical to discretion and comfort when you are carrying a concealed weapon. It's all a little more subtle than "big coats hide more hardware easier than small coats."

First, it's a given that "concealed means concealed." If only 5 percent of the gun is exposed, does that mean it's 95 percent

Jack Webb, shown here checking his Colt Detective Special on an old *Dragnet*, set more fashion trends for CCW people than he probably ever knew.

concealed? No, it means that if someone can see that you're carrying a gun, even if only a small portion of the gun – or the gun's distinctive outline – is visible, the gun is 100 percent "exposed" and 0 percent concealed.

Here are a few random tips from 47 years of carrying a concealed handgun…

Jackets

Learn from LAPD. I hate to keep invoking Hollywood, but get some of the old videos of Jack Webb's *Dragnet* series. You'll note that most of the time, he's wearing black slacks and a tweed sport coat. In the old days of poorly dyed holsters, black dye would wear off the leather and stain the trousers. It didn't show up on black cloth. The solid "hang" of relatively heavy tweed tended not to outline a holstered handgun, and its patterned appearance tended to break up "printing" outlines of a gun beneath the fabric. We see a similar effect with untucked Hawaiian print shirts, checkered garments, etc. Unlike a typical shirt, a tweed or corduroy sport coat has enough substance to its material to often mask the strapping of a shoulder rig's harness, too.

With more casual jackets, something like a plaid hunter's coat works great. The black and red checks catch the eye, and divert attention from gun-shaped bulges.

You don't need James Bond's or Mike Hammer's tailor to conceal your firearm.

Simply get the suitcoat or sport coat slightly larger, i.e, size 44 if you normally wear a size 42. You will get just enough more "drape" to cover a good-size fighting pistol. You will appear to have gained a few pounds through the torso, but won't look like a little boy wearing his daddy's clothing. *This is true of any gun-concealing outer garment, not just sport jackets or suit coats.*

Leave the front of the suit coat or sport coat unfastened as much as possible. This will give a natural, concealing drape to the garment, and will allow the fastest access. With the garment closed in front, you'll have to open it (or pull it up, difficult if not impossible in a garment whose hem falls as low as a sport coat's). If the garment is fastened, fabric is pulled tightly over the gun and tends to outline it, in addition to the slower draw.

Outside pockets of sport jackets and suit coats are a lousy choice for pocket guns. They tend to bulge and sag obviously. Inside breast pockets are a little better, but they will constantly be bumping against your chest and will probably work best in that location with pocket holsters.

Depending on your generation and locale, the term "windbreaker"

Author, (left, his Glock invisible in belly-band under tucked shirt), chats with Scott Jordan at SHOT Show about the Scott-E-Vest.

Scott Jordan demonstrates his hi-tech windbreaker. It looks ordinary…

...until you discover the myriad of built-in pockets for electronic whiz-bangs, many sized just right for guns and related gear, all discreetly hidden from view...

can describe two different garments. The short "Eisenhower" jacket and the heavier "bomber jacket" are less than ideal choices for gun concealment because they are generally cut to stop at the waist or just below, which increases the chance of a hip holster becoming exposed. These styles also tend to have elastic bottom hems, which are contraindicated if you have a gun on or in your belt because the elastic feature pulls the fabric in on the gun and outlines it rather than hiding it.

Nylon jackets of the style known in some places as "warmup jackets" are better, because being "hip length" garments their bottom edges fall much lower, affording better gun concealment.

With any jacket that can close top to bottom, you want to make sure that the bottom portion can be unfastened while the top part remains closed. On a chilly day, when comfort (and sometimes, avoidance of pneumonia!) demands that the chest be covered, you want to be able to get the area below the stomach

...and even a solar panel that folds down in back, for "green" techno-pistol-packers!

to clear so you can reach a gun at your strong side hip. If the coat is zipper front, you want two-way zipper design that can let you unzip the belly part beforehand so you get at that hip holster. If the garment is button front, all the better; button over the chest, but leave everything from the lower edge of the rib cage down unbuttoned.

Nylon windbreakers tend to be "straight cut" and therefore have a straight-down natural drape that conceals large handguns very well. *Caution:* Many such windbreakers will have a drawstring at the bottom. *Remove it!* The loose end of the drawstring can find its way into the trigger guard as you re-holster, setting the stage for an accidental discharge! Don't just tie a knot in the end. Don't just shorten it. *Remove the drawstring!*

Photographer's Vests

Later in this chapter, we'll discuss garments specifically designed for concealing guns. Right now, let's touch on the common fisherman's vest or photographer's vest.

These hit the pistol-packer's fashion mainstream in the 1980s. Light and comfortable depending on material and cut, they give more freedom of movement for things like fist-fighting or shooting from an Isosceles stance than any regular jacket, since they generally don't bind at the shoulders when the arms extend.

Watch out for many of the true lightweight vests, which have mesh on the back and sides for comfort. The gun and holster can become visible through the mesh. They're probably not ideal for shoulder

The tighter your clothes fit, the more snug to the body you need to carry the gun. This is author's full-size SIG P226, in IWB LFI Concealment Rig.

Size of gun vis-à-vis type of clothing help dictate holster choice. Pistol is full-size Dave Lauck 1911 45 with light rail. Holster options are, from left: Kydex OWB for looser-fitting outer garments; Leather Arsenal Quad Concealment with ITB capability for tighter fitting clothes; and Secret Squirrel IWB for when clothing is even "lighter and tighter."

and her bodyguards, who are wearing a uniform that includes a vest that looks remarkably like the ones under discussion, are fighting a losing battle against the Storm Troopers of the evil Empire led by Darth Vader. When the last vest-wearing good guy is shot on sight by the Storm Troopers with ray guns, the princess is captured.

But that "happened long, long ago, on a planet far, far away…"

Vests, like other garments, should be purchased at least one size large, and side vents are to be avoided. Make sure they go down far enough to conceal a hip holstered gun: a surprising number of these, especially the cheap ones, are cut to waist length rather than hip-length.

Shirts

Tucked-in shirts, such as dress shirts, should not be tightly tapered and form-fitting if you're carrying a gun. Even if

holsters, either, since the harness straps can become visible at the armhole of any sleeveless vest. I only know one top gun guy who ever wears a shoulder holster with just a vest, and with a badge and ID card in one pocket, he's not particularly concerned about concealment anyway.

There is a very popular belief in the "gun culture" that because so many of our kind wear these vests, they have become a mark of the gun carrier. Some call them "shoot me first" vests.

I dunno about that. I've been wearing them for more than twenty years, and never had that sort of problem. I've seen them worn (and sold!) in airports. The many pockets and high comfort factor make them great "traveling vests." You'll see them all over the place at Disney World and other "gun-free zones."

I've never heard of a documented case of a "shot him first" case in which a good guy was shot by surprise by a bad guy who "made him" as such. The only such case I've ever seen was fictional.

Remember the first Star Wars movie? Princess Leia

Floral print sport shirts, if they aren't too loud for your taste, are great for concealing guns.

your gun is concealed by an outer garment instead of a holster, a too-tight shirt can bind the upper body and restrict your range of movement if you're fighting for your life … and if you don't see yourself ever fighting for your life, why do you carry a gun in the first place?

If the tucked-in shirt is going to conceal a handgun in a Kramer undershirt, a belly-band, or a "tuckable" holster, it needs to be loose fitting and kind of "blousy" at the appropriate areas, i.e., the shoulder/ armpit region if the gun is there, or at the waist if the gun is at belt level. You want an *opaque* shirt, such as an Oxford fabric. Pinstripes will help break up the outline.

If you carry in a belly-band or tuckable, one of the fastest locations is front cross-draw. Without pulling the shirt loose, you can knife the hand right in there with the movement martial artists call a "spear hand." This generally means leaving the second button above the belt unfastened. A necktie will generally cover this minor breach of style etiquette and let you off with only a warning from the Fashion Police. If you're serious about it, sew that button to the outside and secure that part of the shirtfront opening with a bit of Velcro. However, be advised that the ripping sound will alert people, and may prevent a surreptitious draw or low-profile hand-on-gun state of readiness.

If you decide to carry under an *un-*tucked shirt, concealed carry life just got a whole lot easier for you. Again, whether the shirt is tee or polo or button-front style, get it about one size larger than normal. This is partly to give you more concealing "drape" at the beltline, and partly to give the hem of the garment more range of movement to come up when you have to clear it out of the way to make the draw. A fabric with some stretch to it is a bonus; you want to be able to pull it up high enough to clear the gun. Not just above the butt of the holstered pistol, but high enough for the gun to come up and out and on target without being impeded.

Floral print sport shirts, if they aren't too loud for your taste, are great for concealing guns. Their patterns break up the underlying outlines. Mike Venturino and Roy Huntington at *American Handgunner* magazine have, almost jokingly, raised the profile of this sort of garment among serious CCW folks.

If the untucked shirt has a button front, you want the area of the lowest button to be unfastened. Some such shirts come that way: the Woolrich Elite line offers one. The ancient but still popular *guyebarra* shirt comes that way, perhaps a heritage from a culture where it was common for men to carry pistols in their waistbands. Old style American bowling shirts can still be had that are cut in the same way, with a straight bottom and a generous drape, and sometimes without the lower button and buttonhole in the usual place. Intended to allow range of bending and arm movement for bowling, they turn out to be great for pistol-packing.

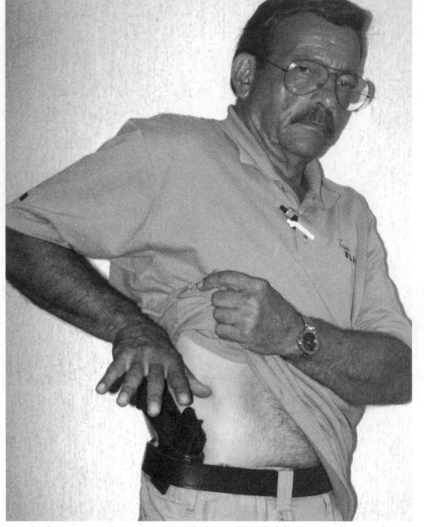

A polo shirt one size large gives enough drape to cover full-size SIG duty pistol in IWB holster, here an LFI Concealment Rig inside a Safariland Velcro belt. Clothing is by Woolrich Elite, on whose factory competition shooting squad, Team Elite, Ayoob shot in 2007.

Pants

If you're carrying inside the waistband, get the trousers two inches larger in the waistband than your actual waist measurement. As discussed elsewhere in this book, doing this adds greatly to your comfort. It also "keeps you honest" by encouraging you to always wear your gun, if only to keep your pants from feeling as if they're about to fall down.

When buying any sort of pants, make sure the belt loops are "gun compatible."

The loops need to be large enough to allow a substantial gun belt, and in appropriate positions to allow the holster to ride exactly where you want it. You'll want the dress gun belt to be a minimum of an inch and a half wide, and loops that will take an inch and three-quarter belt are a plus.

With any sort of belt holster, make sure the belt is wide enough, and fastened snugly enough. Otherwise, the holster will sag downward and the gun butt will tilt outward, severely compromising discreet concealment.

*If you're going to carry inside the waistband, make sure there's room for you **and** the gun and holster, and perhaps a spare magazine pouch, too.* As a rule of thumb, you want the pants two inches wider in the waist than you would normally wear them without a gun in your waistband.

No matter what the men's fashion magazines may say, side vent suit coats and sport coats are permanently "out of style" for those who carry in hip holsters. The gun butt will work its way through the vent and expose itself. A middle of the back holster will do the same with a center vent.

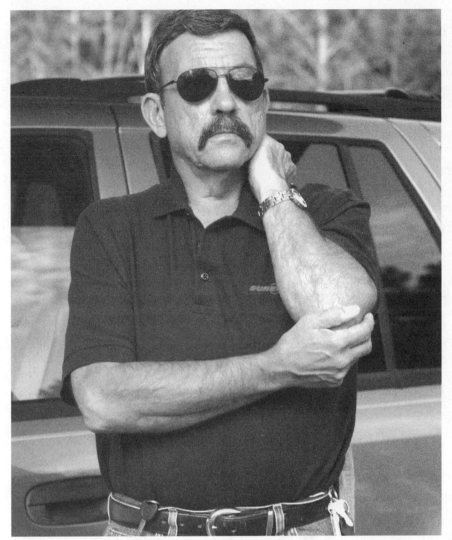

Weapon placement helps you interface with clothing options. Full size Beretta 92 and spare magazine are invisible behind author's hips, but to conceal from sides and rear, he'll need to don that vest he's holding over his shoulder.

Black pants stain less. Again, flash back to those *Dragnet* reruns and notice how often Jack Webb's "Sergeant Friday" is wearing black pants. In the old days, poorly dyed leather "bled" its coloring onto clothing, especially when people got hot and sweaty. Gun oil can drain out from the muzzle end and stain the garment. Black shows it less.

Today's holsters may not "bleed" (the good ones, anyway), but they can still seep gun oil. A big concern is the skeletal Yaqui Slide design. If you've been shooting, each time the gun goes into the holster, carbon on the barrel or slide can transfer onto the trouser fabric. Since that stuff is black, it'll show up less on black pants.

If you might be wearing an ankle holster, you want straight leg cuffs at the very least, and no tapered leg or pegged bottom styles. In jeans or cords, "boot cut" is the minimum that will give you access, and "flared cuffs" are better. Standard American cut men's suit pants and police uniform pants will have the proper cut, and BDU/"cargo" pants also generally have cuffs of sufficiently generous size and shape to work well with an ankle holster.

The pockets of the trousers want to be deep, and made of strong material. A seamstress or clothing store can access replacement pockets made of a heavy fabric called "cotton drill," designed for uniform and work pants. Good quality BDUs (cargo pants) will have these already. You don't need to sew in the canvas and leather pockets that were "custom gun wear" for the gunfighters of long ago. When you are looking at the pants at the clothing store, insert your hand into the front pants pocket with the fingers extended, until the fingertips hit bottom on the pocket. The opening of the pocket should now be up just a little past your wrist. If they pass this test, they're deep enough to properly conceal a snub-nose revolver or a small autoloader in a pocket holster without any of the gun showing.

Pleated casual dress pants of the style popularized by Dockers are "in" at this writing. They drape enough in the thighs that they're ideal for pocket carry, and the cuffs seem to be amenable to ankle holsters as well.

In conventional brands, Carharrt and Wrangler have very strong adherents. The latter company makes "work casual" pants with leather-reinforced pockets that work beautifully with tactical folding knives designed like Sal Glesser's pioneering Spyderco Clipit. Some gun owners prefer not to purchase Dockers or Levis on the grounds that the manufacturers are anti-gun. If that's the case, any designs they have that you like are almost certainly replicated in someone else's product line.

Gun-Specific Clothing

On the October day in 1881 when the Earp faction met the Clantons near the OK Corral, Wyatt Earp put his long-barrel Colt revolver in his coat pocket with his hand on it. It helped him to be among the first to get his weapon into action at the historic "Gunfight at the OK Corral." The mackinaw-style denim coat had just arrived, on special order. Earp had specified an extra-deep, heavy pocket that could discreetly contain a large revolver.

John Wesley Hardin, believed by some to have been the deadliest gunfighter of the Old Frontier, liked to wear a vest he had designed (and possibly made) himself. It had leather gun pockets rib-cage-high on either side, with revolver butts facing forward. It was not a concealment vest; rather, he concealed the vest and the twin revolvers under a coat.

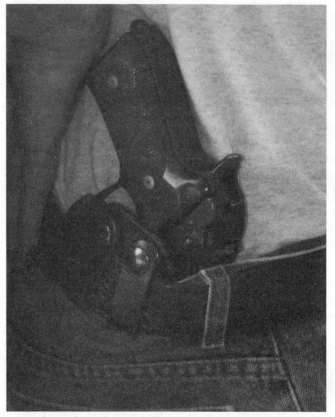

By angling Milt Sparks IWB holster to put butt of Beretta 92G pointing distinctly upward, wearer makes it easier for clothing to cover the pistol discreetly.

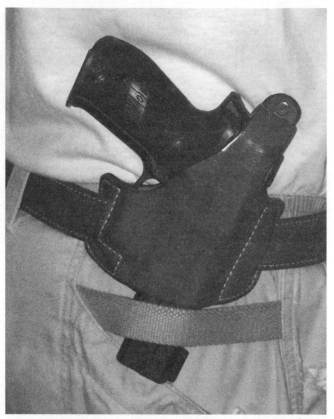

Holster stabilizer strap on 5.11's hugely and deservedly popular BDUs, seen here applied to thumb-break belt-slide by Ted Blocker that holds SIG P226R.

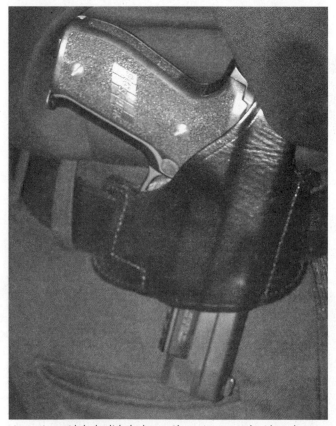

A caution with belt-slide holsters: if gun is covered with carbon from a long session at the range, some of the black crud may wipe off onto your pants.

CCW-ers often carry tactical folding knives with pocket clips as well. These Wrangler jeans have special leather-reinforced pockets for just such practices. Most regular pants quickly get frayed at this spot from the knife clips.

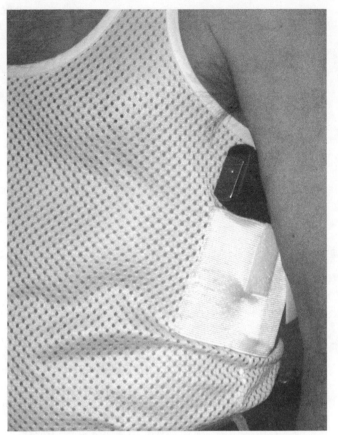

Yes, CCW people have their own special underwear. This undershirt by Greg Kramer, the Confidante, has holster pocket for small handgun sewn in under each armpit. This one holds 9mm Kahr PM9 lightweight subcompact for shoulder holster-like draw through concealing dress shirt.

Yes, clothing expressly designed for gun concealment goes back a long way. Today, it's a small but fascinating cottage industry…and, apparently, a growing one.

Concealed Carry Clothiers has an excellent line that includes models with pockets lined with a semi-stiff synthetic, to hold a small handgun. My favorite in the line is the Tropical, which feels as close as you're going to get to wearing no outer garment at all. This line also offers vests that aren't festooned with pockets, which is much more to some folks tastes than the "tactical" look of a many-pocketed vest.

5.11, with their line formerly known as Royal Robbins, really kicked off the tactical vest market. Their vests are expressly designed for carrying heavy equipment such as radios, guns, and spare ammunition. (For ordinary folks, the elasticized vertical pouches at the rear are perfect for holding water bottles.) The only flaw I can find with them (since they offered a lighter one than their original, which was too heavy for warm weather wear) is that the snap-flap on the inside, designed to hold a gun-carrying system, can catch on the butt of a handgun carried in a belt holster, and slow the draw. If that's a problem, just cut it away and you're good to go. They pioneered the front thigh level pockets that are great for spare magazines and cell phones, and they're no longer on the wrong side. I'm not sold on the band over the rear pocket that's supposed to help stabilize a holster, but they popularized the brilliant concept of deep hip pockets with a diagonal slash that lets the hand get past the holster and into that pocket for one's handkerchief or whatever.

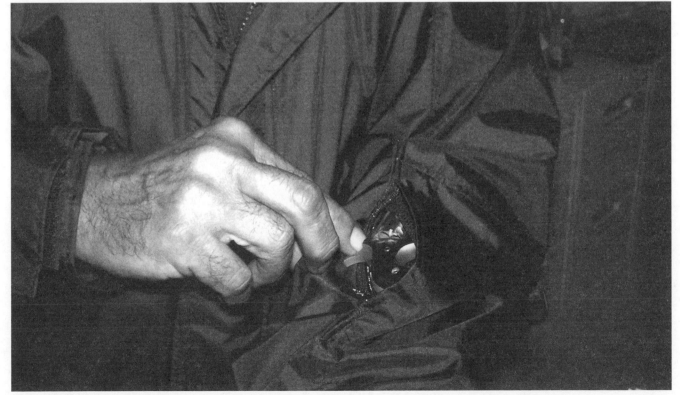

"Got something up your sleeve?" Actually, yes. If you'll look carefully, the tiny sleeve pocket on Scott-E jacket…

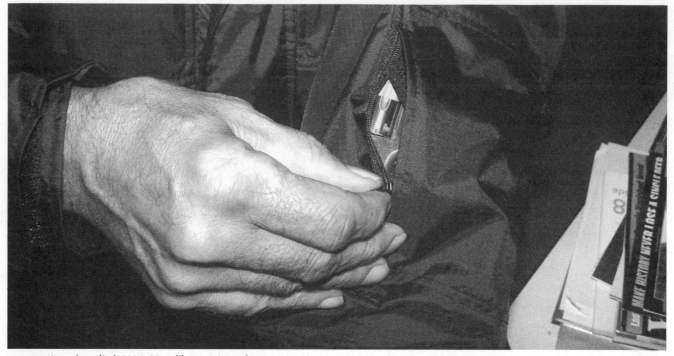

… contains a last-ditch NAA 22-caliber mini-revolver.

EoTac is captained by firearms/ammo industry veteran Fernando Coelho, who brought in a top beta-testing team of real world professionals to help with design. The result is a superb line of pants, shirts, and trousers for those who go armed. The pants can be had in BDU style (one version of which has tiny outer pockets at ankle level, which Velcro shut and can more or less comfortably carry a Kel-Tec 32), or in a Docker's style casual dress pant. Elastic judiciously applied at the waist helps allow for IWB holsters, and the belt loops are well placed. I've found Coelho's weatherproofing superior, with rainwater beading up on the outer surface of the fabric, but with no discomfort that we normally associate with "non-breathing" waterproof clothing. The shirts are comfortable, heavy duty, and sport useful hidden pockets. The casual dress shirt, mentioned above, has a Velcro attachment at the bottom of its buttoned front and just the right amount of clearance for drawing from a hip holster.

If jeans are more to your taste, Blackie Collins designed a neat pair. They're called Toters. Each front pocket is actually two pockets, and reinforced for carrying guns therein. The waist is generously cut for IWB holsters, and the cuffs are just right for ankle rigs. I've worn out two pair, not because they aren't sturdy, but because I found myself wearing them that much. They come with knife pockets, too; Blackie Collins is first and foremost a knife designer.

SIG-Tac has a very good series of "designer gun wear," too. If you carry a long barrel pistol on the hip, the SIG-Tac vest is a great way to go: it's longer than most, and therefore gives such a combination the best possible "coverage."

Scott-E-Vest makes a high-speed, low-drag, way-cool series of garments that he designed originally for "techies." There are pockets for the PDA, the iPod, the cell phone, you name it…tubes for electronics and hidden radios and BlueTooths…and even a fold-out solar back panel that gathers energy for your batteries. While not designed expressly for pistol packers, this line has ingenious hidden pockets that folks in the CCW lifestyle can make use of. Inventor Scott Jordan has some high quality chino-style dress slacks with double hidden pockets similar to the Toters, but in higher style. Magnetic closures hold the "secret pocket" shut, while the parallel pocket beneath it is conventionally open. Material is excellent, and the pocket lining works fine with small handguns in pocket holsters. One of his jackets even comes with a hidden sleeve pouch that's just the right size for an NAA mini-revolver.

Blackhawk also has a new line of tactical wear. I haven't had a chance to work with it much, but it's promising, and the company certainly has both the financial and the human resources to run with the best in the business on this kind of stuff.

Dang…we've got our own boutique wear for pistol packers. The CCW culture has come a *long* way!

> **D**ang…we've got our own boutique wear for pistol packers. The CCW culture has come a *long* way!

IDPA:
HOW IT HELPS THE CONCEALED CARRY PRACTITIONER

In IDPA, you get a chance to watch the best in action, and try to beat them. Here the legendary Jerry Miculek draws his S&W 45 revolver in a blur as he bolts from seated start position en route to winning 2006 IDPA National Championships, Enhanced Service Revolver division.

Founded in 1996, the International Defensive Pistol Association (IDPA) was created so those who carried conventional, concealed handguns would have a venue for testing their skills in deploying them. Its founders were all distinguished alumni of the International Practical Shooting Confederation (IPSC) and members in good standing of that organization's arm in the United States, the U.S. Practical Shooting Association (USPSA).

As in real life, IDPA sometimes gives you targets that are "down but not out." Ken Ortbach "finishes the fight" with flame blooming from his S&W Model 686 4-inch 357 as he wins the 2007 Pennsylvania State Championship, Stock Service Revolver division.

You won't find props this elaborate on your backyard range. At 2006 Nationals, Terri Strayer shoots around an overturned automobile.

Automobiles figure in street gunfights, so they figure in IDPA. Author moves out of path of car as he fires at "armed occupant," using his department-issue Ruger 45 and Safariland security holster, and then…

… in another stage, has to fire from inside the car outward. Note flying glass as 45 slugs smash through rear window. Photos taken at 2007 Pennsylvania State Championships.

In this stage at the 2007 Florida State Championship, Jon Strayer has to fire from elaborately constructed "rocking boat." Weapon is S&W 625 45 ACP, backed with moon clips and Blade-Tech holster. Jon won ESR Champion title.

Forgive all of that alphabet soup, but it helps to know the background. The late, great Jeff Cooper laid the groundwork for IPSC with the open gunfight simulation competition he and his colleagues pioneered in California in the mid-1950s, and Jeff was the prime mover in the creation of IPSC some twenty years later. IPSC started with "street guns" in "street holsters," but because rules were left open to encourage innovation, competitive enthusiasm took over. Soon the gun it took to win a match was a huge pistol with a widened magazine chute big enough to be a flower-pot, an optical sight on top, exotic recoil compensation devices that might blind the shooter if fired from a retention position in real world self-defense, and a pure speed holster so huge it would take Count Dracula's Cape to conceal it.

USPSA eventually caught onto that, and now has competition categories that allow ordinary stock firearms to compete effectively, though concealment is still not required. However, IDPA struck a responsive chord when founded by Bill Wilson and a board that included street-smart Walt Rauch, renowned combat handgun expert Ken Hackathorn, and some other knowledgeable authorities. It remains one of the most popular and fastest-growing handgun games in the country today.

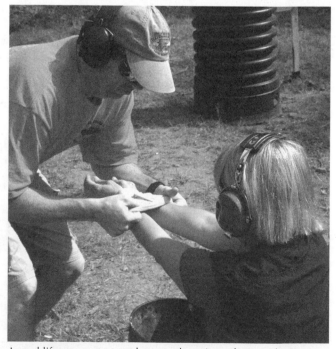

In real life, access to guns has saved captives of criminals. Here, range officer binds hands of FL/GA Regional Woman IDPA Champion Gail Pepin with heavy elastic…

In IDPA as in real life, one hand is often encumbered. Norm Ambrozy fires his S&W M&P 9mm one-handed while maintaining control of "attaché case with priceless contents" with other hand, at 2007 Florida State Championships.

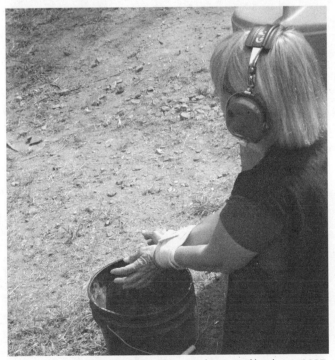

...and she awaits start signal with gun at bottom of bucket at 2007 New England Regional Championships ...

...and on signal, retrieves her 9mm Glock 34 and engages her "armed captors" with her hands still literally bound.

Like real life, IDPA forces you to shoot from less than ideal positions. Here former national champ Tom Yost has to take one foot completely off the ground to get a shot at his last "opponent" at New England Regional Championships, 2007.

IDPA often has night stages. Here, light beam and gun flame combine as author shoots a darkness stage, defending his New England Regional Stock Service Revolver Champion title in 2007. He lost to Jerry Biggs.

IDPA In Context

IDPA's founders and directors are clear on their purpose. *IDPA is a sport and a skill test, not a training course!* Certainly, you can learn from it. But, really, any skill test should be a learning experience.

Understand that you are not necessarily there to be the next national champion. Those titles have been held by some of the greatest combat handgunners in history: Ernest Langdon, Rob Leatham, Jerry Miculek, Dave Sevigny, Scott Warren, and more. As in most competitions, the majority of entrants are going for a personal goal. Perhaps a personal best, perhaps a trophy in their particular class.

Shooting classifications start at Unclassified and go through Novice, Marksman, Sharpshooter, and Expert, all the way up to Master. While IDPA's shooting *classifications* are performance-driven, the organization's shooting *categories* are determined by the type of gun used. It was understood at the beginning that it would not be a level playing field if Competitor A used a 6-shot revolver against Competitor B with an 18-shot Glock 17 on an 18-shot course of fire, even if both contestants were identical in skill. Because IDPA was created during the period of the onerous Clinton Crime Bill that banned manufacture and sale to civilians of magazines of greater than ten-round capacity, this was established as the uppermost limit for auto pistols. That rule remains in force, not to endorse the Clinton concept by any means, but simply to maintain the level playing field that is essential in any sport.

There were once four handgun categories, and for the last few years IDPA has had five, and arguably a sixth. Those categories are as follows, and they pretty much cover anything you're likely to be using in self-defense in the real world.

Stock Service Pistol (SSP). This is the most popular category in the game by far, and has been since IDPA's inception. It encompasses double action semiautomatics of the traditional style, double action only autos, and the Safe Action Glock, which is the single most popular brand in the category. Calibers may be 9mm Parabellum and up.

Custom Defense Pistol (CDP). This is the home of the classic Cooper gun, the single action, cocked and locked 45 auto. Maximum magazine capacity allowed is eight rounds. A minimum power floor of performance is required that is roughly equivalent to 45 ACP hardball. Shooters with single stack, double-action 45 autos often

compete against the single actions in CDP because in SSP, an eleven-shot stage may require them to reload but not the contestant with an 11-shot pistol.

Enhanced Service Pistol (ESP). This category is for single action auto pistols, caliber 9mm and larger. Originally intended for the classic Browning Hi-Power, it tends to be dominated by 9mm, 38 Super, and 40 S&W guns in the 1911 format. It is also the home of the popular Springfield Armory XD, determined by

Like real life, IDPA can get complicated. Here, author jumps off-line from no-shoot target and reaches for GP100 in Blade-tech holster as two radio-controlled, knife-armed targets, visible at right, begin to race forward, ducking sideways on curving rails, at 2006 National Championships.

BATF to be a single-action semiautomatic. No more than 10 rounds per magazine, and no more than 11 rounds in the gun to start.

Stock Service Revolver (SSR). Minimum 38 Special caliber, maximum four-inch barrel length, and firing a rimmed cartridge inserted with speedloaders instead of moon clips. A review of such electronic gun boards as www.smith-wessonforum.com show that an amazing number of people carry four-inch service revolvers concealed daily for self-defense, and more keep them as home defense guns. This is the place to test skill with them. It generally takes a +P 38 load to make the power factor, a minimum figure of 125,000 when velocity is multiplied by bullet weight, the same power floor as in SSP and ESP. The revolver cannot be loaded with more than six rounds at any time.

Enhanced Service Revolver (ESR). When SSR encompassed any six-gun 38-caliber and up, the Smith & Wesson Model 625 revolver kicked butt. That was because it could fire round nose 45 ACP ammo in moon clips, which went into the gun faster than any speedloader could insert rimmed cartridges. Once again, the goal was to level the playing field: these moon clip guns were moved into their own category, ESR. The 625 is *still* the gun to beat there.

Earlier, I said there was arguably a sixth category. That arguable category is Back-Up Gun (BUG). There are *side matches* for these guns, most notably at the National Championships where last year Smith & Wesson provided the Model 640-1 snub-nosed J-frame revolvers that were used in the competition. I shoot IDPA in a lot of places, though, and only one venue has regular BUG stages, and those are usually factored out of the main competition.

A pity, because the two-inch 38 revolver and the small pocket-size auto pistol, the guns that the BUG concept were built around, are perhaps the most popular carry guns out there, yet are not truly represented in mainstream IDPA competition. I for one would like to see it come into its own as a full-fledged gun competition category awarded the same respect as the big autos and revolvers are in IDPA.

What You Get

There's a modest entry fee to join IDPA, and for your first match you don't have to even be a member. After that, a typical local match fee with go about $15 or $20 at this writing. For that, you get to shoot four or six or so live-fire "scenarios" that have been set up elaborately with props. The targets often are "clothed" in tee shirts or similar garb, just as your opponent would likely be in real life. There are cover points that range from automobiles (sometimes fake, sometimes actual cars) to barricades that represent vertical building corners, doors you have

Movement is life in a gunfight, and is required in IDPA. Here, safely holding Glock 34, teenager Randi Rogers sprints toward her next target and the National Woman's Champion title of 2007. Randi, shooting under the monicker "Holy Terror," beat all male contestants at a recent national Cowboy Action Shooting championship.

Shooting on the move is a staple of IDPA, demonstrated here by gunwriter and competitive shooter Chris Christian with S&W M&P at Florida State Championships.

IDPA rewards speed, accuracy, and smoothness. Laura Torres-Reyes, MD displays all three as range officer holds the timer at '07 New England Regional Championships. Pistol is 9mm Glock 34.

to maneuver through, and the whole nine yards. Let your imagination run free: the match designers do. At the last national championship, there was one stage in which an automobile was turned over on its side as part of the scenario.

You might have dummies you have to drag out of the line of fire, and large dolls representing babies you are required to not only carry to safety, but shield with your own body as you do so. You may start pushing a lawn mower, serving food at a barbecue, or burping a "baby" you have to carefully set down before you engage the threat. (If you "spike" the baby like a football, you get the dreaded twenty-second Failure To Do Right penalty added to your time. When I was match director one year for the Mid-Winter Regional IDPA Championship at Smith & Wesson Academy's fine facility in Massachusetts, I had to uphold a range officer's penalty on a contestant who used the "baby" as a human shield between him and the bad guy targets. Sorry, fella, that just ain't the spirit of the defensive handgun game…)

There are moving targets. Pop-up targets. "Gravity turners" that may only expose themselves for a fraction of a second. Steel knockdowns and cardboard silhouettes alike. Because having to shoot vicious animals is a very real scenario for both armed citizens and cops, the cardboard silhouette targets will occasionally be turned over on their sides to represent vicious dogs, or a wolf pack. A friend of mine won the Wisconsin IDPA Championship shooting matches like that, and when he was on patrol one day and had to shoot a wolf that was menacing a group of little girls, he was able to achieve 100-percent hit potential with his department-issue Beretta 92 and kill the beast before fangs reached flesh. He got a commendation out of the deal. He'll tell you that, yes, IDPA is "job-related."

It would cost you a fortune in time and money to set all those scenarios up for yourself. Fifteen or twenty bucks to have someone set it up for you, and time you and score you as you go through? That, brothers and sisters, is a *helluva* deal. Look at some of the props we had to work with at the 2007 Pennsylvania State Championship hosted by the Ontelaunee Sportsmen's Club, where some of the photos illustrating this article were taken.

The Concealed Weapon Factor

Most IDPA stages will start with the gun concealed. This is one of its most important benefits to the CCW shooter. Where is your gun likely to be when a deadly fight starts if you're not a cop, soldier, or security professional? Why, under a concealing garment. IDPA, *and IDPA alone among the major, established handgun sports*, requires you to begin with your hands away from your body, and *actually get the clothing out of the way and draw the damn thing from concealment!*

Now, this doesn't happen 100 percent of the time, but it's good for maybe 90 percent. In the Classifier shoot (about which more later) that IDPA rules require every member to shoot once a year, no concealment is worn. This is because the range safety officers are assessing pure skill, and they know they'll have a lot of new shooters, and for safety reasons they want to see what the hands are doing when the draw of a loaded handgun is underway. In matches, there will also be stages where the shooter starts (as is often

IDPA doesn't address only man-to-man conflict. Here, at '07 PA state shoot, the target array is a "dog pack attack," with knife-armed humanoid target on a swinger at far left.

the case in real life) with the gun in a drawer, an attaché case, a backpack, or lying on the ground. In one memorable match, there was a stage where the gun was in a lock box, and the shooter was given the punch-in combination just before the start signal sounded.

I've also been at some matches where brutally hot weather caused the match sponsors to forego the concealment requirement in the name of shooter safety: their concern was heatstroke. That was the case in a match I recently shot at the Central Florida Rifle & Pistol Club in Orlando, FL, where the thermometer was at 97 degrees, the humidity was close to max, and the "heat index" was well over a hundred.

One other exception is that those who carry openly at work (uniformed cops and soldiers, for instance) are allowed to forego the concealment requirement. However, the holster must be suitable for uniform wear and worn with all safety/security devices fastened, and if it's on a police duty belt, there better

IDPA is "the concealed carry competition sport." David Sevigny, shown here winning the 2006 National Championship with G34, began IDPA shooting to sharpen his skill with the smaller Glock pistol he was licensed to carry concealed.

be handcuffs in the belt pouches. Having shot this way with my department issue double action .45 and Safariland level II security holster, I can tell you that it gives one no competitive advantage over an open-top speed holster concealed under a photographer's vest.

The Use of Cover Factor

History shows us that when bad tactics get good guys killed in gunfights, the failure to use available cover is usually the single biggest of the fatal errors. In IDPA, you are required to have at least half of your upper body behind "cover" if such replicated cover is available on that stage, and your whole lower body behind it as well.

One direction in which competitive shooting went wrong insofar as being a positive learning experience for those who took handguns into harm's way, was in emphasizing speed of shot placement over use of cover. In the real world, as any firefight survivor can tell you, the bullets are going in both directions. The goal is not to shoot the bad guy; the goal is not to get shot. Shooting the bad guy is merely one of your options in achieving the goal of survival.

The emphasis on use of cover in IDPA is, to this reviewer's mind, one of the strongest aspects of the game as far as its value to the person who carries a gun "for real." I was certified as an IDPA Safety Officer several years ago under Mike Briggs, and recently audited another such class by Florida's IDPA go-to guy, Lance Biddle. Both emphasized the importance of staying true to the core concepts of IDPA by assessing penalties on shooters who exposed themselves to what in real life would be incoming fire, unnecessarily. It was good to see. It shows me that, then and now, IDPA is about *Defensive* Shooting more than it's about Defensive *Shooting*.

Real World Factors

The timer is digitally ticking away the seconds. A bunch of people are watching you. Is there stress? *Oh, yeah!* Not necessarily the full-blown fight or flight response that occurs in the true near death experience of the kind you carry a gun to ward off, but yes, there can be big-time stress.

At another fast-paced match of another nature (the first Bianchi Cup in 1979), I found myself on the same relay with a famous big city cop who had survived a number of deadly shootouts. As we walked side-by-side from one stage to another, he said, "(Expletive deleted), I've never felt stress like this in any of my (expletive deleted) gunfights!"

I asked him, "Why do you think that is?"

He replied, rapidly (and, I think, from the heart) "Because there wasn't all this (expletive deleted) time to build up to it, and there weren't all these (expletive deleted) people watching you!"

No, it's not the same as getting shot at and knowing that life can end for you in the next instant. But, ya know what? It *does* condition you to ignore extraneous things and focus on the tasks you need to accomplish right now. History tells us that men and women who focus on such tasks in such terribly dangerous moments are the ones who are most likely to accomplish those tasks, and to survive the threat to their life.

At about fifteen or twenty bucks a dose at local IDPA matches, that's *awfully* cheap for "preventive medicine" that conditions you to function when

your hands are shaking, your tongue is stuck to the roof of your mouth, and you're so deep in alligators that you can't remember that your original intention was to drain the swamp, *and there is a loaded gun in your hand that you must fire **safely**, swiftly, and accurately!*

The Awkwardness of the Real World

One thing I appreciate about IDPA is that it recognizes that while we all love to shoot from our strongest position so we perform well and look good, the real world has an unfortunate way of catching us off guard in awkward positions. IDPA course designers like to start you and me off in such awkward positions. "It's a good thing."

In just the last few months of IDPA shooting, I've had to do the following.

"Shoot through a window from the front seat of the car." I remember the falling glass coming into my field of view as the Ruger 45 came back on target for the next shot. That would be pretty expensive to replicate in my back yard. At the Pennsylvania State IDPA Championships, it came with a moderate entry fee for ten separate stages.

"Draw the gun from this or that odd place." It could happen. My review of the gunfights of Lance Thomas, perhaps the most accomplished Armed Citizen Gunfighter of the 20th Century, didn't show any that started with him making a classic draw from a holster "on Main Street in Dodge City at high noon." In every case, he grabbed one of the several guns he had secreted in tactical locations in his watch shop, to shoot the many armed robbers he put down.

"Grab the gun and shoot while on your back/on your belly/on your knees." Been there, done that in IDPA. It's a real good idea for your brain to be able to say "Been there, done that" when you find yourself in such a position and about to die if you don't get a gun into action and shoot back, right now.

"Expose only what needs to be exposed to aim and fire." The great combat pistol champ Ray Chapman pioneered the concept of coming up on the ball of the opposite foot just enough to get you to where "you can shoot him with impunity, but he'll have a tough time shooting you." This works on the street, and it works – not altogether coincidentally – in IDPA.

"How much do I need the rest of that ammo?" Several shots have been fired. Like most people in actual gunfights, you lost count when it went past three or four. Do you speedload your pistol and leave the few live rounds in the magazine on the ground, or do you take a little extra time to retain that partial magazine before you snap in a fresh one, in case you need those last few rounds as the fight goes on?

"Speed reload" versus "tactical reload" versus "reload with retention" is an argument that can go all night between trained professionals looking at the issue from different, but equally relevant, sides. After having to debate this issue more than any other with its members, IDPA has gone to "any IDPA-approved reload technique" for most matches, and this has cut the Gordian knot. However, the 90-shot Classifier course covers both "tac loads" and "emergency (slide-lock) reloads," as well as shooting while moving forward and back, multiple targets, head-shot failure-drills, shooting from both tall vertical and low horizontal cover, and left-hand-only, right-hand-only, *and* two-handed shooting. It is one of the most challenging and comprehensive skill tests you will find.

Specialty Categories

IDPA has categories for high individuals of certain categories: high female, high cop, high soldier, high geezer, etc. These are determined from among *all five gun categories combined,* so you would be wise if you are shooting to win one of these particular awards to use a gun that holds 11 rounds, which puts you in SSP or ESP. There are enough occasional 10- and 11-round stages that guns which have to be reloaded before that many shots are fired will put you at the "have to climb uphill" end of the playing field. Several years ago, I managed to win the Senior Championship at the Mid-Winter Nationals at Smith & Wesson Academy, which were directed by Ken Hackathorn at the time. I did it with an Al Greco-tuned S&W Model 625 45 ACP revolver. But the lesson to learn is, that in all these years, that's the *only* time I've been able to do that with a 6-shot revolver against 9- and 11-shot autos against a highly skilled field. I just had one of those perfect days when everything seemed to go right for me. That is *never* guaranteed. Not at the range, and not on the street.

Don't let anyone else be the role model as to what you'll shoot. Determine your goals, and shoot with the best gun for the job. Personally, I'm a full-time use of force instructor and a part-time cop, and since my students come in with all the different gun types, I shoot with them all. My personal favorite is Stock Service Revolver category. I like the challenge: it's kind of like shooting a single shot or a muzzle-loader during regular deer season. Of course, it also makes it more likely that I'll win the particular gun category, since way more folks shoot autos than revolvers, so there are fewer competitors to beat.

Determine your goals, and shoot with the best gun for the job.

If I was a full-time cop, I would shoot mostly with my duty gun and duty holster, and one time out of every three or four, with my off-duty gun and leather. And if you're an armed citizen getting into this to fine-tune the skills you'll use once the potentially deadly encounter truly comes down to shooting, your smartest course of action is to use the guns you actually carry on the street, the guns you actually keep at home to ward off home invaders.

"You pays your money, and you takes your choice." If you are there to test *your* skill with the handgun *you* are most likely to be using when you have to fire to defend your life or the lives of other innocent people, then *you* decide what you will compete with.

Personally, I'm geared more to training than to competition, and I've found IDPA to be the most useful competitive venue available to me for testing and analyzing the relevant skills. To see if it will be the same for you, check out the organization at www.idpa.com, where you will find references to IDPA-affiliated groups reasonably near you.

Good luck. Keep it all in perspective. And, stay safe!

FINAL ADVICE

This small-frame S&W 357 was used by the young woman who carries it to ward off two assailants, with no blood shed on either side. Concealed carry was a practice she learned from her mom and dad, and it saved her.

Whether I'm finishing a book or finishing a class, there's a voice in the back of my mind yelling, "Dammit, there wasn't time to cover it all!" I suppose I'll be thinking the same thing on my deathbed. Hell, I suppose we'll *all* be thinking that on our deathbeds.

This is a life study. I've written several books and literally thousands of articles on this, and *still* haven't covered it all. For instance, this book touched little on defensive shooting techniques and skills. For that I'd recommend *The Gun Digest Book of Combat Handgunnery, 6th Edition*, from Krause. In the book you're holding, there wasn't space to go into the different gun platforms in detail, but

Ayoob testifies on behalf of shall-issue concealed carry legislation at a State House. If we don't fight for our rights, he warns, we'll lose them.

The Gun Digest Book of … series covers that nicely. My old friend, colleague, and fellow shooting competitor Patrick Sweeney did a great job covering the 1911, the Glock, and the Smith & Wesson line to name three, and I did the Beretta and SIG books. If you own the given brand or are thinking of acquiring it, you'll find the appropriate book from that series useful.

Almost half a century of carrying a loaded, concealed handgun has taught me a few things. Let me say adieu with a final sharing of discoveries.

■ **Never take safety for granted.** You and yours will constantly be in the presence of a loaded, lethal weapon. Kinda like driving a car. Familiarity absolutely does breed contempt. Never lower your guard or your level of care, and think like an engineer: put multiple safety procedures in place, and follow them religiously.

■ **Live in a state of relaxed alertness.** The late, great Col. Jeff Cooper called this Condition Yellow. At any given moment, you know what's going on around you, who's near you, and where you are. He said that a well-adjusted man or woman should be able to spend their entire waking life in Yellow with no adverse psychological effects. I've found it's even better than that. It makes you a people-watcher. You see the good, life-affirming things around you that you were missing before.

■ **Stay current with the topic.** Read the periodicals, particularly *American Handgunner* and *Combat Handguns*. Take classes. There are more good firearms/self-defense training programs available today than ever. We're talking about skills that degrade easily if not refreshed. Don't limit those classes to guns and combat. Adult ed courses in body language, deviant human behavior, and criminology can be rich mines of useful self-defense knowledge.

■ **Commit to always carrying.** If we knew when we were going to need a gun, we'd change our plans and go somewhere safer. Danger comes from out of nowhere and doesn't limit itself to "bad areas." Mass murders take place at good schools, upscale malls, and family restaurants in nice neighborhoods. The only way to make sure the gun will always be there when you need it is to always carry it. Go online to www.handgunlaw.us and commit to getting all the permits you can. The more places you can legally carry, the safer you'll be.

■ **Be prepared, in your heart and mind, to use deadly force if necessary.** It's a long search of the soul, but a critically important one. If you don't know for certain that you can kill a violent attacker if you have to, you're likely to hesitate at the worst possible time, and he'll kill you and yours instead. Ironically, because predators have a finely tuned sense of what is and is not prey, that commitment seems to transmit. Thus, an irony: the person prepared to kill is less likely to have to do so. The great majority of situations in which armed citizens drew down on criminal suspects have ended with no bloodshed, because the predators sensed they were about to die and either surrendered or fled. They won't surrender or flee if they sense hesitation on the part of their opponent. In LFI classes, I explain the worst of the aftermath and how to deal with it, so the student can get that out of the way and be prepared to act instantly if the moment ever comes. If you haven't sorted it out beforehand, the fight will happen too fast for you to come to terms with the cosmic act of ending another human life.

■ **Fight to keep your rights and privileges.** There are those in this society who work in a tireless, well-funded, concerted effort to deprive you and your children of the right to self-protection. You have a genuine duty to "you and yours" to fight that. Whether or not you appreciate the National Rifle Association, join and support the NRA: they literally coined the term "armed citizen," and they are the strongest voice for those citizens' rights in Washington. Personally, I have served for many years on the board of trustees of the Second Amendment Foundation, and do what I can to support the highly effective grassroots gun-owners' groups at the state level. This is about civil rights. It's about human rights. The great authority on the common law, Lord Blackstone, said "Self-defense is the highest of all human rights." Work hard to keep it, because powerful forces don't want you and your descendants to have it.

■ **Maintain a logical perspective.** I don't know if you in particular are going to need what's in these pages. I do know that some of you are. My paternal grandfather came to these shores in the year 1896, and in every generation since, at least one member of my linear family has been saved from death or great bodily harm by the ability to produce a loaded handgun when attacked on the street. And even if that never happens to you, your commitment to concealed carry will have bought you a lifetime of peace of mind, and there's no dollar price to put on something that precious.

I'm out of time. You're not. Continue your learning in this life study. Share it with others. Fight to keep your rights and privileges.

Good luck. Stay safe, and keep your loved ones safe.

-- *Massad Ayoob,* December 2007

KEY THINGS

It is wise for the individual who lawfully carries a concealed handgun in public to keep a few things foremost in mind.

Know the laws governing concealed carry *where you are at any given time,* **and follow them religiously.** "Gun crimes" committed by those licensed to carry are extremely rare, but of those that occur, a huge percentage involve people who simply "forgot they were armed" when they entered an area where the practice was legally forbidden.

Concealed means concealed. Yes, I know it's a trite and hackneyed phrase, but it carries a lot of truth. Our society is such, like it or not, that the presence of an obviously lethal weapon in the hands of someone not readily identifiable as an "official protector" frighten people. Someday, if you haven't already, you'll buy a newspaper or a candy bar from a convenience store clerk who was terrorized by an armed robber who menacingly drew his coat back to reveal a weapon. If you accidentally do the same, can you blame her for her predictable reaction? The results won't be good for either of you.

Keep it quiet. The fewer people who know you carry a gun, the better. You don't want to be caught up in the middle of an armed robbery where the multiple offenders with drawn guns hold all the cards, and have a terrified victim look at you and scream, "My God, you've got a gun, *do* something!"

The potential for false accusations is endless. You don't want an employee you fired for incompetence to vengefully go to the police and swear out a complaint saying, "And then my boss pulled out a snub-nose .38 from inside his shirt and pointed it between my eyes!" When the police come and find you carrying that kind of gun in just that place, you're behind the eight-ball. I've seen a false accusation of aggravated assault leveled at a man solely because another motorist, in a state of road rage, spotted the NRA decal on his car, correctly assumed he would have a gun with him, and told the police falsely that the good guy had pointed a gun at him without provocation. It took that good man about fifty grand in non-refundable legal fees and costs to win an acquittal on the felony charges.

Don't carry a "CCW" badge. Sold in great numbers to well-meaning CCW permit-holders, these are seen by police and prosecutors (and the general public and the jury pool) as "fake badges." At best you look like a wanna-be trying to play cop. At worst, you fit the profile of criminals from home invaders to child molesters who impersonate a police officer in the course of heinous offenses. That's not a profile you ever want to fit.

Avoid trouble more than ever. Under the "higher standard of care" principle, the armed private citizen is seen as having a particular duty to avoid conflicts – shouting matches, upraised middle fingers, curses – and is expected to de-escalate rather than "keep the ball rolling," let alone offering provocation.

Gain familiarity and competence with your weapon and carry system. A life or death situation is no time for fumbling. Practice with empty or dummy guns to gain smooth speed of draw from concealment. Some supervised live fire speed work (training, or an IDPA competition) will boost both confidence and competence with your concealed handgun. Train and practice as frequently as you can, to make the mechanics of drawing (and, if necessary, firing) as much second nature as possible.

Prepare for the totality of the circumstances. Make sure that those most likely to be with you if an armed encounter takes place know what to do. Always have a plan in case you have to remove your weapon and secure it, which can arise from anything from an unexpected trip to the Courthouse for routine paperwork, to an auto accident in which you had to be transported to a hospital by ambulance.

Be vigilant about gun safety. Familiarity breeds contempt. Put layer after layer of safety into your daily handling and carrying practices. Remember Jeff Cooper's Four Rules. (1) All guns are always (considered) loaded. (2) Never point the gun at anything you are not prepared to see destroyed. (3) Never touch the trigger until the gun is on target and you are in the act of intentionally firing. (4) Always be certain of your target and what is behind it. Remember that the responsibility to keep your weapon out of incompetent and/or unauthorized hands falls solely upon *you.*

Remember why you carry. The gun is there to protect your loved ones, and to keep you alive to return to them. Just as its presence is a constant reminder of your responsibilities, let the presence of that deadly weapon also be a constant reminder of the importance of the loved ones in your life. Consciously or subconsciously, this recognition is one reason that those who carry guns seem to be among not only the most responsible people in this society, but the most caring and compassionate.

GET A GRIP ON POWERFUL PERFORMANCE

The Gun Digest® Book of the Glock
A Comprehensive Review: Design, History, Use
2nd Edition
by Patrick Sweeney

Glock's dynamic presence in military and law enforcement circles around the world, including being the choice arm of 65 percent of all U.S. law enforcement agencies, speaks to its innovative design and durability. This new edition of the Gun Digest Book® of the Glock delivers the reliable and detailed model and production data you've come to expect from Gun Digest, along with an extensive equipment guide of the newest models, plus step-by-step illustrations demonstrating ways to maintain and accessorize a Glock. Get the go-to guide of Glock gear and goods!

Softcover • 8-1/4 x 10-7/8 • 336 pages
300 b&w photos
Item# Z1926 • $27.99

Standard Catalog of® Colt Firearms
by Rick Sapp

Colt may not be making as many new models as it once did, but the value of what's out there is on the rise; creating a need for reliable details, up-to-date values and comprehensive Colt historical data. With this bold, beautiful and useful book you gain 500 large-format color photos of Colt firearms and modern Colt clones, certified pricing in up to five grades of condition, serial number data, details about intensely interesting (Tommy guns) and trendy (Anaconda, and .28 Supers) models, plus historical details to help with identifying Colt classics.

Softcover • 8-1/4 x 10-7/8 • 288 pages
450 color photos
Item# Z0931 • $29.99

The Gun Digest® Book of the 1911, Volume 2
by Patrick Sweeney

The Gun Digest® Book of The 1911, Volume 2 gives you expanded information for using and upgrading the 1911, including reviews of the latest models, new factory ammunition and test-fire evaluations for 17 pistols. Plus, you gain technical specifications including trigger pull, chamber depth and weight for this new collection of pistols. This second volume of the two-book set completes the story of the 1911, while inspiring to discover more hands-on details on your own.

Softcover • 8-1/2 x 11 • 327 pages
350 b&w photos
Item# VIIPT • $27.99

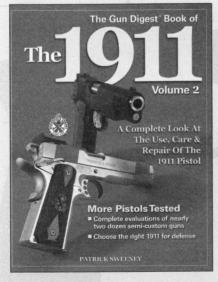

Krause Publications
P.O. Box 5009,
Iola, WI 54945-5009
www.krausebooks.com

Order directly from the publisher by calling **800-258-0929** M-F 8 am – 5 pm
Online at **www.krausebooks.com** or from booksellers nationwide.
Please reference offer **GNB8** with all direct-to publisher orders.
Gun News • Sales • Prices and More at **www.gundigestmagazine.com**.

MORE TIPS, AND TECHNIQUES FROM THE EXPERTS

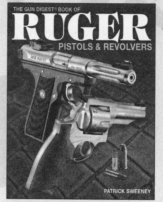

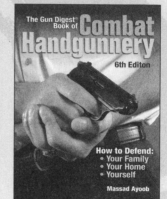

The Gun Digest® Book of Automatic Pistols Assembly/Disassembly
J.B. Wood
Expert gunsmith J.B. Woods delivers the latest in cleaning, care and customizing advice and instruction for automatic pistol disassembly in this detailed guide.
Softcover • 8-1/4 x 10-7/8
752 pages • 4,000 b&w illus.
Item# Z0737 • $34.99

The Gun Digest® Book of Ruger Pistols and Revolvers
Patrick Sweeney
Get the most out of your Ruger by reviewing current real-world performance test results and load data, and expanding your expert understanding of Ruger functionality.
Softcover • 8-1/4 x 10-7/8
304 pages
600 b&w photos & illus.
Item# Z0736 • $27.99

The Gun Digest® Book of Combat Handgunnery
6th Edition
Massad Ayoob
Discover practical, life-saving instruction for handgun self defense from the nation's most recognized expert in the subject.
Softcover • 8-1/4 x 10-7/8
256 pages • 500 b&w photos
Item# Z0880 • $24.99

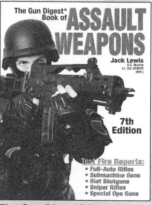

The Gun Digest® Book of Assault Weapons
7th Edition
by Jack Lewis
Review optimum coverage of the most common and available assault weapons on the market with more performance results, hard to find application data, and the latest trend information.
Softcover • 8-1/4 x 10-7/8
256 pages • 350 color photos
Item# Z0769 • $26.99

Armed America
Portraits of Gun Owners in Their Homes
by Kyle Cassidy
Travel with photographer Kyle Cassidy across America as he looks for the answer to one question: Why do you own a gun? Meet a few of the millions of U.S. gun owners, in their own homes, and in their own words.
Hardcover with Jacket • 12 x 9
208 pages • 200 color photos
Item# Z0956 • $30.00

Standard Catalog of® Smith & Wesson
3rd Edition
Jim Supica and Richard Nahas
Identify and appreciate any Smith & Wesson firearm more with the easy-to-locate listings, rarely seen production data and historical details and more than 350 color photos featured in this definitive guide!
Hardcover • 8-¼ x 10-7/8
384 pages • 350+ color photos
Item# FSW03 • $39.99

Krause Publications
P.O. Box 5009,
Iola, WI 54945-5009
www.krausebooks.com

Order directly from the publisher by calling **800-258-0929** M-F 8 am – 5 pm
Online at **www.krausebooks.com** or from booksellers nationwide.
Please reference offer **GNB8** with all direct-to publisher orders.
Get the latest arms action and news at **www.gundigestmagazine.com**.